Reconstructing Contexts

Reconstructing Contexts

The Aims and Principles
of Archaeo-Historicism

ROBERT D. HUME

OXFORD
UNIVERSITY PRESS

OXFORD
UNIVERSITY PRESS

Great Clarendon Street, Oxford OX2 6DP

Oxford University Press is a department of the University of Oxford.
It furthers the University's objective of excellence in research, scholarship,
and education by publishing worldwide in

Oxford New York

Athens Auckland Bangkok Bogotá Buenos Aires Calcutta
Cape Town Chennai Dar es Salaam Delhi Florence Hong Kong Istanbul
Karachi Kuala Lumpur Madrid Melbourne Mexico City Mumbai
Nairobi Paris São Paulo Singapore Taipei Tokyo Toronto Warsaw

with associated companies in Berlin Ibadan

Oxford is a registered trade mark of Oxford University Press
in the UK and in certain other countries

Published in the United States
by Oxford University Press Inc., New York

British Library Cataloguing in Publication Data

Data available

Library of Congress Cataloging in Publication Data

Hume, Robert D.
Reconstructing contexts: the aims and principles of archaeo-
historicism / Robert D. Hume
Includes bibliographical references and index;
1. English literature—History and criticism—Theory, etc.
2. Literature and History—Great Britain—History. 3. Literature—
History and Criticism—Theory, etc. 4. Music—History and
criticism. 5. Historicism. I. Title.
PR25.H86 1999 820.9—dc21 98-39762
ISBN 0-19-818632-0

1 3 5 7 9 10 8 6 4 2

Typeset by Vera A. Keep, Cheltenham
Printed in Great Britain
on acid-free paper by
Bookcraft Ltd.
Midsomer Norton, Somerset

Preface

A BOOK with a coinage in the title needs to start with an explanation of what that coinage is designed to convey. 'Historicism' has been given a bewildering variety of meanings, but is used here in a common one: an attempt to understand historical materials in their own context. The prefix is intended to suggest: (1) archives; (2) the Greek *archaiologia*, or discussion of antiquity; (3) archaeology, meaning 'scientific'—I prefer to say 'systematic'—'study of historic or prehistoric peoples and their cultures by analysis of their artefacts, inscriptions, and monuments'. Archaeo-Historicism as I understand it and have practised it is a scholarly method by which one attempts—across formidable barriers—to recreate the events and outlook of an earlier period. If such reconstruction is to be anything more than wildly impressionistic (or worse), then it must be grounded in hard evidence handled according to strict rules. This book seeks to identify legitimate objects for historical reconstruction and to propose procedures and principles by which this sort of work can properly be pursued.

In one sense, this is a book of 'theory': I am talking about what Archaeo-Historicism can aspire to do and how it should be practised, not actually practising it. I feel a bit defensive about this, as I am far from happy about hot-air theorists who talk endlessly about what 'ought' to be done without ever getting round to doing it. I see this book, however, as a systematic explanation of the principles of a kind of work practised by many twentieth-century scholars. I have been publishing historical scholarship in books and articles for the past quarter century, and anyone who wishes to see what I have in mind (or wants to attack the sort of work that results) is cordially invited to devour—and if so inclined, to denounce—Hume's *Opera omnia*. I would point in particular to *Henry Fielding and the London Theatre, 1728–1737* and Volume I of *Italian Opera in Late Eighteenth-Century London* (the latter written in collaboration with Curtis Price and Judith Milhous) as examples of the sort of heavily documented reconstruction I am trying to theorize here. But if this is a book of theory (I would prefer to say 'methodology'), I trust that it is by no means an abstract one. I have kept it short, and I have tried to make it clear. I have used a large number of examples of actual problems and actual scholarship. Many of these are matters I have worked on myself. I have used them not because I wish to play the peacock or because I think them especially important, but because I have (I hope) a thorough grasp of the primary material and methodological problems at issue.

The examples of good and bad historical scholarship proffered in this book inevitably reflect my own knowledge and ignorance. I am a specialist in the literature and theatre history of Britain in the period 1660 to 1800, and I am an American. The kinds of evidence that survive in my areas of speciality, and the practical and theoretical problems the scholar must confront, are inevitably a bit different than those faced by specialists in medieval literature, Elizabethan manuscript poetry, or the Irish Renaissance. I am well aware that a reader in Australia, New Zealand, India, South Africa, or Canada will probably feel that I am offensively ignorant of the literatures and histories of those countries. I would argue, however, that even fully granting the practical and national differences involved, most of the principles expounded in this book can be readily translated into other periods and countries. I would further argue that a medievalist or an Australian can carry out such translation more effectively than I could. I have, therefore, basically stuck with territories where I have some first-hand knowledge, convinced that the methodological principles extracted from areas familiar to me can be readily applied to others.

Practice without theory is blind, as Marx observes: how is one to know what one is trying to do or by what rules and methods it can legitimately be done? Abstract theory, however, seems equally misguided: theory is useful only if it 'works'—that is, if it leads to results that can in some fashion be confirmed or validated in whatever territory the theory is held to apply. From the standpoint of what J. G. A. Pocock calls the 'working historian' (and I count myself such a historian of theatre and culture), a useful theory needs to tell us four things: (1) aim; (2) working procedures—i.e. 'method'; (3) the limita-

tions and failures of the method; and (4) how the method
connects and fails to connect to other methods that might be
chosen and employed. By no coincidence, these issues are the
focuses for the four chapters of this book. I am deeply suspicious of any 'theorist' who is not prepared to address all four
of these issues. I do not fancy the role of snake-oil salesman. A
theorist who does not try to display all that is wrong with his or
her theory (as well as what is right) must be either a fool or a
fraud. A substantial portion of this book is devoted to the
shortcomings and problems inherent in Archaeo-Historicism.
The problems are both numerous and serious. The method
applies only to appropriate subjects, and only where sufficient
evidence can be found. I have written this book to try to show
what can be done and how it should be done, but also to delimit
as clearly as possible what should not be attempted (and why). I
do not regard 'historical reconstruction' as a panacea. It is not
for all critics and scholars, and it works badly (or not at all) for
many subjects. My argument is essentially that it should be one
choice, and that when wisely and skilfully applied, it can yield
important results.

Some comments are in order concerning the nature of this
book and my assumptions in writing it. This is not a 'primer'.
Good scholarship cannot be reduced to such formulae any
more than good criticism can. Rather, this book is an attempt
to theorize a particular method. It offers an examination of
the assumptions, principles, and limits of a sharply defined
approach to the reconstruction of past viewpoints. My aim is to
analyse a method that has been long practised by many scholars
(albeit without much theoretical scrutiny). My stress is on the
aims and procedures of this method; I have no desire to fight
with my predecessors over philosophical issues, or to criticize
other methods. Some readers of my manuscript have been disappointed that I have not done battle with Derrida, Foucault,
and Greenblatt. Actually, I admire all these writers. I would
describe even Foucault and Greenblatt, however, as 'cultural theorists' engaged in enterprises radically different from
Archaeo-Historicism as I conceive it, and hence not centrally
relevant to my argument. My concern here is how a certain
kind of historicism can be practised. I originally planned whole
chapters on 'The Discrimination of Historicisms' and 'Philo-

sophical Objections'; on reflection, I have compressed these discussions to very short compass.

Any serious work of scholarship or criticism should surprise its author in the course of research and composition. In the light of friends' comments on my draft, I wish to mention two developments totally unanticipated on my part. First, my changed response to Hans Robert Jauss's 'Literary History as a Challenge to Literary Theory'. I read this celebrated essay when it appeared in *New Literary History* more than twenty-five years ago, and reread it with approval in the mid-eighties. Reconsidering it closely now, I am disconcerted to find that it does *not* supply (as I had rather supposed it did) any sort of basis for the kind of scholarship I am trying to describe. The essay remains widely admired and cited, but I have felt obliged to register my doubts and disagreements in Chapter 1. Second, my rediscovery of R. S. Crane, whose work I admired as a student in the 1960s and had basically forgotten about. Rereading Crane, I realized that he grappled with all sorts of problems that continue to haunt me, and wrote about them with a rigour and good sense from which I had much to learn. A friend who had not read Crane asked 'Why do you keep quoting an obsolete and forgotten neo-Aristotelian?' Crane's neo-Aristotelian and 'Chicago Critic' sides hold little interest for me, but his essays on historical method seem to me lastingly important considerations of issues that remain current and urgent in the later 1990s. Whether a reader approves or disapproves of this book, I hope that one of its results will be to call attention to Crane's profoundly stimulating work.

Launching my reader into the thickets of the arguments that follow, I should like to make four basic points about the assumptions and limits that seem to me crucial in understanding Archaeo-Historicism. (1) A method devoted to historical reconstruction depends on 'evidence', and in the absence of satisfactory evidence, the method cannot work properly and should not be used. Most historical theorists have treated evidence as something that falls out of the sky when needed. I would argue, on the contrary, that finding evidence (particularly before the nineteenth century) is often extremely difficult or just plain impossible, and that therefore the kind of argument one can validly attempt to make is radically limited by the nature of the evidence, if any. (2) Archaeo-Historicism is not a specifically 'literary' method at all, since it can be used to recreate 'historical viewpoint' in any realm for which evidence can be found. Archaeo-Historicism uses texts and other artefacts, and can be employed to interpret them, but it is not inherently textual except in the philosophic sense that every subject of investigation can be conceived as textual. (3) Archaeo-Historicism flatly denies the plausibility of 'literary history' so called: only very limited explanatory narratives can be justified (for example, the history of an institution like a theatre company). The idea that 'literature' has a separate history that makes sense in its own terms seems to me inherently fatuous, for if one expands coverage to incorporate all the relevant factors, one would be writing a history of the universe, not of 'literature'. (4) Archaeo-Historicism neither denies nor rests upon the possibility of causal explanation; such explanation is by no means central to what it tries to do. One can recreate *viewpoint* without claiming to explain *why* everything happens.

A number of people have read drafts, answered questions, or otherwise assisted me in this project. For such help I wish to express my particular gratitude to Julie Annas, Paul D. Cannan, Don-John Dugas, William Ingram, John T. Harwood, Kathryn Hume, J. R. de J. Jackson, Paulina Kewes, Matthew J. Kinservik, Harold Love, Judith Milhous, Richard Strier, and Amy Elizabeth Smith. Two anonymous readers for Oxford University Press gave me prompt, friendly, probing responses that greatly assisted me in putting my arguments into final form. Bonnie Blackburn has been a marvellous copy editor.

This book was completed and seen to press during a sabbatical year spent as a Visiting Research Fellow at the Institute of Historical Research (University of London). I am grateful to the Institute and its staff, and in particular to Professor Patrick K. O'Brien, the Director, for their hospitality and good offices.

I have drawn freely throughout this book on material first published in 'Texts Within Contexts: Notes Toward a Historical Method', *Philological Quarterly*, 71 (1992), 69–100. I am grateful to the editor for his permission to make this use of my earlier exploration of problems in historical method.

R.D.H.

Contents

I

Historicism and Archaeo-Historicism

THE PRIMARY object of literary criticism and scholarship is to explain texts. Many things can be done to facilitate this enterprise, and larger-scale forms of cultural criticism can be carried out as a result of it—but 'reading literature' is at the heart of the enterprise. In this respect study of literature and the arts differs sharply from history *per se*. Where the literary scholar has an artefact to confront, the historian must attempt to imagine a vanished past from such evidence as remains. A literary scholar may work at the level of philological nuts and bolts or at the rarefied heights of cultural theory, but the enterprise takes its thrust from texts.

'Explaining a text' can mean very different things. The critic may (1) clarify verbal meaning; (2) offer clarification of communication apparently designed by the author; (3) investigate the documented or probable interpretation and response of the original or later audiences; (4) refer to a conceptual construct outside the text as a means of making sense of it; or (5) analyse the text in terms of present-day ideology or sensibility. The first is classic New Criticism. The first and second are often treated as much the same thing in practice. Any of the first four *may* be a 'historicist' enterprise, though only the third is necessarily so. A 'conceptual construct outside the text' might be anything from seventeenth-century puritanism to Lacanian psychology. My concern here is with interpreting texts by means of reference to contexts in which we no longer live. Or to be more precise, my aim is to analyse the methodological problems that underlie any attempt to recreate the contexts that might be used for the explanation of 'old' works.

The primary object of Archaeo-Historicism is to reconstruct historical contexts. I might more properly say 'construct' rather than 'reconstruct' because the past is gone: we are building the best simulacrum we can from such 'traces' as remain. This is far from an objective or scientific enterprise: we choose to make the effort, we do the building, and we bring the construct into being to serve *our* purposes. Nonetheless, as I conceive the enterprise, we strive to replicate as closely as possible the events, values, circumstances, judgements, and *Weltanschauung* of a particular past time and place.[1] This need not be an antiquarian enterprise. The past begins every time the clock ticks, and reconstructing the 1980s presents challenges as formidable in their way as those posed by the 1680s.

Several questions need to be addressed at the outset of this investigation. How does Archaeo-Historicism relate to other notions of historicism? Why should we attempt to construct such contexts? Is this enterprise philosophically justifiable? How can we bridge the gap between past and present—and in particular how do we confront the possibilities and limitations laid down by Jauss? What kinds of scholarship and criticism does Archaeo-Historicism comprise?

Concepts of Historicism

'Historicism' has been used in such contradictory ways that anyone proposing to employ the term needs to provide some clarification. A recent commentator observes that the word

can designate any one of the following beliefs: that the meaning of a text is to be found through the reconstruction of the history of its reception; that the meaning of a text is to be found by reconstructing the historical context in which it appeared; that language and culture constantly change and therefore meanings are always relative; that history reveals laws or cycles from which predictions can be made; and

[1] I need to make an important terminological point here at the outset. The archaeo-historicist aims in one sense to 'recreate' or 'reconstruct' the past and is honour-bound to stay strictly within the limits of available evidence. The *result*, however, can only be an *ex post facto* construction, not the past itself. I have therefore freely used both 'reconstruct' and 'construct' (and 'reconstruction' and 'construction') in describing the enterprise and its results, trying to favour 're-' when primarily concerned with the aim, and 'construct' or 'construction' when emphasizing the inevitably artificial nature of the results. This is probably bad philosophy, but in these terms I think both 'construct' and 'reconstruct' can legitimately be applied to the archaeo-historicist enterprise.

that the diversity of the past and relativity of the observer's position make it impossible to reconstruct past meanings.[2]

The contradictions are dizzying, but the concepts behind the principal definitions will repay some attention. In current popular usage, 'historicism' often means little more than criticism with 'a historical dimension', which is to say that almost anything qualifies.[3] Older definitions are more provocative.

1. A long tradition treats *Historismus* (in English, historism or historicism) as a doctrine of individuality. Different 'ages' have their own characteristics, and therefore works written within those ages reflect their origins. The term was coined by Friedrich Meinecke to describe doctrines held by Goethe, Schleiermacher, and von Ranke denying the possibility of general laws in history. Vico and Erich Auerbach are among the more celebrated adherents of this view. The thrust is more negative than positive, the point being denial of universals, but an obvious corollary is that one can investigate the origins of literary works, both genetically in terms of authors and more broadly in terms of parent culture and original audience.

2. Marx believed that both economics and history could and should be raised to the level of rigorous sciences.[4] This has not worked out as well as he hoped, but for a considerable time both Marxists and those historians who adopted science as a model imagined that history would some day reach a point at which it could establish 'laws' and 'cycles' that would allow prediction of the future. This curious delusion was savaged by Karl R. Popper in *The Poverty of Historicism*.[5] Popper insisted (sensibly enough) that 'it is impossible for us to predict the future course of history'. He defined historicism as the assumption that 'historical prediction' is the 'principal aim' of 'the social sciences', to be achieved by 'discovering the "rhythms" or the "patterns", or the "laws" or the "trends" that underlie

[2] Wendell V. Harris, 'The Discourse of Literary Criticism and Theory', *Social Epistemology*, 10 (1996), 75–88 at 81. For a convenient survey of meanings from the Enlightenment to the present, see Paul Hamilton, *Historicism* (London: Routledge, 1996).
[3] Hayden White, 'New Historicism: A Comment', in H. Aram Veeser (ed.), *The New Historicism* (London: Routledge, 1989), 293.
[4] For discussion, see Georg G. Iggers, *New Directions in European Historiography* (Middletown, Conn.: Wesleyan University Press, 1975), 125.
[5] (Boston: Beacon Press, 1957); the following quotations are from pp. ix, 3.

the evolution of history'. Popper was attacking social theory as embodied in Marxist and Fascist experiments whose proponents had claimed for them a kind of manifest destiny. No one in the present generation has imagined that historians were about to discover or invent a crystal ball, and this very overblown and negative meaning for historicism can probably now be safely ignored, the pretensions of economists and practitioners of 'future studies' notwithstanding.

3. Many uses of historicism prior to the 1950s imply acute and even crippling relativism in the judgement of any work, belief, or institution. A striking late example occurs in the Introduction to J. Hillis Miller's *The Disappearance of God*: 'The central factor in historicism is an assumption of the relativity of any particular life or culture. . . . Historicism does not mean merely an awareness of the contradictory diversity of cultures and attitudes . . . [but rather] the loss of faith in the possibility of ever discovering the right and true culture . . . philosophy or religion. . . . The modern historicist . . . doubts the absolute validity of any world view or philosophy.'[6] The implications for the interpreter of literature are unsettling. As Harris summarizes the problem, 'If a literary work is only to be understood in its own historical period, and if the mentalities of periods differ substantially, can the work be relevant if read in a way not originally intended, and should it be so read?'[7] And indeed one may ask if a work *can* be accurately read in its original sense by a reader coming from a totally different period.

Thus—until very recently at least—the implication of a 'historicist' position could be either that meaning resides in historical context and *can* be reconstructed, or alternatively that meaning resides in historical context and hence *cannot* be reconstructed because past contexts are inaccessible and unrecapturable. In the last fifteen years, most self-proclaimed historicists of all stripes have believed that original meaning can be to some degree recuperated—but poststructuralists have denied the possibility with great vigour. Common usage in the 1990s generally implies an attempt to return to original contexts in order to reconstruct the meaning of a work at the time of its

[6] (Cambridge, Mass.: Harvard University Press, 1963), 9–10.
[7] Wendell V. Harris, *Dictionary of Concepts in Literary Criticism and Theory* (Westport, Conn.: Greenwood, 1992), 146.

composition and initial reception. The philosophical validity and practical feasibility of such an enterprise, however, remain under sharp challenge.

Old and New Historicism

In both concept and terminology the appearance of the New Historicism in the early 1980s is an unfortunate complication. Lack of clarity as to what is meant by New Historicism is equalled only by confusion about the Old Historicism that it was presumably rebelling against. Stephen Greenblatt has pointed (rather implausibly) to Dover Wilson, and many stones have been thrown at E. M. W. Tillyard's *The Elizabethan World Picture* (1943) as an instance of simplistic intellectual history, but so far as I am aware no theory of Old Historicism was ever promulgated. By process of inference one may discover that it comprises philology, genre history, biography, contextual *explication de texte*, and all forms of boring archival research. Three things made New Historicism of the 1980s different, at least in the eyes of members of the club: (1) The belief that no period is intellectually monolithic, and that 'tensions' should be sought; (2) the admission that no historical scholar can be wholly impartial; all investigators are influenced by their own backgrounds and circumstances; (3) particular attention to 'power' as a motivating and explanatory force.[8]

In retrospect, this seems an extremely shaky basis for a method.[9] Large numbers of Old Historicist books and articles had demonstrated the ferocious clashes and rifts in every period of literary history. Few scholars now believe in objectivity. 'Power' can be an exciting interpretive paradigm, but it is hardly a universal key to human behaviour, and it is basically ahistorical. The work that has emerged under the label New Historicism has often been stimulating, but seldom truly historical. David Perkins calls the use of context 'ornamental', and

---

[8] *The Power of Forms in the English Renaissance*, ed. Stephen Greenblatt (Norman, Okla.: Pilgrim, 1982), 3–6.

[9] For a friendly but trenchant critique of the theoretical shortcomings of New Historicism as propounded by Greenblatt, see Richard Strier, *Resistant Structures: Particularity, Radicalism, and Renaissance Texts* (Berkeley: University of California Press, 1995), ch. 4.

he is right.[10] At least as it started out, the enterprise was far more critical than contextual.

What sort of criticism was it? Three basic kinds of reading need to be distinguished. *Close reading*—New Criticism as once was. *Contextual reading*—that is, historicist reading in which the critic attempts to reconstruct original meanings. *Theorized reading*, in which the critic employs analytic tools from outside the context in which the work was written. Close reading finds few kind words these days, but it is still necessarily and rightly a staple of undergraduate education, and both contextual and theorized readings rely for their point on the difference between what they can offer and what can be obtained from a simple reading of the text. Considered against this matrix, the degree to which 'New Historicism' is a terrible misnomer becomes clear, for in its classic 1980s form it imported twentieth-century theories and paradigms into historical contexts.

From the vantage point of the later 1990s, New Historicism seems largely to have evaporated as a distinct enterprise. The 1980s practitioners of New Historicism—I am thinking particularly of Greenblatt here—have always struck me as carrying out a text-based form of close reading, not as engaging in a serious attempt to investigate original contexts. I agree with Howard Felperin that 'American new historicism . . . is not genuinely *historical* or seriously political either.'[11] From my point of view, a basic tenet of historicism must be that it rejects arbitrary selection and demands investigation of a wide range of background materials—or at the very least, rigorous justification of selectivity. The critical results of New Historicism have often been valuable, but essentially as a kind of comparatist New Criticism, with some New Left ideological trimmings and notions of subversion borrowed from deconstruction.[12] Most such studies have little to do with systematic contextual scholarship.

Deriding the clichés of the 1980s is easy enough. Thomas McFarland says that New Historicism 'was formed from the

---

[10] David Perkins, *Is Literary History Possible?* (Baltimore: Johns Hopkins University Press, 1992), 149.

[11] *The Uses of the Canon: Elizabethan Literature and Contemporary Theory* (Oxford: Clarendon Press, 1990), 155.

[12] See Alan Liu, 'The Power of Formalism: The New Historicism', *ELH* 56 (1989), 721–71.

detritus of the collision between Derrida and Foucault' and 'has become a fashion of the intellectual day in part because it makes scant demand upon the learning of the commentator: a significant anecdote to be deconstructed, and a small knowledge of Marx as a reference for values, set one up as a practising New Historicist quite nicely'.[13] As a caricature of early practice, this has a point, but in the present decade a great deal of work calling itself New Historicist is neither superficial in its historicity nor doctrinaire in its presentation of ideology and power. David Bevington correctly observes that 'we often have trouble distinguishing "New" from "Old" Historicism'.[14] Whether most of the genuinely contextual investigations of the present day that announce themselves as New Historicist should be so designated is highly questionable. The label now means practically nothing. Greenblatt later proposed 'cultural poetics' (whatever that may mean) as a better term, and the time seems ripe to abandon 'New Historicism' altogether. Popular usage tends to take on a life of its own, but critics might do well to try to adopt a more logical terminology. Building systematic cultural contexts for interpretation, 'cultural poetics', and 'cultural materialism' are manifestly different enterprises and should be kept terminologically distinct. Given the chaotic and contradictory history of 'historicism' as a term, I am proposing 'Archaeo-Historicism' as a more explicit label for context-building and contextual interpretation.

Why Practise Archaeo-Historicism?

Why indeed? A justification must rest on three premises, all open to challenge: that literature is worth reading; that older books remain valuable; and that we can and should attempt to read with an awareness of the perspective of the original audience.

Traditional justifications for reading 'great literature' have come to be suspect in recent years.[15] I have no desire to rehearse

---

[13] *TLS*, 6–12 Apr. 1990, 381.

[14] 'Varieties of Historicism: "Beyond the Infinite and Boundless Reach"', *Modern Philology*, 93 (1995), 73–88.

[15] Stephen J. Greenblatt dismisses the 'liberal humanist' position with contempt. See *Learning to Curse: Essays in Early Modern Culture* (New York: Routledge, 1990), ch. 9.

the sick-making platitudes of yore, but I am prepared to argue that if one reads, teaches, and writes about 'old' literature, one must either find intrinsic aesthetic or moral value in it *or* believe that one can discover important cultural truths by analysing it. If one subscribes to neither position, then the only rationale I can imagine is personal advantage in terms of tenure, promotion, and self-glory. A non-scholar may read for a great variety of reasons: simple pleasure and entertainment; the discovery of others' insights; vicarious experience; the challenge of encountering very different outlooks. Reading puts one in touch with other people's feelings and viewpoints. Ultimately, one reads as a process of self-discovery, to expand (perhaps sometimes to limit) one's sense of oneself as a human being.

Literature is commentary on human experience. As values and culture change, however, reading older texts becomes more difficult, complicated by our distance from the original interpretive context. When an author created or adapted the story, characters, and words, he or she could assume knowledge and attitudes shared by the designed audience that would be brought into play when experiencing them. Jerome McGann's principle of 'critical historicism' tells us that even the greatest masterpieces quickly become dated, situated as they inevitably are in the circumstances of their genesis.[16] Why then bother with such dated stuff? Why not look at recent films or soap operas? They too comment on human experience. Or if we are going to read old books, why not simply read them from the vantage point of the present?

I would answer by arguing that if the essential justification for serious reading is self-knowledge (personal and cultural), then we need to get beyond a complacent enjoyment of the present. Any generation occupies a transient place in history and culture, and to make much sense of our circumstances, we need perspective obtainable only by going outside our own condition—temporally and culturally. From literature we learn two sobering truths:

1. How different the past is from the present.
2. How similar the present is to the past.

---

[16] Jerome J. McGann, 'The Meaning of *The Ancient Mariner*', *Critical Inquiry*, 8 (1981), 35–67.

In this simple paradox lies a considerable point. Teaching literature both old and recent, I am always astonished how close we
can find ourselves to people in the remote past, and how distant
we can seem from people in the almost present. My students are
incredulous when I tell them that the state of Massachusetts
legalized contraceptives for married women in the year 1966—
the year my wife and I got married in that state. Does literature
of the 1950s reflect radically different views of premarital sex,
pregnancy, and abortion than students now take for granted? In
a word, yes. But computers and heart transplants and abortion
on demand do not make obsolete the hopes, fears, ambitions,
and suffering of characters in Homer. When we discover kinship
across many centuries and major cultural barriers, we enlarge
our sense of human potentialities. We are also confronted with
the transience of values and customs that we might otherwise
accept as ineluctable parts of the universe. To wish to speak
with the dead is far from foolish. 'As you are, I was. As I am,
you shall be.' The glories of the present are highly unlikely to be
any more lasting than the glories of the past. R. S. Crane asks
'What . . . is the profit to be derived?' from study of the past.
His answer is simple and wry: 'the cultivation of a less dogmatic
attachment to the conventions and prejudices of one's own
age'.[17]

How do we get across the barriers that time erects between us
and the books of the past? Archaeo-Historicism as I practise it
attempts to reconstruct specific contexts that permit the present-
day interpreter to make sense of the cultural artefacts of the
past and the conditions in which they were produced. Things
do change. When I teach *Hamlet* my undergraduates ask 'Did
Shakespeare believe in ghosts?' 'What did the Elizabethan audience think of revenge?' 'What did it think of marrying a dead
brother's widow?' 'Why did Hamlet not become King if his
father had been King?' 'Did the audience believe Ophelia should
obey her father?' A historicist investigation can supply good
answers to the third and fourth questions, and can offer helpful
context on the vogue for revenge tragedy. On ghosts and patriarchal authority, it produces a cornucopia of contextual information, but no very satisfactory answers.

[17] 'History versus Criticism in the Study of Literature', in *The Idea of the
Humanities*, 2 vols. (Chicago: University of Chicago Press, 1967), ii. 11.

Historicism is no cure-all. Neither should it be regarded as a way of finding 'right readings'. This is a pernicious idea. Even if we were able to document an author's intentions and the responses of the original audience, we should not feel bound to limit ourselves to that set of meanings. Obviously I do not agree with Wellek and Warren when they say that 'If we should really be able to reconstruct the meaning which *Hamlet* held for its contemporary audience, we would merely impoverish it.'[18] I do, however, agree that to try to restrict interpreters to original contextual meaning would be direly to impoverish literature — indeed, to render it virtually pointless. I flatly deny Jonathan Culler's assertion that the object of a 'historical approach' is 'to control the meaning of rich and complex works by ruling out possible meanings as historically inappropriate'.[19] Declaring a reading ahistorical does not rule it out except for the most fanatic antiquarian. Rather, a historical reading gives us a base-line from which to work, a starting point. Understanding the intrinsic and contextual meanings yields a vital and exciting sense of difference between the author's perspective and ours; it also supplies a comparative basis on which to appreciate the powers and possibilities of theorized readings. A historical reading, however, presupposes the existence of a pertinent context from which to generate it. Unless we are prepared to take our contexts ready-made off the shelf from the likes of Tillyard, we need to devote considerable thought to the process of context-making and the ground rules by which it may be carried out.

In common parlance, a historian asks what has happened in the past and attempts to enquire why it happened. The goal of a cultural historian is more narrowly circumscribed, but relies likewise on the feasibility of comprehending past thought. Archaeo-Historicism, as I conceive it, is devoted to the reconstruction of historical events and viewpoint from primary materials. Possessed of such a reconstruction, one can attempt to read poems, plays, novels, operas, or paintings in the light of authorial viewpoint and the assumptions, knowledge, and expectations of the original audience. More broadly, one can attempt to understand the lives, choices, failures, and intel-

[18] René Wellek and Austin Warren, *Theory of Literature* (1949; London: Jonathan Cape, 1961), 34.
[19] *On Deconstruction* (London: Routledge & Kegan Paul, 1983), 129.

lectual assumptions of the artists. These are fine-sounding goals indeed, but is the venture legitimate? Anyone familiar with even the rudiments of poststructuralist literary theory can think of an abundance of reasons for declaring any historicist enterprise a snare and a delusion. We must consider some of these objections.

Objections in Principle

First, nothing exists; second, even if anything exists, it is unknowable; third, even if anything can be known, it cannot be communicated to others by language.

Gorgias of Leontini, quoted by Sextus Empiricus[20]

Archaeo-Historicism rests on the proposition that historical knowledge is possible. If such a belief is merely a pitiful remnant of positivist delusion, then the sooner we abandon the enterprise, the better. Objections to the practice of any sort of historicism are of two basic kinds. One is broadly philosophical. Phenomenologists insist that the necessary knowledge is unobtainable—and that even if it were obtainable language could not communicate it effectively. A less sweeping but equally damning set of objections stems from a concept of history derived from physical science. An astonishing proportion of twentieth-century philosophy of history is devoted to grappling with demands that history produce 'proof' under 'general laws', which it has almost entirely failed to do. Just how damaging are these objections?

The phenomenological position—'hermeticism', as Wendell Harris dubs it—rests on a denial that language connects with reality. It also insists that language is too slippery to support reliable communication.[21] These have been fashionable positions among literary poststructuralists of the past twenty years. Let us consider the second point first. Language is our only

---

[20] Sextus Empiricus, *Against the Logicians*, 1. 65 (translation rephrased), Loeb Classical Library *Sextus Empiricus*, trans. R. G. Bury (Cambridge, Mass.: Harvard University Press, 1935), 35.

[21] Harris contrasts 'hermetics' with 'hermeneutics' (the latter dedicated to the proposition that communication about reality is possible). See *Literary Meaning* (London: Macmillan, 1996), chs. 1–5.

extensive means of conceptual communication—but does it really work? Whether it does or does not, one is inclined to take elaborate negative arguments with more than a grain of salt. As many an exasperated traditionalist has observed, why write books if one does not believe that they can be understood? Hermeticists publish prolifically, and they object to being misunderstood or misrepresented. One must therefore doubt that they believe exactly what they say. The limitations of language are a genuine problem, but 'difficult' is not the same as 'impossible'. Can human beings communicate with one another? Obviously we do all the time—sometimes incompletely or imperfectly, but usually with a fair degree of success. Like the rest of us, radical-sceptic poststructuralists can usually get what they order for dinner in a restaurant, judge the mood of a spouse at a glance without even waiting for words, and get into hot arguments over abstract principles. If language suffices to explain how to make a bomb or practise transcendental meditation (which it demonstrably does), then language will suffice to discuss the date of *Hamlet* or the effect of Dickens's childhood on him as a writer. The limits of language are an important philosophical and practical problem, but claiming that language cannot support serious critical or historical analysis is about as sensible as maintaining the truth of Zeno's paradox.

The connection of language to reality seems to me another false issue. Old historicists are regularly taken to task for 'realism' and epistemological innocence, but who in the last half-century has seriously imagined that 'reality' is open to the objective inspection of the humanist? Anyone who has read Kant has presumably accepted the unknowability of the *Ding an sich*. Our inability to know reality with certainty does not mean that no reality exists. For the practising historian the crux is not whether we know reality-as-it-really-is, but whether our experience of reality is adequately replicable from person to person. Granted, our senses can be treacherous, and language is inexact and full of traps. Scientists can, however, repeat experimental observations. Humanists can likewise discover substantial areas in which sensory experience appears to be fairly uniform from person to person and can be communicated in language in ways that convey useful and predictive information.

(Stoves may be hot.)[22] Whether a historian can construct a reliable simulacrum of the past is a separate problem. The unknowability of reality *per se* is really not an issue. As a theoretical proposition, it is undeniable, but what matters is whether human perception of reality is reasonably constant from person to person—and it is.

The philosophy of history has long been stormy ground, and it will probably remain so. For the cultural historian what matters is whether credible arguments can still be made for the knowability of history. As a serious and systematic attempt to justify the premises that underlie the practice of history, I would recommend Murray G. Murphey's recent *Philosophical Foundations of Historical Knowledge*.[23] Murphey commences his investigation by admitting the problems:

History is generally agreed to be a type of factual knowledge. But since history deals with things and events that no longer exist, it has not been easy to fit history into the mould of classical empiricism. Idealists have therefore seen in history an example of factual knowledge for which empiricist theories could not account, and empiricists have responded by trying to force historical knowledge to fit the model of physics. Neither attempt has been particularly successful. More recently, some philosophers have endorsed essentially literary claims, arguing that history is a narrative art which is—somehow—nevertheless true. ... The field has thus become a battleground over which a variety of dubious armies have skirmished. In short, it is fair to say that the philosophy of history is currently something of a mess. (pp. ix–x)

Murphey's response to this chaotic and unsatisfactory state of affairs is to attempt to substantiate what he considers the 'essential' premises underlying the study of history. These he states as follows:

1. There is a real world of which true knowledge is possible.
2. There are other persons who have minds.
3. It is possible for one person to know what another person thinks.

[22] I am indebted here to Robert Scholes's useful concept of 'pragmatic presence': human beings may never be fully 'present' to one another, but pragmatic presence is sufficient to enable communication to work between them. See 'Deconstruction and Communication', *Critical Inquiry*, 14 (1988), 278–95, esp. 288–9.

[23] (Albany: State University of New York Press, 1994). Murphey has substantially modified the position he took in *Our Knowledge of the Historical Past* (Indianapolis: Bobbs-Merrill, 1973).

4. A language spoken by one person can be correctly interpreted by someone from outside that linguistic community, and a text in one language can be translated into an approximately equivalent text in another language of comparable resources.

5. There exists a past in which human beings lived and acted.

6. We can have some accurate knowledge of the past.

7. Members of one culture can understand members of other cultures, including members of antecedent states of their own culture.

8. Human action is causally explainable.

In nearly 350 pages Murphey attempts 'to investigate the grounds for accepting these eight premises' (p. xi). His prose is mercifully lucid, and anyone interested in philosophical justification of historicist practice will find much food for thought. Personally I find most of the arguments persuasive (but then I would). No doubt a dedicated phenomenologist would be inclined to bicker with every page. I refer to Murphey because he makes a powerful argument for accepting premises that justify and legitimize historical study. A wrongheaded philosopher he may be, but he is by no means a poor innocent literary positivist, wandering about at the wrong end of a century that has left his species behind. Many of his arguments are grounded in references to recent studies in perception and cognition—which I make no pretence of being able to judge, but which interestingly parallel Norman Holland's insistence that 'The New Cryptics' base their notions of language on outdated linguistics and the sort of hermetic logic by which Hegel proved that there can be no more than seven planets. Test Derrida and Saussure against 'the real world' and they *fail*.[24]

I believe that a historicist (in my sense of the term) does more or less need to subscribe to the premises Murphey lays down. I would make qualifications in items 1, 5, and 8. I am Kantian enough to squirm at 'true knowledge' of the 'real world'. To say 'replicable knowledge' that is 'verifiable in the sensory terms available to us' does not seem to me merely a technical quibble if we are going to be philosophical. On no. 5 I cannot accept the present tense: the past *existed*, but it no longer 'exists' except as

[24] Norman N. Holland, *The Critical I* (New York: Columbia University Press, 1992), 149, 166.

a variety of very incomplete 'traces' (as Marc Bloch terms them).[25] The distinction makes an enormous difference to the practice of history, and to the differentiation of history from physical science. On no. 8 I shall basically reserve my arguments for Chapter 3, but I will say here that I think Murphey is overstating his case. To say that human action has causes is one thing; to say that we can identify them is something else — especially when the action took place in the remote past. Many historians have seen causal explanation as the object of the whole enterprise, but for the purposes I am pursuing here, it is no more than a desirable possibility, and by no means always feasible. Such qualifications aside, Murphey's premisses do pretty well lay down the essential conditions for the possibility of historical study.

If historical inquiry is not rendered futile by our entrapment in sense data and our reliance on language, then what exactly do we ask of the historian in practice? What is to be accomplished? Virtually all theorists of history demand 'explanation' rather than merely chronology, but what constitutes satisfactory explanation? Historians have long suffered from a dangerous hankering to be as precise and rigorous as physicists, and more than half a century ago historical theory took a terrible wrong turn when Hempel published 'The Function of General Laws in History'.[26] Historians spent the next thirty years trying to get out from under the demands that follow from Hempel's attempt to impose on history the logical structure of explanation he found in physics. The gist of the 'covering law model' is simplicity itself: explanation can be achieved 'by subsuming what is to be explained under a general law'.[27]

[25] Marc Bloch, *The Historian's Craft* (orig. French 1949), trans. Peter Putnam (New York: Knopf, 1953), ch. 2, esp. pp. 54–5. Bloch speaks of 'résidus' and 'une connaissance par traces' (*Apologie pour l'histoire ou métier d'historien* (Paris: Librairie Armand Colin, 1949), 20–1. Putnam translates the latter as 'tracks', but the original French term seems at least as good.
[26] Carl G. Hempel, 'The Function of General Laws in History', *Journal of Philosophy*, 39 (1942), 35–48. For reconsiderations of this episode in the theory of history, see Raymond Martin, *The Past within Us: An Empirical Approach to Philosophy of History* (Princeton: Princeton University Press, 1989), and Arthur C. Danto, 'The Decline and Fall of the Analytical Philosophy of History', in Frank Ankersmit and Hans Kellner (eds.), *A New Philosophy of History* (Chicago: University of Chicago Press, 1995), 70–85.
[27] William Dray, *Laws and Explanation in History* (London: Oxford University Press, 1957), 1.

In the cold aftermath of repentance at leisure, this is manifestly a lunatic idea. If history has general 'laws', they are not of the sort to be found in classical physics. Physical science attempts to deal with something more or less available in the present; history attempts to explain a past now unrecapturable except via extrapolation from traces. The degree to which billiard balls can be used to explain human behaviour is evidently limited. More than a century ago Dilthey rightly distinguished between physical science (concerned with causal *explanation* of present phenomena) and history (concerned with *comprehension* of a vanished past). Proof in science presumes the possibility of repetition and predictability: results that cannot be replicated are suspect in the extreme. Whatever may constitute proof in history, neither experimental repetition nor predictability have any significant part in it.

I have read fairly extensively in mid-century historical theory: the classic studies, and some others I have found of interest, are listed in the bibliography. They make a cautionary tale. Highly intelligent and vastly erudite scholars labour heroically to get history out from under a burden it cannot bear, and to do so without actually admitting that it is sloppy, impressionistic, subjective, and hopelessly inferior to science. William Dray devotes a whole book to arguing that a covering law is not a '*necessary* condition of giving an explanation' (22). Getting from single instance to pertinent law is a major stretch. Dray argues, sensibly enough, that causal analysis need not invoke causal laws, but that historical understanding can be 'empathetic'. 'Rational explanation' can be carried out '*from the evidence*. To get inside Disraeli's shoes the historian does not simply ask himself: "What would I have done?" . . . he reads Disraeli's dispatches, his letters, his speeches . . . in the hope of appreciating the problem as Disraeli saw it' (129). This is a reasonable position, but it leaves the historian woefully short of proof. One-right-explanation has continued to exercise a powerful appeal. As late as 1972, writing in support of 'scientific study of history', Lee Benson quotes approvingly from a classic article on causation: 'verification involves not only confirmation but the exclusion or disproof of alternative hypotheses'.[28] The

---

[28] Lee Benson, *Toward the Scientific Study of History* (Philadelphia: J. B. Lippincott, 1972), 96–7. He is quoting Morris R. Cohen, 'Causation and its Application to History', *Journal of the History of Ideas*, 3 (1942), 12–29.

simpler parts of physics may work this way, but human behaviour does not, as Clifford Geertz wryly admits as late as
1983, when he says that social scientists have still only partially
'freed themselves . . . from dreams of social physics—covering
laws, unified science, operationalism, and all that'.[29]

Many historians have found the attractions of the scientific
model overwhelming. The tidy rigours of Popper's analysis of
the process of scientific discovery undeniably have an appeal. 'I
shall certainly admit a system as empirical or scientific only if it
is capable of being *tested* by experience. These considerations
suggest that not the *verifiability* but the *falsifiability* of a system
is to be taken as a criterion of demarcation.'[30] Beautiful in its
way, yes; pertinent, no. The first step towards valid historical
practice must be to abandon false pretentions. Writing in the
mid-1970s, Goldstein attempted to show 'that history is an
epistemically licit discipline which deserves to be taken seriously
on its own terms'—that is, not subject to the demands of empirical verification. He says flatly at the outset that

the initially unpromising epistemological conditions of history are entirely owing to the fact that the claims to knowledge with which it
emerges can never be subject to perceptual confirmation. . . . No activities of historical research are in any way perceptual, or sensory. So it is
really not to be expected that history could satisfy criteria of factuality,
reference, objectivity, and truth.[31]

By mid-century standards, these were dire admissions, but they
are both accurate and necessary. Goldstein says that 'the purpose of history is the constitution of past events' (p. xx), taking
the term 'constitution' from phenomenologists to get away from
that 'historical realism' which presumes that

the real past as it was when it was being lived is the touchstone against
which to test for truth or falsity the products of historical constitution.
It is my contention that historical realism is utterly false to the nature of
historical constitution. (pp. xxi–xxii)

[29] Clifford Geertz, 'Blurred Genres: The Reconfiguration of Social Thought', in
Local Knowledge: Further Essays in Interpretive Anthropology (New York: Basic
Books, 1983), ch. 1, p. 23.
[30] Karl R. Popper, *The Logic of Scientific Discovery* (London: Hutchinson, 1959),
40.
[31] Leon J. Goldstein, *Historical Knowing* (Austin: University of Texas Press,
1976), pp. xi, xiii.

Again, quite right: the past is gone and cannot be invoked directly to serve as a touchstone—this must be one of the most basic principles of historical study.

History is not science. Whatever forms of proof and verification the historian may be able to practise, double-blind clinical trials and the like will not enter into them. Sir Isaiah Berlin observed that 'in a developed natural science we consider it more rational to put our confidence in general propositions or laws than in specific phenomena . . . [but] this rule does not seem to operate successfully in history'.[32] So what is to be done? How dire a problem is the inaccessibility of the past? Oakeshott says rather forbiddingly that 'what is sundered from present experience is sundered from experience altogether. A fixed and finished past, divorced from and uninfluenced by the present, is a past divorced from evidence . . . and is consequently nothing and unknowable.' The conclusion he draws, however, is by no means despairing: '"what really happened"' must be 'replaced by "what the evidence obliges us to believe"'.[33] As with the unknowability of the *Ding an sich*, the inaccessibility of the actual past represents a significant limitation and barrier, but by no means a ruinous one. The historian and the archaeo-historicist are left to practise their craft on traces of a vanished past. They may do so with care and rigour, or quite otherwise. But the unscientific nature of the evidence and the enterprise is not a serious liability, if indeed it is any liability at all.

Practical Considerations: Contra Jauss

Historicist scholarship rests on the presumption that in some fashion we can bridge the gap between past and present. Can this actually be done, and if so, how? Few scholars now retain an innocent faith in the inherent value of laundry lists, but remarkably little theory has been written in this realm. When the subject of bridging the gap arises, what almost always follows is

[32] 'The Concept of Scientific History' (1960), repr. in *Concepts and Categories: Philosophical Essays by Isaiah Berlin*, ed. Henry Hardy (New York: Viking, 1979), 103–42 at 111.
[33] Michael Oakeshott, *Experience and its Modes* (1933; Cambridge: Cambridge University Press, 1966), 107–8.

reference to Hans Robert Jauss, and in particular to his essay published in English as 'Literary History as a Challenge to Literary Theory'.[34] Now almost thirty years old, it remains interesting and provocative, though it has been more cited than actually influential. Various criticisms of the piece have appeared in print, but I am not aware of any serious theoretical or practical critique of it. Jauss is in fact proposing a kind of enterprise radically different from mine, but the area of overlap is sufficient to make close scrutiny desirable.[35]

Attempting to assess the program Jauss proposes, one must start by recognizing that what he wants to do is re-establish a basis for writing sequential literary *history*. His starting point is something like the classic nineteenth-century 'national history' of literature. He abjures Gervinus's notion that the literary historian is to discover '"the one basic idea that permeates precisely that series of events that he took upon himself as his object"', and he is not prepared to subscribe to teleological principles in the fashion of Schiller (6). Marilyn Butler complains, however, that he would merely 'replace the old linear narrative of literary history with an endlessly proliferating series of case studies showing how the same work has been received by different readers over time'—and she has a point.[36] An assumption more deeply buried in the subtext until the very end of the essay is Jauss's belief that what the present-day historical critic most needs to discover is 'that properly *socially formative* function that belongs to literature' (45). This imposes a system of quasi-Marxist value judgement that no archaeo-historicist could willingly accept. Jauss never explains or justifies his commitment to linear history of literature in isolation: literary history seems to be A Good Thing, presumably because it will show us that literature is 'formative' as well as merely mimetic (11, 14). From my point of view, Jauss seems dangerously committed to the assumption that literature is developmental and

[34] First published in *New Literary History* in 1969. I quote from the version that serves as ch. 1 of *Toward an Aesthetic of Reception*, trans. Timothy Bahti, intro. by Paul de Man (Minneapolis: University of Minnesota Press, 1982).

[35] For a lucid assessment of Jauss's work through the early 1980s, see Robert C. Holub, *Reception Theory* (London: Methuen, 1984), esp. 53–82.

[36] Marilyn Butler, 'Against Tradition: The Case for a Particularized Historical Method', in Jerome J. McGann (ed.), *Historical Studies and Literary Criticism* (Madison: University of Wisconsin Press, 1985), 25–47 at 36.

that 'horizontal change' should yield what might be called 'progress'. But such objections do not really touch the central thrust of Jauss's essay, which argues that 'reception and influence' should have equal weight with the 'aesthetics of production and representation' in our study of literature. He puts forward seven 'theses' in response to 'the question as to how literary history can today be methodologically grounded and written anew' (20). The problem that most exercises him, however, is clearly 'the gap between literature and history, between aesthetic and historical knowledge' (45). We need therefore to scrutinize his theses.

Thesis 1 asks for *'the grounding of the traditional aesthetics of production and representation in an aesthetics of reception and influence'* (20; my emphasis throughout). We may certainly agree that 'A literary work is not an object that stands by itself and that offers the same view to each reader in each period' (21). Jauss emphasizes the 'dialogical character of the literary work'—another proposition that we may accept, though with the reservation that he is singularly vague here and elsewhere about the actual process of work–reader interaction. What really happens when a flesh-and-blood twentieth-century reader engages with a seventeenth-century text?[37] Much depends on the particulars of the reader, and on his or her notion of how 'reading' should be carried out.

Thesis 2 says that *'the analysis of the literary experience of the reader avoids the threatening pitfalls of psychology if it describes the reception and the influence of a work within the objectifiable system of expectations that arises for each work in the historical moment of its appearance, from a pre-understanding of the genre'* (22). An ill-disposed paraphrase might say 'we can avoid awkward reality by sticking with a purely hypothetical reception'. Nowhere in the essay does Jauss ever suggest that we might obtain direct testimony from real readers, living or dead. Yet surely if such testimony exists it should always be used, however contradictory it might be—or

---

[37] Jauss does furnish a detailed example of reading in ch. 5, 'The Poetic Text within the Change of Horizons of Reading: The Example of Baudelaire's "Spleen II"'. His principal concern, however, is with the difference between 'a first, aesthetically perceptual reading' and a 'second, retrospectively interpretive reading', against which he contrasts a 'third, historical reading' that starts with the horizon of expectations implicit in the poem and concludes with his own reading (139).

however hard on the scholar's pet theories. I find the notion of an '*objectifiable* system of expectations' seriously disturbing. Exactly what does this mean? Who supplies this system of expectations anyway? Do I get Dryden on the Ouija board? Do I check the library to see if one of Tillyard's ideological descendants can provide a pertinent handbook? Short of such expedients, I presume that the investigating scholar is responsible for *constructing* a relevant system of expectations. 'Objectifiable' sounds marvellously pure, rational, and scientific, but any constructed context is necessarily selective. One hopes it will be documented and the principles of selectivity carefully explained, but the whole process is far more personal, biased, and insanitary than Jauss is admitting.

Thesis 3 says that '*Reconstructed in this way, the horizon of expectations of a work allows one to determine its artistic character by the kind and the degree of its influence on a presupposed audience*' (25). I have all kinds of problems here. Jauss has said virtually nothing about *how* one reconstructs a horizon of expectations. Why would one not determine 'artistic character' from the text rather than from hypothetical influence on a 'presupposed' audience? Who 'presupposes' this audience, and how? Why not study impact on a real audience if evidence exists? The phrase 'allows one to determine' depersonalizes an operation that seems anything but impersonal. What this really says is that 'I' (or someone equally biased and fallible) can manufacture a historical-reception paradigm for a hypothetical audience and use it as a basis for analysing the 'work'. Well, so I can. But how is this different from all sorts of discredited ventures of half a century ago—for example, Balachandra Rajan's *Paradise Lost and the Seventeenth-Century Reader* (1947)?[38]

Thesis 4 says that '*The reconstruction of the horizon of expectations, in the face of which a work was created and received in the past, enables one on the other hand to pose questions that the text gave an answer to, and thereby to discover how the contemporary reader could have viewed and understood the work*' (28). My first question concerns 'the' horizon of expectations. Whose? The author's? That of an ideal reader implied by the text? That of actual contemporary readers of the time?

[38] Of its kind, not a bad book.

Throughout this essay Jauss emphasizes the importance of 'new-ness': 'The distance between the horizon of expectations and the work, between the familiarity of previous aesthetic experience and the "horizontal change" demanded by the reception of the new work' is crucial to his sense of quality. A work that demands no 'horizontal change' is merely popular entertainment—'culinary', as Jauss says (25), borrowing from Brecht. Here he is not only failing to maintain his own important distinction between the 'horizons of expectations' of the author and the audience, but he is procrustean in assuming a uniformitarian audience. Not all readers came to *Paradise Lost* with the same horizon of expectations, and an account of 'reception' that does not take chaotically differing expectations and responses into account can only be something like nonsense. As a number of critics have observed, this is one of Jauss's weakest points. 'The contemporary reader' is a multi-headed beast, and this ugly truth cannot be evaded except at the upper reaches of abstract theory.

Thesis 5 says that '*The theory of the aesthetics of reception ... demands that one insert the individual work into its "literary series" to recognize its historical position.*' Further, '*in the step from a history of the reception of works to an eventful history of literature, the latter manifests itself as a process in which the passive reception is on the part of authors*' (32). Both propositions are reasonable: we study each work in relation to its predecessors and in relation to the successors influenced by it. Contemplating the resultant chains of works, we are rightly conscious of their influence (or lack of it) on the writers of new works.

Thesis 6 says that '*achievements made in linguistics*' and '*methodological interrelation of diachronic and synchronic analysis*' are '*the occasion for overcoming the diachronic perspective*' (36). Neither the linguistic achievements nor the 'methodological interrelation' is clearly specified. 'Overcoming the diachronic perspective' seems to mean that the gap between the modern scholar's horizon of expectations and that of his or her subject matter (in the seventeenth century, let us say) has somehow been bridged, eliminated, or otherwise done away with. But what does this really *mean*? Has the modern scholar somehow entered into the seventeenth-century outlook? Has that outlook by some means been imported into a twentieth-century intellectual laboratory? If the twentieth-century scholar has somehow teleported him or herself into the seventeenth-century horizon of expectations, are there not all sorts of twentieth-century ideas, outlooks, and prejudices imported too? And is this not a serious contamination of the subject matter? An early historicist like Eichhorn can tell the student to 'forget ... the century in which you are living and the knowledge which it gives you', but surely Jauss would regard this as bad advice, and impracticable to boot.[39]

Thesis 7 states that *'the task of literary history is thus only completed when literary production is not only represented synchronically and diachronically in the succession of its systems, but also seen as "special history" in its own unique relationship to "general history"'* (39). Leaving aside as (perhaps) mere technical details any difficulties in the synchronic and diachronic representation of literary production, I would question here both 'special history' and 'general history'. Early in the essay, Jauss said bluntly (and to my mind rightly) that 'the history of literature, like that of art, can no longer maintain the "appearance of its independence" when one has realized that its production presupposes the material production and social praxis of human beings' (10). In thesis 7 he seems to be assuming that attention to 'active life-process' in the study of reception justifies writing an 'independent' history of literature. Treating such a separate history (if it can be validly written) in relation to 'general history' does not seem unreasonable, but who provides said general history? If we are having the devil's own time writing (let alone justifying) mere history of literature, who are the geniuses providing the comforting bedrock of general history to which we can relate our puny but improving literary efforts? If I write a 'special history' of eighteenth-century British fiction, to whom do I apply for the concomitant general history?

Standing back and contemplating Jauss's project, I find it of little use in establishing practical procedures for a historicist scholar. His devotion to a very coherent (I would say over-tidy) kind of linear narrative history need not be much of an issue,

[39] J. G. Eichhorn, *Einleitung ins Alte Testament* (2nd edn., 1787), ii. 345, trans. Jerome J. McGann, in *Social Values and Poetic Acts: The Historical Judgment of Literary Work* (Cambridge, Mass.: Harvard University Press, 1988), 14.

but on other grounds he is wide open to challenge. René Wellek expressed doubt as to 'how Jauss can bridge the gap between the implied audience in a work and the actual reactions of an audience in history'.[40] The answer is that Jauss ignores the whole problem of real audiences, even when hard evidence about their reactions can readily be found. He seems to have devoted no thought at all to the actual composition of the audience. David Perkins rightly complains that 'Jauss pays far too little attention to . . . race, gender, class',[41] but his failure to confront other kinds of human heterogeneity is even more damaging.

The phrase 'horizon of expectations' has come into common usage, and it is helpful in reminding us of the drastic differences between (say) seventeenth- and twentieth-century readers. Jauss is almost totally silent about the practicalities of how we (re)-construct the earlier outlook—or how we conceive and define our own. If anything, he is worse on what happens when the two are brought together in a 'mediated' collision that is some-how to produce enlightenment. In what I consider the key passage in the essay, Jauss quotes Hans-Georg Gadamer:

In a continuation of Collingwood's thesis that 'one can understand a text only when one has understood the question to which it is an answer', Gadamer demonstrates that the reconstructed question can no longer stand within its original horizon because this historical horizon is always already enveloped within the horizon of the present: 'Under-standing is always the process of the fusion of these horizons that we suppose to exist by themselves.' (29–30)

Like Coleridge's 'dissolves, diffuses, and dissipates, in order to recreate', this sounds wonderful, but what precisely does it *mean*? What is 'fusion'? How does it work? 'Fusion' seems to imply an overmapping, a conjoining of some sort—but does this not seriously distort the 'horizon' we have laboriously con-structed for the earlier period? Granting that the historian can-not wholly escape his or her horizon, should not some effort be made to minimize the degree to which it coerces or distorts what it is fusing with? On all such matters Jauss is silent.

---

[40] *The Attack on Literature and Other Essays* (Chapel Hill: University of North Carolina Press, 1982), 49–50.
[41] *Is Literary History Possible?*, 27.

If we turn for help to Paul de Man's introduction to *Toward an Aesthetic of Reception*, we will not discover a great deal. De Man says that 'a dialectic of understanding . . . is built within the very process of literary history' (p. xii). He likens this to the dialogue between an analyst and a patient in psychoanalysis, and then tells us that 'the two "horizons", that of individual experience and that of methodical understanding, can engage each other and they will undergo modifications in the process, though none of the experiences may ever become fully explicit'. As in Jauss himself, human agency seems largely to have evaporated at a critical point. In what sense do the two horizons 'engage each other'? Engage how? To what end? Surely the modern historian or critic, having first reconstructed or borrowed ready-made the earlier horizon, then attempts to enter into it, to bring it to life imaginatively, to adopt as far as possible the outlook of the earlier period? The historian's own horizon may be employed for purposes of contrast or interrogation, and it certainly helps drive the investigation being performed and supplies questions that are asked.

In any case, Jauss stops dead just at the point at which the historian is most eager to know what occurs next. 'Understanding' is said to be the result of 'fusion', but what kind of understanding of what object? We mediate between the two horizons; they fuse; and what happens then? Presumably some sort of comprehension of the earlier outlook has been achieved, but how is it to be used? A sceptic might be excused for concluding that Jauss has given us a highfalutin' version of a commonplace: the historian, inevitably contaminated by his or her own period, attempts to reconstruct an earlier mindset and enter into it imaginatively.[42]

The Objects of Archaeo-Historicism

History, Collingwood tells us, is essentially the re-enactment of past thought. The historian conducts 'a kind of research or inquiry' that may permit the investigator 'to answer questions

---

[42] For a friendly but sceptical critique of Jauss's later work, see David H. Richter, *The Progress of Romance: Literary Historiography and the Gothic Novel* (Columbus: Ohio State University Press, 1996), ch. 2.

about human actions done in the past'.[43] How do we get from the rarefied heights of philosophical abstraction to the concerns of the 'working historian' and the student of literature? The best procedure is to sketch (and supply examples of) the various sorts of scholarship that a cultural archaeo-historicist can attempt. At this point I shall pass very lightly over both procedures and methodological problems, which will be the subject of Chapters 2 and 3.

As I conceive the enterprise, Archaeo-Historicism comprises *both* the reconstruction of context and the interpretation of texts within the context thus assembled. The object, however, is not to pretend that we are (say) seventeenth-century readers, which would be both fallacious and silly. I must disavow LaCapra's dismissive characterization of 'the sort of historicism that is still prevalent among professional historians, one [that] attempts to understand the past in its own terms and for its own sake, as if the past simply had its own terms and was there for its own sake'.[44] 'In its own terms' (insofar as possible) yes; 'for its own sake' absolutely not. One reads the culture of the past with attention to its original integrity for much the reason that one troubles to understand fellow human beings in the present: not to do so leaves you trapped in your own mindset. Reading the past 'for its own sake' is antiquarianism.

A serious historicist enterprise is much more than an inquiry into origins, though it is certainly that.[45] What then are the things an archaeo-historicist might attempt to do? Obvious possibilities include philological groundwork, editing texts, biographical investigation of writers, collection of documents pertaining to the creation or reception of texts, and intellectual history of the sort that attempts to reconstruct the outlook of particular readers or groups of hypothesized readers. Equally valid is a 'reading', either of a text considered in the light of

[43] R. G. Collingwood, *The Idea of History* (rev. edn.), ed. Jan van der Dussen (Oxford: Clarendon Press, 1993), 9. For elucidation of Collingwood's concept of history, see William H. Dray, *History as Re-enactment: R. G. Collingwood's Idea of History* (Oxford: Clarendon Press, 1995).

[44] Dominick LaCapra, *Soundings in Critical Theory* (Ithaca: Cornell University Press, 1989), 195.

[45] 'Historicism is a general term we now apply to those nineteenth-century genetic methods whose subject was ancient texts and whose avowed purpose was to interpret them on their own terms.' McGann, *Social Values*, 14.

context or of a text for which the particulars of reception can be documented. Many of the things that may be usefully done do not directly involve reading texts. I do, however, want to insist that the ultimate point of the venture, at least in the realm of literature, has to do with making sense of texts—though one may then extend this understanding in building a broader sense of cultural context at a particular point in the past.

In all literary interpretation there is an inescapable tension between text and context. We have the words of the text (or we hope we do). Contexts are far cloudier—constructs, not givens, and their claims tend to overlap and conflict. (Derrida is too extreme but not altogether foolish when he denies the possibility of determining what context is relevant.)[46] Context exerts a powerful effect on the mindset of the author and so contributes to the shaping of the text. Context helps shape the expectations and responses of the original audience and powerfully affects their decoding of the text. The same holds true for each generation of later readers, ourselves included. Insofar as the present-day interpreter is concerned with 'significance' as well as verbal 'meaning' (in E. D. Hirsch's sense), context becomes even more important.[47] Meaning inheres in the text, but significance resides in the reader. A practical difficulty is that one cannot pay complete attention to both text and context at the same time. One can go back and forth between them, but one cannot carry out both textual and contextual enterprises simultaneously.

All this is very abstract. The importance of context is evident in an example. Suppose that *Absalom and Achitophel* were written and published in 1675. Of course this is ridiculous: without the Exclusion Crisis Dryden would not have written his elaborate (but technically indirect) allegory of Charles II, Monmouth, and Shaftesbury. But this is my point: what a recension of this biblical story would have 'meant' in 1675 is utterly different from what it 'meant' in 1681. Read today it becomes, inevitably, yet a different poem, necessarily deciphered with the aid of footnotes and historical reconstruction. Even a ruthlessly doctrinaire New Critic (if such a being still exists) would grant the need for a bit of historical orientation in approaching

[46] Jacques Derrida, 'Signature Event Context', *Glyph*, 1 (1977), 172–97 at 174.
[47] E. D. Hirsch, Jr., *The Aims of Interpretation* (Chicago: University of Chicago Press, 1976), esp. 1–13.

Dryden's poem, but his or her interpretation would centre on the structure and rhetoric of the poem. A historicist reader, committed to interpretation in the light of original contexts, might turn to Dryden's poetic or political background, to politics, to contemporary Whig and Tory propaganda, or to the angry counter-attacks that Dryden provoked. A non-historical reader might inquire what the poem now means 'to us' (not much, for most readers), or might bring present-day critical tools to bear. Specifically sited though the poem is in 1681, it seems wide open to any deconstructionist sufficiently attuned to historical circumstances to pay attention to the enormous strains and problems that Dryden so tidily papers over. Dryden himself, I suspect, would have held that *Absalom and Achitophel* was timeless because the same kinds of politics and politicians would recur in every age—not a point of view common among twentieth-century readers.

Two points need to be made about historicist method here. First, the object is 'truth'. Even to mention 'truth' is probably to provoke derision: every good poststructuralist knows that signifiers being what they are, there can be no truth, and we would have no way of apprehending it if there were any. Perhaps I should withdraw so flagrant a red flag, lest I be unnecessarily gored by hermeticist bulls. I am trying merely to make a practical point. What is at issue is the necessity of documentation and verifiability. If we are reconstructing a context, we must supply the best hard evidence we can find. And we must footnote it with sufficient exactitude that a successor can review what we have done, confident that the same evidence is in play. The successor may confirm our conclusion, or dispute it on logical or interpretive grounds, or add new evidence, or challenge the inclusion of old evidence—but the question is very simply whether the evidence supports the conclusion.

At a bedrock level, Archaeo-Historicism lends itself to right/ wrong conclusions: *Paradise Lost* was or was not first published in 1667. Very quickly, however, one gets beyond fact, and into constructed contexts and logical inferences. Even in centuries where evidence is relatively ample, speculation becomes inevitable—always subject to revision in the light of new evidence or improved interpretation. The point is not to restrict oneself to statements that can be footnoted with a reference to a document in the Public Record Office. Rather, the archaeo-historicist is committed to the fullest possible documentation and rigorous rules for the handling of evidence. There is a longstanding concept in British and American criminal law: to convict, a jury must be convinced that the case has been proved beyond 'reasonable doubt'. Metaphysical certitude is not required. In civil cases, establishing a balance of probability on one side or the other is regarded as sufficient. A scholar may or may not be able to arrive even at this sort of verdict. Our evidence often fails to support more than tentative or provisional conclusions. If, however, the commitment of the scholar is not to the discovery of what is both *true* and *documentable*, then there is no point at all to the enterprise.[48]

The second point about method is that the approach has to be 'bottom up' rather than 'top down'. By this I mean that while one starts with a method—Archaeo-Historicism—one approaches a subject with no prior commitment to any theory by which the primary material is to be organized or explained.[49] Good things can be done by cultural materialists or Freudians or Lacanians or Jungians or feminists or deconstructionists (or interpreters of whatever stripe)—but in each instance a pre-judgement has been made as how best to analyse the subject matter. In short, a conceptual structure has been imported and will serve as the scholar's 'machine'. A genuine archaeo-historicist is debarred from any such procedure. He or she aims *to reconstruct the viewpoint of the time*, and must attempt to do so in whatever terms the original inhabitants thought and worked.

I am not trying to execute a sneaky return to the comforts of positivism here. I agree with Bruce McConachie's insistence that 'The historian . . . never starts with the facts. He . . . starts with his values, which must guide him in the framing of questions significant for him.'[50] The archaeo-historicist comes to his or her chosen territory with the advantages and disadvantages of a present-day horizon of expectations. Acute awareness of *our*

---

[48] Historians owe a substantial (often unacknowledged) debt to legal history for their concepts of proof in assessing evidence.

[49] For further clarification of the principles at issue here, see 'Method versus Theory' at the start of Ch. 4.

[50] 'Towards a Postpositivist Theatre History', *Theatre Journal*, 37 (1985), 465–86 at 468.

interests and value judgements is indeed vital, for much of what is interesting in the results of historical study lies in 'them versus us' differences. But as we set about reconstructing (say) a theatrical context for the 1590s, we need to look at as wide a range as possible of the artefacts of the time. Our aim, after all, is to comprehend the outlook of the full spectrum of Shakespeare's contemporaries. This is hard at best, but cannot be well done if we are simply imposing our own terms and interests. We cannot pretend to 'objectivity', but we need make no such claim. We are entering someone else's territory: we can do so as jackbooted imperialists or as respectful tourists, not uncritical but attempting to cultivate the negative capability that will allow us to enter sympathetically into outlooks remote from our own.

The historicist enterprise as I conceive it encompasses at least four broadly different kinds of scholarly/critical activity. Directly or indirectly, all four stem from a desire to illuminate text from context. The archaeo-historicist may (1) collect primary materials; (2) put them together and interpret them; (3) build larger contexts from texts themselves; or (4) attempt to read particular texts in the light of a reconstructed context. Let us consider some particulars.

The Collection of New Facts and Primary Materials

Archaeo-historicists aim to discover new documents and to bring neglected ones to attention. If interpreters are to do more than quibble over well-known texts and problems, then we must avoid playing our games with old counters. Airy theorists sometimes indulge in foolish slurs on 'journeyman work in archives', but we need facts to keep our field alive and changing, and those facts mostly come out of archives. Few members of literature departments have any training in archival research—a result of longstanding emphasis first on 'reading' and then on 'theory'. Let anyone who thinks archival research is easy visit the Public Record Office in London and see what he or she can come up with. Finding important new evidence about any particular subject can be difficult, or just plain impossible. Wildcat oil drillers must budget for a fair number of dry holes, and so must even a highly experienced historical scholar. How many people have prospected for Shakespeare documents, and how many have ever been discovered? Short of a miracle, we probably have most of what is to be found in that field. Flashy discoveries are few and far between. Someone may yet turn up a box of Dryden letters, or a juicy diary, but the chances are against it. Yet the possibility of significant advance through contextual research is evident if we compare James Winn's *John Dryden and his World* (1987) with its predecessor, Charles Ward's *The Life of John Dryden* (1961). Winn made few discoveries, but he was able to shed a great deal of light on both Dryden and his texts by broadening his focus to the world in which Dryden lived. This emphasis on the circumstances in which Dryden worked (personal, political, economic, literary, intellectual) adds enormously to our comprehension of what he wrote, why he wrote it, and how various groups of readers in his time would have read it.

Very occasionally, huge caches of unknown material come to light. The discovery of the Boswell papers at Auchinleck, or Leslie Hotson's identification of more than one hundred theatre-related Chancery lawsuits from the period 1660–1710 are famous examples.[51] Such windfalls are the exception: most facts get accumulated scrap by scrap, and only when one is able to put the disparate bits together does much that is exciting or useful emerge. Facts come in many forms. One might discover new evidence about the size of Handel's opera orchestra, or a new ground plan of a theatre, or a document outlining a grammar school curriculum in the 1720s, or a letter to a publisher, or a new manuscript of a poem, or a neglected political pamphlet. Each scrappy bit may (or may not) eventually contribute usefully to an enormous and forever incomplete jigsaw puzzle. All bits are not created equal: there are important discoveries and meaningless ones. Many critics suppose that major discoveries are a thing of the past, but this is not true. Like compound interest, discoveries build upon themselves. Nothing much seems to happen in most years, but at the end of any decade we somehow know a lot more than we did at the beginning. And occasionally a Rose theatre site comes to light, discrediting old verities and forcing us to rethink our theories of Renaissance theatre architecture from new evidence.

[51] David Buchanan, *The Treasure of Auchinleck: The Story of the Boswell Papers* (New York: McGraw-Hill, 1974); Leslie Hotson, *The Commonwealth and Restoration Stage* (Cambridge, Mass.: Harvard University Press, 1928).

At a very basic level historical scholarship provides texts and access. If we are studying Milton's intellectual context, we need (for a start) to have a solid idea what was written and published in the 1640s and 1650s. The 'Wing' *Short-Title Catalogue* tells us what was published and where to find it—and the electronic search capacities now available in the CD-ROM version spectacularly increase our access to the data. For extensive commentary on life, literature, society, and politics in the 1770s and 1780s, one can hardly do better than start with the massive *Yale Edition of Horace Walpole's Correspondence* (48 vols., 1937–83) and *The Papers of Benjamin Franklin* (32 vols. in print since 1959, with another ten or so to go), both done out of Yale over a period of decades. Such lists and editions do not happen by accident. Compiling such monuments is monstrously laborious, but they change the nature of what is *possible* in scholarship in a way that no interpretation ever can.

The Rose theatre site notwithstanding, discoveries have long been difficult in the Renaissance and earlier periods. For the eighteenth century and later, however, we live in a time of extraordinary discoveries. The ESTC alone opens whole new worlds to any critic eager to get beyond the traditional Great Works canon—and does not even require knowledge of elementary palaeography. Clever readings come and go (most vanishing without trace in short order), but a new *fact* adds to a permanent store of knowledge. Here is a tiny example. What did playwrights earn from their plays in the later eighteenth century? In particular, what did they earn from publication? A lawsuit by Arthur Murphy against his publisher specifies copyright prices for seven plays and two revisions—and proves that when Murphy tried publishing at his own risk he made £8 rather than his usual £150.[52] Trivial in itself—but perhaps a useful building block for a later scholar. We should also remember that difficult as discoveries in the remote past now seem, the past is constantly growing. The 'recent present' quickly becomes the past, and its surviving traces become archival matter. The correspondence and financial records that a publisher discards

[52] The source is PRO E 112/1649, no. 2392 (an equity lawsuit in the Court of Exchequer). See Judith Milhous and Robert D. Hume, 'Profits from Play Publication: The Evidence of *Murphy v. Vaillant*', *Studies in Bibliography*, 51 (1998), 213–29.

today to save filing space might well (if somehow preserved) come to be regarded as a treasure trove in the not-so-distant future.

The Construction of Contexts from Historical Evidence

A 'fact' is not much use unless it answers a question. We have long known that Colley Cibber was paid £105 for copyright of *The Provok'd Husband* (1728), but this does not help us much unless we have a sense of what the sum was worth and what other plays fetched from publishers. We take our orchestra list or our theatre ground plan or our grammar school curriculum and compare it with others. We ask what kinds of classical allusions a graduate of the grammar school could understand —and see what this implies about reading *Tom Jones*.[53] The archaeo-historicist attempts to add new facts to old, and to see what then changes in the total picture. The nitty-gritty scraps must somehow be synthesized into a coherent picture. This is a high-risk enterprise, and the dangers will be considered in detail in Chapter 3. There is, however, no doubt about the aim: one of the historicist's principal objects is to build detailed and reliable reconstructions of context.

What kind of education did authors and readers have? What was widely read? What were the economics of publishing? What were the effects of newspapers on the reading public? Of a magazine such as *The Gentleman's Journal* in the 1690s? What were the religious, political, social, sexual, and marital assumptions of various parts of the public? What was money worth? What did one learn from a university education? What did women of various classes learn from the education available to them? How did changeable scenery work? Important books might be written on any of these topics or many more. A synthesis of historical evidence may be as narrow and technical as Edward A. Langhans's *Restoration Promptbooks* (1981). Alternatively, a synthesis may be as panoramic as Pat Rogers's *Grub Street: Studies in a Subculture* (1972), which does a fine job of creating a sense of one of the worlds against which we need to consider Pope and Swift.

[53] See Nancy A. Mace, *Henry Fielding's Novels and the Classical Tradition* (Newark: University of Delaware Press, 1996).

Two recent books that I greatly admire may serve to convey some sense of contextual possibilities. Dryden's *Absalom and Achitophel* has been written about many times in many ways, but usually from rather limited perspectives. Phillip Harth's *Pen for a Party: Dryden's Tory Propaganda in its Contexts* (1993) recontextualizes the poem, based on research that was very much bottom-up: Harth started by attempting to read *everything* printed in England in 1681 that has survived. Obviously a large part of this reading never appears directly in his book. Another scholar might quibble over the privileging of one text or the exclusion of another—but Harth read the lot and established a sense of political, social, literary, and religious milieu thoroughly grounded in primary documents. Documentation is no substitute for intelligent analysis, and time will be the test of Harth's conclusions. For my money, however, he offers a persuasive account of what Dryden did and why he did it. The context is richly substantiated in primary sources; it does not appear to reflect overtidy simplifications; and it 'makes sense'. Another archaeo-historical venture that has excited my admiration is David Foxon's *Alexander Pope and the Early Eighteenth-Century Book Trade* (1991). 'Print culture' is a particularly promising realm for historicist investigation: New Critics and theorists alike have shunned so grubby and bibliographic a business, sordidly concerned with mere money and the physical. But most authors do have to sell books, and some of them are greatly concerned with the physical appearance and layout of their work. Print technology, sales, distribution, piracy, and copyright law exert enormous influence on what gets published and whether it gets read. Pope—for example— did not write in an ivory tower, and even a good modern biography such as Maynard Mack's cannot do full justice to the impact of the trade on his work. Literature is more than aesthetics.

Making Contexts from Literary Texts

Historical scholars construct 'background' contexts. They also build 'generic' contexts. When someone attempts to explain changes in generic norms we are over a boundary into 'literary history'. These are three quite separate enterprises and should not be confused.

One potentially useful context is the sum of texts. The great dangers here lie in selectivity and in imagining that we can 'explain' change. To write 'the history of the novel to 1800', we can take some of the texts we choose to define as novels and string them together in what is presumed to be a meaningful way. The dangers of circularity are obvious: we are liable to construct a pattern out of a handful of favourite examples, thereby distorting our understanding of some works while entirely excluding others from consideration. I am extremely sceptical about 'telling the story' varieties of 'literary history', a problem to which we shall return. Part of the disrepute under which old historicism has laboured in recent years stems from its association with simpleminded narrative history. If we disavow that kind of enterprise—literary history in the style of Albert C. Baugh's *A Literary History of England* (1948)—what remains to us in the realm of textual context?

One possibility is to try to develop a complex picture of a genre over a relatively manageable time span. Jerry C. Beasley's *Novels of the 1740s* (1982) is a sound example. Another approach is to extrapolate 'intellectual climate' from an assortment of texts. John Sitter's *Literary Loneliness in Mid-Eighteenth-Century England* (1982) illustrates such a venture. Either may be done well or badly, but both enterprises are methodologically defensible. Two caveats should be entered. First, the broader the subject or the more selective the treatment, the higher the risk of falsification. Secondly, one must be ever attentive to contradictions and disagreements. No useful theory of the novel is going to resolve the formal differences between Fielding and Sterne. No meaningful sense of 'climate' is going to get away from the fact that the 1660s were a time of hope for Dryden, of alienation and discontent for Milton. All *Age of X* studies are basically procrustean nonsense, whether *X* is 'neoclassicism' or 'reason' or 'romanticism' or 'Samuel Johnson', and no matter how learned the author. The allegedly 'defining characteristic' may be widely present, may be significant—but such a definition can only be a severe distortion and oversimplification. Homogeneous context (one might unkindly say homogenized context) is bad context.

A good reason for moving from text to context (not merely vice versa) is that texts affect context as well as emerging from it. Each new text becomes part of its context, *and changes it.* Swift was doubtless strange, baffling, and offensive to part of his audience; *A Tale of a Tub* must have blown some minds in 1704. But its publication altered the ambience of the world in which he wrote. Historicists are often accused of being uniformitarian. Applying context to text, one tends to look for a spectrum of 'normal' assumptions and potential responses — that is, to be conscious of the assumptions common to many readers. Going the other way, from text to context, helps sensitize us to the original, the abnormal, and the subversive: we become aware of the potential power of individual challenge to cultural norms. Historicists need not be levellers: who is better situated to recognize genuine originality?

The Application of Context to Text

The *textual interpretive* part of Archaeo-Historicism occurs when we attempt to alter our understanding of a particular text by reading it in the light of context. Such an enterprise presupposes a close reading of the text itself. Beyond that, we are rapidly enmeshed in methodological difficulties. Exactly how does 'reading' work, and reading of old texts in particular? We can footnote topical allusions and sketch 'background', but *context does not determine meaning.* Context can merely help us judge possible meanings for various interpreters. Michael McKeon is quite right when he insists that to situate a work 'against a background' is not to 'historicize' it.[54] Contexts are constructed, and one can seldom prove the relevance of context to text, let alone demonstrate that the work is an expression of context. Consider two very different examples. Dryden's *Cleomenes* (1692) concerns the pathetic death of an exiled king. The likelihood that Dryden was inviting application to the exiled James II seems overwhelming: performance was held up by Queen Mary, and some passages may have been dropped when it was given. Why was the play allowed at all? Did the censor miss the point? Did he think the play toothless? Or did the

[54] 'Historicizing *Absalom and Achitophel*', in Felicity Nussbaum and Laura Brown (eds.), *The New Eighteenth Century* (London: Methuen, 1987), 37.

government calculate that only Jacobites would respond to the play this way and that banning it would merely create a furore that would sell a lot of printed copies? Thomas Pynchon's *Gravity's Rainbow* is a different case. A historical novel centred in the 1940s, it expresses 1960s sensibility and was published in 1973. Ideologically, the book is much more about the sixties than the forties, and a reading in the 1990s will almost inevitably be influenced by the reader's view of what now seems a quaint and bygone outlook. The novel fairly reeks of the Vietnam era, and yet how does one prove that this is what makes the book what it is?

To bring text and context together we must ask questions— and they are *our* questions. For example:

Why did the author write what he or she wrote?
What audience(s) did the author address?
What are the interpretive implications of the work's allusions and implied intellectual context?
What reactions did the work generate around the time of its original publication or performance?
How would various members of the original audience (as best we can reconstruct it) have understood the work or reacted to it?
What do we learn from parallels to and differences from related works at about the same time?

If we happen to possess extensive information about reception it may be helpful, though of course it neither says what the text means nor dictates a reading for any particular reader or group of readers, let alone all readers of the time.

Evidence is often sparse or non-existent. My students ask me, 'What did Shakespeare's audience think about *King Lear*?' I would like to say, for a start, that they would naturally have found the division of the kingdom dangerous and ill-advised. Then again, neither Kent nor Gloucester (nor anyone else) criticizes Lear at the time for the division. Did Shakespeare assume that criticism was supererogatory? Assume that the audience would treat the politics of the situation as irrelevant to a kind of historical fairy tale? We are in very different circumstances if we ask how Richardson's readers responded to *Clarissa*, since we possess a plenitude of evidence. Those responses are, to be sure, often discordant, internally contradictory, and arguably based on distorted understandings of what Richardson appears to have been trying to say. In this case we possess three major sets of his revisions, made in frustration as the author realized how little control he had been able to exercise over his readers' responses.

Contextual interpretation comes in many varieties: biographical, generic, reception history, broader intellectual history. Exemplars that have impressed me include Maynard Mack's *The Garden and the City: Retirement and Politics in the Later Poetry of Pope 1731-1743* (1969—biographical); Fredson Bowers's classic *Elizabethan Revenge Tragedy* (1940—generic); Ralph Cohen's *The Art of Discrimination: Thomson's 'The Seasons' and the Language of Criticism* (1964—reception history), and Ruth Smith's *Handel's Oratorios and Eighteenth-Century Thought* (1995—intellectual history). These studies vary considerably in the degree to which they 'read text': the borderline between supplying context and applying context is not precise. In each instance, however, one's grasp of major texts changes substantially in the light of the context that is constructed. In practice one rarely meets a 'pure' form of any of these four historicist enterprises, so I turn at this juncture to a particular case to illustrate what a historicist might do with it.

The Example of The Country-Wife

The many contradictory interpretations of Wycherley's play of 1675 are an embarrassment in the field of late seventeenth-century drama. Much of the difficulty lies in the plethora of simplistic interpreters who insist upon finding a single 'correct' meaning in a text that is manifestly susceptible to a wide range of meanings in performance and is not reducible to a tidy formula such as 'the idea of friendship' or 'the exposure of folly'.[55] Depending on directorial choices, the play can easily be staged as a romp, as a celebration of libertinism, or as a satire on libertinism, all within the verbal limits of the original text.

[55] See Judith Milhous and Robert D. Hume, *Producible Interpretation: Eight English Plays, 1675-1707* (Carbondale: Southern Illinois University Press, 1985), ch. 3.

Add the complications posed by spectators of varied sensibility, and you get no very fixed meaning for Wycherley's play. What can a historicist try to do with this text?

We can look at reputed sources—bits of Molière (which concern only small parts of the text). At Wycherley's biography (personal facts are sparse). At pamphlets on sex and marriage from the 1670s (mostly very moralistic). At conduct books (exceedingly moralistic). At contemporary reactions (few are recorded, but Wycherley says the Maids of Honour had a fit and boycotted his work). At Wycherley's earlier plays (which prove radically different). At his next and last play, *The Plain-Dealer* (itself hotly disputed). We can usefully survey a flock of other sex-comedies of the mid-1670s, and we can look as well at some of the more romantic comedies from the same years. Wycherley wrote, we will soon discover, as one who had leapt upon the bandwagon of sex-comedy, but that was by no means the dominant form in 1675. We should certainly look at the original cast: Charles Hart played heroes, and his taking Horner strongly implies a positive view of a libertine hero in the first production. Overall, contextual evidence is sparse. We lack letter and diary commentary, and there were no newspaper or pamphlet reactions. We may lament this the less in that the possession of such evidence in other cases—for example, concerning Steele's *The Conscious Lovers* in 1722—gives us a great deal more to play with, but solves few interpretive problems.

We know that *The Country-Wife* was popular (and remained so for several decades); we have Wycherley's word (in *The Plain-Dealer*) that there was moral outcry in 1675. What did 'the seventeenth-century reader' (or playgoer) think of the play? We arrive here at a methodological crux. The fatuity of this question is perhaps more obvious if we ask what the 'twentieth-century reader' thinks of it. What reader would that be? Messrs Robert D. Hume and Aubrey Williams, if taken jointly, constitute a rather incompatible reader, and they are by no means unique in their disagreements. Rose Zimbardo thinks the play is a satire on lust, and Anthony Kaufman finds Horner psychologically sick. But C. D. Cecil sees the play as a comic celebration of a libertine ideal, and Virginia Ogden Birdsall regards Horner as a positive model, a representation of 'life force triumphant' and 'élan vital' who is 'a wholly positive and creative

comic hero . . . squarely on the side of health, of freedom, and
. . . of honesty'.[56] The fraternity boys in my classes love the play
(thinking that Wycherley has depicted male-chauvinist heaven);
most of the women in my classes now find it offensively im-
moral, or sexist, or both.

The 'twentieth-century reader' turns out to be alarmingly
schizophrenic. Have we any good reason to suppose that the
seventeenth-century reader or playgoer was less so? Among
those who might have attended the first run are the famously
libertine Earl of Rochester; the stuffy, moral John Evelyn;
the raunchy and moralistic Samuel Pepys; and the libertine
playwright-cum-feminist Aphra Behn. I would be surprised to
learn from newly discovered diaries that they all emerged from
the theatre with precisely the same reactions.

Concerning historicist approaches to *The Country-Wife* I
would offer several observations. Finding new facts about the
play and its reception is at least difficult and very likely impossible. We could easily construct various relevant contexts—
author, contemporary plays, pamphlets, hypothetical varieties
of spectators, original cast—most of which have been little
used by interpreters. No full-dress attempt at a historicist interpretation of the play has ever been made. Various contexts have
been appealed to, but only in passing. A systematic contextual
reading would *not*, of course, yield a single interpretation. On
the contrary, awareness of the varied audience should produce a
complex sense of contradictory meanings.

Attempts to relate text to context have almost always falsified
the context by presuming that Wycherley's play was more
typical than it really was. Extrapolation from this text and a
few others has produced a myth of a libertine comedy—variously condemned (Macaulay), excused as a satire (Zimbardo),
and regarded as a moral model for our time (Birdsall). A less
selective treatment of 1670s plays demonstrates that the sex-
comedies of Wycherley and Etherege were quite atypical and
that the vogue for such plays was relatively brief.[57] This

---

[56] *Wild Civility: The English Comic Spirit on the Restoration Stage* (Bloomington:
Indiana University Press, 1970), 136, 156.

[57] I have demonstrated this point at length in '"The Change in Comedy": Cynical
versus Exemplary Comedy on the London Stage, 1675–1693', *Essays in Theatre*, 1
(1983), 101–18.

becomes a fact of some importance when we come to ask what it implies about interpretation of the play in its original context. Wycherley's play was probably less an expression of a dominant court libertine ethos than it was an attempt to shock *les bourgeoises*.

I offer the example of *The Country-Wife* in order to stress three points. First, the contextual evidence is likely to be scrappy and inconclusive, but is still well worth investigation. Secondly, the historicist is going to have to allow for plural meanings in texts: the seriousness with which Wycherley presented libertinism is not determinable and is subject to drastic variation in performance. And thirdly, the historicist is going to have to grapple with the complexities in meaning created by radically heterogeneous readers and audiences. Appeal to historicist materials is likely to complicate, not to simplify, the resulting interpretation.

Validation

Before plunging into the complexities of practice in Chapter 2 I wish to make a simple but vital point.

> Archaeo-Historicism is based on the premiss that any conclusion (contextual or interpretive) is subject to factual and logical challenge.

A practitioner must therefore accept strict rules of documentation and argument. If we say that Shakespeare's plays were written by Sir Francis Bacon, or that Dryden was a Pyrrhonist, or that Handel's opera company was financially viable in the 1720s, then we must be prepared to show that the statement is borne out by such evidence as can currently be found. We cannot appeal to laboratory results, and our data may be woefully limited. What we quite reasonably believe in one decade may be discredited in the next. Granting all the limitations of historical evidence, there can be no possible point to this enterprise if it is carried out on the theory that nothing is true and that therefore anything goes.

Statements about genesis, context, and reception must be backed up by hard documentation, or they are worthless. Like the bad old positivist homilies about impartiality and object-ivity, this is easy to say, hard to make meaningful in practice. 'Seek and ye shall find' is not one of the happier truths of this business: critics and scholars alike will somehow manage to turn up evidence to 'support their case'. R. S. Crane observes truly that 'a lawyer intent only on finding such evidence as will support his brief' is 'a bad model'.[58] (I will concede that the barrister-model is more acceptable if the critic or scholar an-nounces openly that he or she is adopting the role of advocate.) Where 'the guiding principle is a will to believe', the concept of verification goes out the window. And if results are not sub-mitted to a serious process of challenge and validation, they are no more than fairy stories to amuse us.

A good place to turn for practical advice is Crane, whose essays on historical method contain much wisdom and have been shamefully neglected. He is very blunt about the hit-or-miss, back-and-forth nature of the process: 'first we have to guess and then we test our guesses'. In making a guess, we are exploring a hypothesis, trying it out. Falling in love with it is a bad idea. Karl Popper has rightly said (in the context of science) that 'to ensure that only the fittest theories survive, their struggle for life must be made severe'.[59] Part of this process must involve our entertaining alternatives as seriously as pos-sible. Crane recommends (1) that we treat alternative hypo-theses as though they were of our own devising, and (2) that we try to treat our own hypothesis as though it were by someone else and attempt to refute it. The eye of parental love being what it is, this is exceedingly difficult. In principle the scholarly refereeing process ought to help, but it rarely does. Here is where one needs a true friend — not one who exclaims 'oh lovely, do publish' but one who kindly but firmly points out every easy assumption, every logical fallacy, and all omissions and errors in fact. Such friends being in short supply, a truly serious scholar tries to learn to be ruthlessly self-critical.

Archaeo-Historicism aims at truth. The most damning thing

---

[58] 'On Hypotheses in Historical Criticism', in *The Idea of the Humanities*, ii. 241. Crane comments that there are 'many widely variant or even contradictory interpre-tations of *Hamlet* . . . but I know of none, however absurd I may think it . . . for which the writer has not been able to find an ample body of according evidence in Shakespeare's text' (242).

[59] Popper, *Poverty of Historicism*, 134.

I know about the early practice of New Historicism is the degree to which its adherents succumbed to the easy acceptance of blanket relativism. Jane Marcus says 'the "ism" signifies philosophical cynicism about what can be known about reality, past or present', and adds that 'As a literary critical practice, New Historicism names itself as an operation upon a text with no pretensions toward "truth value"'.[60] In the introduction to the volume in which her essay appears, the editor sums up Hayden White's 'Comment' on the rest of the contents thus: 'White concedes that the New Historicism leaves intact no theoretical basis on which to call to account even the most spurious historical revisions' (p. x). This seems not merely a 'concession' but rather a profoundly damaging charge. I do not, in fact, believe that many self-described New Historicists of the past decade would endorse such a position. If we cannot invalidate the 'spurious', then we are in a world in which Holocaust-denial is as intellectually respectable as anything else.

Archaeo-Historicism is not science and should not try to pretend to be science. The nature of the subject matter is radically different, and so are the aims. Physical observation and prediction are quite different from empathetic comprehension of the human. But unless we are prepared to treat historical scholarship as a form of poetic self-expression, not subject to factual challenge or validation, then we have to accept some basic rules. Evidence must be obtainable, and it must be fully and accurately represented. Hypotheses may be floated with no more than tentative proof, but they are always subject to factual and logical challenge, and they will be modified and replaced as additional evidence and further analysis dictate. Truth must always be the aim, but in practice the extent and nature of evidence force us to acknowledge a spectrum from 'strong truth' to 'weak truth' to unresolvable doubt. The strong version seeks truth as an absolute (however rarely it can be established). The weak version must be more concerned with eliminating error. An honest historicist must admit that all too often only the weak version is practicable—or perhaps no version at all. One can say 'this cannot be so' much more easily than 'this must be so'. This seems to me true for readings as well as contexts.

[60] 'The Asylums of Antaeus: Women, War, and Madness—Is there a Feminist Fetishism?' in Veeser (ed.), *The New Historicism*, 132–51 at 132.

Umberto Eco illustrates the difference well when he demurs from the elder Rossetti's Rosicrucian reading of Dante.[61] Any method must always be subject to review and improvement. I believe, however, that Archaeo-Historicism is fully viable and useful right now. I confess to being acutely allergic to 'pie-someday' kinds of theorizing. To say that criticism 'will' be able to do something, or that wonderful results will emerge as soon as we finish building the machine, seem to me a sorry form of cop-out. By all means let us criticize current practice, but then let us forthwith produce better work, not rest satisfied with admonitions to our successors. A theorist who tells us what we 'should' do needs to point to successful examples of such work—or better yet to provide them.

[61] Umberto Eco, 'Overinterpreting Texts', in *Interpretation and Overinterpretation*, ed. Stefan Collini (Cambridge: Cambridge University Press, 1992), 45–66, esp. 52–60.

2

The Practice of Archaeo-Historicism

History-writing is not story-telling but problem solving.

David Hackett Fischer[1]

ARCHAEO-HISTORICISM offers us a very clear sense of purpose. We aim to reconstruct past events and viewpoints, and to use our constructions in aid of contextual interpretation. The theoretical and practical problems involved in carrying out those purposes, however, present considerable difficulties. Where do we start? Where do we get our questions? How do we acquire evidence? How do we reconstruct contexts? How do we enter a 'foreign' horizon of expectations, and what happens when we do? How do we take account of the radical diversity of any historical audience? How do we carry out contextual analysis of texts? How do we test context-constructions and interpretations?

No tidy answers can be supplied. What follows is basically a survey of the sorts of things archaeo-historicists do, with practical commentary on assumptions, objectives, and pitfalls. The survey proceeds from 'arriving at questions' to 'testing results', but I would not want to imply that historical research ever proceeds in so neat and structured a way: flailing about in the dark in a state of confusion and misdirection has always featured largely in my own enterprises. Neither do I mean to suggest that any one archaeo-historicist book (let alone article) would be likely to involve all the seven processes discussed here.

At the outset, let me restate and defend a crucial principle. *The historicist's primary commitment is to the recreation of the viewpoints of the people he or she studies.* I readily acknowledge that all of us are situated in our own world and that we cannot simply shed it like a snake skin. We carry our own ideological luggage, and given the inaccessibility of the past, we are

---

[1] *Historians' Fallacies: Toward a Logic of Historical Thought* (New York: Harper and Row, 1970), p. xii.

permanently estranged from it in important ways. Granted. The crux is whether we can to a substantial degree bridge the gap or otherwise overcome the barriers that separate us from the objects of our study. Obviously I believe that we can. I would liken the enterprise to learning a foreign language in adulthood. Aptitude helps (and varies vastly from person to person). Persistence helps. Total immersion helps, though one cannot go to the past as one can go to France. One will never speak the language exactly like a native, but some people can come reasonably close. One need not abandon or deny one's own language, and one may ultimately achieve a high level of comfort with the idiomatic structures of both. To 'think in' a foreign language *is* possible for some people. So with the dedicated historicist. He or she will endeavour to reconstruct and enter into the viewpoints of the past, attempting to do so as well as possible even while knowing that it can never be done completely. One will always be conscious of the gap (and one needs to be conscious of it), but some people can learn to feel profoundly at home on both sides of it.

Arriving at Questions

Where does a historicist scholar start? Not with a *tabula rasa*. Reading some not-so-ancient historical theory, one might imagine that the scholar is parachuted into *terra incognita* in a state of pure innocence. Alas, one does not commence as a passive data-receptor amidst a flood of signifiers rich in inherent meaning. Rather, one sets out with the knowledge, likes, and dislikes that got one into the field in the first place. Even an unfledged beginner has usually taken courses, written papers, read some primary sources and secondary scholarship or criticism. Quite apart from our own late twentieth-century values and prejudices (and our individual quirks), we cannot even begin to think about identifying a subject on which to work, let alone arrive at a focal question, until we have considerable familiarity with the territory.

There are two reasons to write scholarly books and articles. One is to make new information available to colleagues in the field. The other is to change—improve, we hope—our understanding of texts, contexts, problems, or issues that are already known and have been studied. Reinterpretation is often aided by new information, and new information is of no use unless it will ultimately assist with better interpretation. *Serious scholarship and criticism change our understanding of the subject.* Or they try to. One can write 'introductory' surveys for students or the general reader, but if there is no original argument this is merely commercial busywork. A scholar attempting to make a contribution to human knowledge needs to subscribe to a simple credo:

No *problem, no point.*

If there is no difficulty in understanding something, then there is no need to proffer a solution. If it ain't broke, don't fix it. I have read many intelligent, erudite, elegantly written books and articles in which I could discover no substantial point: the author did not really appear to be trying to change our understanding of the subject. What was said may well be true, but does it matter? A scholar needs to start by explaining the current state of understanding, and then tell us what is wrong or inadequate about it. What evidence is left out of account? What is misinterpreted? How can we improve our understanding?

One may choose a field for all sorts of reasons. One adores Victorian novels. One links up with a great thesis supervisor who accepts only Colonial American subjects. One might (if lucky) inherit a box of manuscripts from one's great-grandfather, or buy them at a jumble sale. Having by whatever process arrived in a territory, one goes looking for gaps and puzzles. Would Wycherley have been seen in his own time as a court-wit libertine or as a moral satirist? How do the religious views of *In Memoriam* fit into the spectrum of mid-nineteenth-century beliefs? What women were writing in eighteenth-century America? Having asked such a question, one looks to see what one's predecessors have done with the subject. Arriving at a focal question is a muddy, often circular process in which one takes a step forwards, a step sideways, three steps back, and turns unexpectedly in a different direction. However logical, tidy, and structured the result may be, the process of establishing a sense of purpose is almost always inefficient and irrational. I have directed enough theses to know that the good ones change and grow along the way, often substantially altering their focal point. So do my own books. Gertrude Stein was right: 'What is the question?' is exactly what we need to know, and there is nothing harder or more crucial in scholarship than arriving at a good one.

A basic methodological problem is how to position oneself in relation to one's predecessors. This is true both before and after one has arrived at a provisional focal question. One sometimes strongly disagrees with a predecessor, and on occasion one may actually get one's focus from a clash between predecessors. But one can hardly avoid being substantially influenced, whether positively or negatively. Facts, questions, attitudes, assumptions—all come to us from secondary sources. This is inevitable, indeed desirable. To refuse to accept the advances of our forebears would leave each of us in the position of having to reinvent the wheel. So we learn from earlier scholars—but what keeps us from trapping ourselves in their limitations? Critics spent many decades feuding pointlessly over morality in 'Restoration comedy', for example—a squabble I now wish I had stayed well clear of.

What attitude should we adopt towards our predecessors? Joseph Donohue has argued that a scholar is obliged to be 'deferential to tradition' (though adding that 'deference . . . falls well this side of idolatry').[2] I strongly disagree. Respect and courtesy are appropriate, but 'deference' seems the wrong attitude. If we accept our predecessors' conclusions, what can we change? If we do not ask new questions, then we confine ourselves to crumbs and bickering. I would argue that we need to read prior scholarship in a highly critical and sceptical spirit, granting it *provisional* acceptance only when it seems to stand up under rigorous challenge. Assuming that something is right because it is famous or standard—or because backtracking and checking up on it would be a great nuisance—is bad methodology.

We inevitably learn from predecessors and rely on them, but we cannot trust them, and especially not blindly. Particulars one can check up on; 'outlook' is a much bigger problem. A

[2] 'Evidence and Documentation', in Thomas Postlewait and Bruce A. McConachie (eds.), *Interpreting the Theatrical Past: Essays in the Historiography of Performance* (Iowa City: University of Iowa Press, 1989), 177–97 at 194.

historical scholar trying to conduct an investigation will waste huge amounts of time and is liable to ghastly errors if he or she is not profoundly steeped in the primary and secondary materials of the subject. A thorough grounding in primary and secondary materials cannot be dispensed with, but a corollary result is almost inevitably entrapment in the outlook of one's predecessors. Thus Hume's Paradox: the better trained the historian, the more difficult original thought becomes.

Once one has acquired a mindset, changing it becomes very hard.[3] Part of such a mindset is the questions we think right to ask and the things we presume can (or cannot) be done. Here is a tiny example. Many years ago my collaborator Judith Milhous succeeded in constructing a pay scale for actors in the late seventeenth century.[4] After reading her draft I commented that she had been terribly polite in refraining from pointing out that the editors of The London Stage had stated categorically that the reconstruction of such a pay scale was 'impossible'. She blurted, 'I'd forgotten that. If I'd thought it was impossible I would never have tried to do it.' Precisely—this is why a historical scholar must maintain a rigorously sceptical attitude towards the facts, questions, logic, and conclusions of even the most respected predecessor.

I am particularly conscious of the issue of 'training' because I am so deficient in it. I have devoted almost my whole career to theatre and opera history, but my formal academic training was almost entirely in aesthetics and the history of criticism. I had virtually no courses in (or other exposure to) drama, theatre architecture, acting theory, scene design, accounting history, palaeography, archival scholarship, or legal records—which are what I have spent my life working in. I have wasted vast amounts of time and made many embarrassing errors out of sheer unadulterated ignorance. I have often wished that I had a proper, systematic grounding in all these areas: self-taught on the fly is a scary basis from which to pronounce. But not having learnt what is 'right' has often been an advantage. I have asked

---

[3] As I use them, 'mindset' and 'viewpoint' are closely related, but the latter tends to be narrower and more particular, the former a more complex combination of assumptions and responses.

[4] Published in 'United Company Finances, 1682–1692', Theatre Research International, 7 (1981–2), 37–53.

many foolish questions, and plenty of unanswerable ones, but also some good ones that a properly educated person would never have bothered to explore.

Since history is problem-solving, our choice of questions dictates the quality of the scholarship we write. Choice of subject and nature of answer are inevitably affected by the value judgements and assumed patterns of meaning that we bring to our work. Why work on Swift instead of Stephen Duck? Why work on Katherine Philips or 'Ephelia' instead of Dryden? These are choices arising from the scholar's mindset. At present scholars are very conscious of canons and value judgements, rather less so of 'pattern' assumptions. A famous instance is E. K. Chambers's *The Mediaeval Stage* (1903). He traces a very satisfying evolution from simple forms to complex ones—selecting his data on the basis of the Darwinian theory popular at the time in scientific circles. The resulting interpretation wound up nicely illustrating the pertinence of Darwinian evolution to literary forms, but only because the pattern had been imposed, not because it was really there. This methodological disaster was not fully understood until O. B. Hardison exposed it in the 1960s.[5] The case is worth the attention of anyone interested in borrowing trendy methodology across disciplinary lines. Chambers wrote a long time ago. But what about the tree emblazoned on the cover of my paperback edition of Ian Watt's *The Rise of the Novel* (1957)?[6] It seems a very accurate symbol of the same sort of organicist assumptions, and we are still struggling to get out from under the pernicious influence of evolutionary views of the novel. A question that invites appeal to theory from another period starts to take us beyond the bounds of our method.

The archaeo-historicist is committed to reconstituting the patterns and structures recognized and used in whatever period is at issue. Are we debarred from employing any others? Not at all, but the ahistorical nature of the paradigms or categories needs to be very clearly admitted. I have, for example, constructed my own generic categories for describing late seventeenth-century plays—because those in use at the time

---

[5] O. B. Hardison, Jr., *Christian Rite and Christian Drama in the Middle Ages* (Baltimore: Johns Hopkins Press, 1965).

[6] Repr. Berkeley: University of California Press, 1964.

were primitive, reductive, and misleading.[7] I would argue that a truly historical investigation can introduce all sorts of 'outside' concepts and theories, but must also demonstrate clearly how people of the time thought about whatever is at issue. Late seventeenth-century dramatic theory is remarkably disjunct from contemporary practice, but it was part of how people thought about plays and cannot legitimately be ignored.

The value and potency of a question are closely bound up with its subject. What makes a subject important? This depends radically on the eye of the beholder. For scholarly significance, however, the potentiality for *change* is vital. One hopes to show either that a familiar topic should be viewed in a new way or that a neglected one offers unsuspected riches. Breaking out of the traditional canon has yielded relatively few masterpieces, but has greatly enriched our sense of the turmoil and diversity of our literary past—not to mention the huge windows opened on that past by attention to women writers and gender issues.

A provocative question is a wedge that the historical scholar can use to get into territory that has seemed well understood—or not important. Here is an example I particularly admire. Every late seventeenth-century scholar knows that genteel amateurs circulated poetry in manuscript, but in point of fact many kinds of documents were circulated in manuscript (rather than printed for distribution). Printing had been established for upwards of two hundred years; it was cheap; it was relatively lightly regulated—but somehow until very recently no scholar thought to inquire seriously *why* manuscript dissemination persisted, and not just for indecent poems circulated by 'court wits'. Harold Love's *Scribal Publication in Seventeenth-Century England* (1993) is a landmark study because it focuses on an important cultural phenomenon that had been virtually ignored except by a few textual scholars who looked at manuscripts in order to construct stemmata and texts. The broader significance of the phenomenon had gone virtually unrecognized.

'Why were MSS still being circulated in late seventeenth-century England?' is an awfully good question, if one stops and thinks about it. A historically inclined scholar proceeds by asking a question and then standing back to reconsider it. Have

[7] *The Development of English Drama in the Late Seventeenth Century* (Oxford: Clarendon Press, 1976).

answers been proposed? Is the question answerable, and if not why not? If answers can be imagined, do they have interesting implications? Is pertinent evidence readily available, and if not, might it be found? Exciting questions are not difficult to imagine. What did Shakespeare's audience think of monarchy? How were attitudes towards kingship and patriarchy changing in the reign of Charles II? What did the 1840s reading public think of industrialization? Each has major implications for reading important texts, and quite a lot of evidence could readily be found. Whether two scholars would select the same evidence or arrive at identical conclusions if they did so is another matter. One normally begins, however, with a provocative question, and then tries to come up with enough evidence to tackle it. Alternatively, one may go hunting for new primary material that will dictate questions one did not know could be asked.

Acquiring Evidence

A reader of texts can pick one and read it, but an archaeo-historicist requires context. Unfortunately, contexts do not grow on trees, nor can they be made from sows' ears. You do not have to want to know what the original audience thought of *Hamlet* to find yourself stymied. Two radically different procedures are open to the archaeo-historicist. These are

1. Pick a topic and scour the world for every scrap of pertinent evidence.

2. Go trawling for whatever seems interesting and work on what you find.

Having done both, I will testify that I prefer the latter, but there are advantages and disadvantages to both. Let me offer an example of each from my own experience.

I have always loved Fielding, and in 1973 I started collecting material towards a book on his decade as a dramatist. I hunted for material in all sorts of libraries, famous and obscure. The resultant book rests heavily on a reading of other 1730s plays and a detailed reconstruction of the theatre world of that decade, but I found little new documentation directly on Fielding.[8] Not

[8] *Henry Fielding and the London Theatre, 1728–1737* (Oxford: Clarendon Press, 1988).

much seems to have survived (few letters, no diaries, virtually no personal papers), and expert scholars have hunted for Fielding material for many decades. Such value as the book has rests largely on its intensive use of contextualization, recreating the financial, managerial, and generic circumstances in which Fielding worked. Only a handful of the primary sources I cite were unknown or previously unused.

In 1985—looking for Fielding material but interested also in Handel's connection with Covent Garden in the 1730s—I went to the Bedford Estates Office and discovered six large cartons stuffed with unknown manuscripts about Italian opera in London in the 1790s. I had never worked seriously past 1737 and had not the slightest intention of doing so. I 'discovered' this cache (the richest documentation ever found for any London theatre prior to the middle of the nineteenth century) because the Duke of Bedford's archivist said to me 'Since you are interested in opera, you will want to see our Pantheon papers.' I felt no interest whatever: I had totally forgotten, if I ever knew, that Wyatt's Pantheon was briefly converted into an opera house after the destruction of the King's Theatre, Haymarket, by fire in 1789. I did have enough sense to be polite to an archivist who wanted to show me something.

What does one do with thousands of pages of documentation on a subject one knows nothing about? The Bedford papers include correspondence for an exciting company that tried to hire Mozart; daily receipts; a unique costume book with every item of clothing for every role in the company's operas and ballets; weekly bills from scene painters—a staggering and intimidating level of detail. One can tiptoe away and stick to the 1730s; one can write an article pointing out the existence of the archive; or one can change one's life to pursue the discovery. Two collaborators and I quickly discovered that the Bedford papers would be only the beginning of the documentation we would have to absorb and distil from. By the 1790s there were many newspapers in London, and they published a lot about opera. Operatic pamphlets were numerous. Casting our nets in the Public Record Office, we found some forty opera-related lawsuits in the period at issue containing many tens of thousands of words of testimony. What we had projected as one substantial volume soon had to be reconceived as two fat ones.

In order to make sense of the material all three of us had to acquire a thorough grounding in a period of which we knew virtually nothing at the start. What we saw as a five-year byway in our careers now looks like a fifteen-year basic change of direction.[9]

I should add a comment here about where discoveries get made. A. H. Scouten and I found a 'lost' seventeenth-century play in manuscript right in the Folger Shakespeare Library (where it had been puzzled over and catalogued, but remained unrecognized).[10] I have also found and published a variety of important theatre-history documents in long-catalogued British Library collections (Additional and Egerton manuscripts). Such repositories have naturally been picked over by a large number of scholars for many decades. Exciting discoveries are, therefore, likelier to be made either in archives where cataloguing is rudimentary (the Public Record Office) or in relatively little-known and underutilized collections (the Bedford Estates Office). The difficulties of the PRO are such that it is certain to remain a prime trawling ground for several decades at the least.[11] A lot of future discoveries, however, will emerge from less intensively prospected territories. The Huntington is superbly catalogued and much used, but the Humanities Research Center at the

---

[9] Curtis Price, Judith Milhous, and Robert D. Hume, *Italian Opera in Late Eighteenth-Century London*, i: *The King's Theatre, Haymarket, 1778–1791* (Oxford: Clarendon Press, 1995). Volume ii, *The Pantheon Opera and its Aftermath, 1790–1795*, by Judith Milhous, Gabriella Dideriksen, and Robert D. Hume, is now substantially complete.

[10] Sir Robert Howard and George Villiers, Second Duke of Buckingham, *The Country Gentleman*, ed. Arthur H. Scouten and Robert D. Hume (Philadelphia: University of Pennsylvania Press, 1976), edited from Folger MS V.b. 228.

[11] Major groups of documents remain virtually unknown and unused. Few scholars have realized, for example, that from the 17th c. to the abolition of the Court of Exchequer in 1841 virtually any lawsuit that could be brought in Chancery could equally well be brought in Exchequer, and a great many were. Chancery remains a treasure trove for students of almost any subject, but because Exchequer has been so neglected, it now offers some quite extraordinary material even on notable people and much-studied subjects. For an account of the organization of materials in Exchequer and illustration of the kinds of material that can be found, see Judith Milhous and Robert D. Hume, 'Eighteenth-Century Equity Lawsuits in the Court of Exchequer as a Source for Historical Research', *Historical Research*, 70 (1997), 231–46. The difficulties of finding and using Chancery material are notorious, but have been substantially reduced by the appearance of Henry Horwitz, *Chancery Equity Records and Proceedings 1600–1800* (Public Record Office Handbook 27, 1995). Horwitz is now at work on a similar volume concerning Exchequer.

University of Texas is both rich in recent acquisitions and decidedly underutilized. At least a hundred visiting scholars must have rooted through the holdings of the Bodleian for every one who has trekked to Leeds to investigate the holdings of the Brotherton Collection. County Record Offices in Britain remain incredibly underexplored. Specialty collections of all sorts continue to attract only a trickle of investigators: I suspect they contain a lot of paydirt, particularly some of the religious libraries virtually unfrequented by literary scholars. Who knows what English manuscripts may be sitting peacefully in major and minor Continental libraries? Fish in a stream where you are elbow-to-elbow with a horde of other anglers and you probably won't catch a lot. But other possibilities exist.

If you start with a subject or a question rather than with a massive archival discovery, how ought you to proceed? If the issue is generic norms in fiction at the outset of Dickens's career, clearly you need to know what novels (old and new) were being read in the 1830s. If your problem concerns the reception of *Ulysses* in the United States before the book became legal, then you require access to a lot of scattered and ephemeral comments in books, articles, reviews, letters, and diaries. A database on 1830s fiction is reasonably easy to assemble; uncatalogued and uncollected ephemera are not.

As a first step, determine how far you can rely on your predecessors. If a bibliography of some sort exists, check its accuracy. Is it exhaustive? What does it omit or neglect? If the first decade of Shaw's playwriting intrigues you, then you are in luck: virtually all the books and pamphlets about London theatre from the 1890s can be found in 'Arnott and Robinson'.[12] This admirable bibliography, however, lists published materials (not manuscripts), and it excludes articles in magazines and newspapers, as well as reviews. If you look for seventeenth-century comments on theatrical performances, you will quickly discover that beyond Pepys, relatively few survive. Modern authorities quote a few famous ones over and over. To add to this stock, one might try reading MS letters and diaries in the

---

[12] James Fullarton Arnott and John William Robinson, *English Theatrical Literature 1559–1900: A Bibliography* (London: Society for Theatre Research, 1970), which incorporates Robert W. Lowe's *A Bibliographical Account of English Theatrical Literature* (1888).

British Library, or digging through items reported by the Historical Manuscripts Commission. If your experience is at all like
mine, you will discover that a month's hard labour can yield
little or nothing. Life is short, and most manuscripts cannot be
read very fast. Realistically, most historical investigations will
rest substantially on the findings of others.

To return to primary documents in all cases would be folly:
clearly we should make use of the work of our predecessors. We
must, however, test them to see how far we should trust them. If
you want to know what plays were performed at Drury Lane
and Covent Garden in the 1740s, you can turn to *The London
Stage, 1660–1800*.[13] Scholarly reviews will inform you that this
is a magnificent and highly accurate reference work, which is
true. If you back-check against the newspaper advertisements
which are the basis for the daily performance calendar, you will
find virtually 100 per cent completeness and accuracy, though
performance details are reported in a format that sometimes
obliterates important information, particularly about song,
dance, and special features. Reading the *Daily Advertiser* page
by page, however, you would soon realize that most 'fringe'
performances have been silently omitted from *The London
Stage*. This is editorial policy, and it is by no means indefensible,
but it does mean that some plays and performances have simply
been erased from the record—which is disconcerting. Reading
through part 2 (1700–1729) you will find a lot of concerts, but
almost none for the rest of the century. This is not because there
were no concerts (which were booming), but rather because the
editors decided in the course of publication that they consumed
too much space and excluded them—an editorial decision not
clearly announced. Try counting the number of times David
Garrick performed Hamlet, and you will discover that the full
cast for a play is usually reported only once per season at each
theatre. Later performances will say 'As 10 October' (or whatever), with amendments as necessary. One can in fact figure out
how many times Garrick played Hamlet, but not quickly or
easily (and not from the indexes). Turn to the massive synoptic
Index (1979) and you will find a lot of performances of *The
Tempest* under 'Shakespeare'. What the *Index* does not tell you

---

[13] Five parts in 11 vols; ed. Emmett L. Avery *et al.* (Carbondale: Southern Illinois
University Press, 1960–8).

(and nor do most entries in the text) is that this was not Shakespeare's play, but rather the Dryden–Davenant–Shadwell opera of 1674. Woe betide the innocent who fails to realize what is never said: the *Index* records all Shakespeare adaptations under Shakespeare *if* the title is unchanged, but under the adapter if the title is different. My point is simply that even the best reference books have quirks, gaps, oddities—and worse. To try to do eighteenth-century theatre history without *The London Stage* would be perfectly mad, but you are courting disaster if you use it blindly.

Anyone who reviews an edition needs to collate a bit of the text against the reported copytext. Even a few pages will tend to reveal plain error if it is there. Often more important, such a sample will show the user exactly what the editorial policy has done to the original text. Likewise any scholar who uses a bibliography, a reference compilation, or a database of any sort needs to do some trial checking to establish its level of accuracy and identify its omissions and pitfalls. Verify twenty-five items in the bibliography of any monograph, and you should know whether it is riddled with errors. Omissions are harder to check, but one is well advised to derive a list of out-of-the-way items from another source and see if they show up. I have hardly ever encountered a bibliographic representation of primary source material that was not sprinkled with landmines.

How much context is enough? At one extreme, we may be dealing with terribly scanty evidence. At another, our problem may be how to whittle down to a scale at which presentation of the evidence is feasible.[14] Dearth and Plethora both present problems. In the Renaissance, and indeed as late as the first half of the eighteenth century, almost every scrap is treasured. I have printed (and solemnly analysed) scratch sheets and stray jottings. As one gets towards the nineteenth century and beyond, the difficulty is quite different. The documentation in the Pantheon papers (let alone in newspapers, pamphlets, and legal records) is so massive that we could not possibly print as much as 2 per cent of what we have collected. The problem is to select a fair representation from an overabundance of primary material.

[14] For some cogent comments on evidence and lacunae, see Edward Hallett Carr, *What is History?* (London: Macmillan, 1961), ch. 1.

In the realm of Dearth one must try to make valid extrapolations and generalizations from scraps. The problem is nicely encapsulated in an old cartoon by Sempé. A woman stands staring at the fragmentary remains of what was once an Ionic column. In her mind's eye she has recreated the entire Acropolis with all its occupants and neighbouring buildings.[15] Would that we could! In a sense, this is what the archaeo-historicist aims to do. Palaeontologists can perhaps do something of the sort with isolated dinosaur bones. But not all remnants of columns were once cornerstones of the Parthenon; literary materials are rather different; and imagination must not be allowed to run riot. In the world of Dearth we wonder what constitutes a valid extrapolation; in the realm of Plethora we attempt to justify radical selection and synopsis.

No tidy, formulaic answer can be given in reply to the query 'how much context is enough?' For what they may be worth, I offer two rules of thumb. First, virtually regardless of what the context is and what the nature of the evidence, strains and contradictions ought to show up. People differ and no period is monolithic. Was everyone sorry when Charles I got his head chopped off? Did every Victorian patriarch believe wholeheartedly in The Family and The Queen? If context as we piece it together is accurately representative of what was really there, we must expect divergence and disagreement. Documenting what was illegal or widely disapproved of may be difficult or impossible. (Prosecutions for sodomy can be tabulated, but what proportion of male homosexual activity they represent is impossible to know.) Secondly, if you are fortunate enough to have a fair amount of evidence, one indication of sufficiency is patterns that repeat. Oddball cases may appear from time to time, but if your evidence falls within certain categories again and again, then very likely further evidence will too, at least until moving forward in time creates change. A parallel case in bibliography concerns the number of copies you must collate in order to turn up in-press corrections, if any. In theory, a hundred copies might prove identical on a Hinman collator before the hundred and first displayed significant resetting. In practice, checking five or at most ten copies will usually reveal such resetting.

[15] Sempé, *La grande panique* (Paris: Denoël, 1966), fos. [51ᵛ–52ʳ].

Whether you have a lot of evidence or a little, you have to ask yourself what is *reliable*. (One view is that we should believe nothing unless it is impressively footnoted with a reference to a Chancery document in the PRO. Considering the packs of lies to be found in Chancery lawsuits, this is a discomfiting notion of proof.) Historians rightly urge the use of eyewitness accounts or at least testimony from as close to the events in question as possible. This is common sense: the theatrical anecdotes published by Thomas Davies in the 1780s had probably evolved a bit in the course of the half-century or more he had been collecting and improving them. But personal participation in an event does not mean that a person will remember it accurately even a day later, let alone understand it. ('He who plays a part in an historic event never understands its significance' says Tolstoy.)[16] Contradictions can be disconcerting. Was Dorimant in Etherege's *The Man of Mode* (1676) a personal picture of one of the court rakes? A letter dated three days after the première by the theatrically well-connected Peter Killigrew says that 'Mr. Batterton under the name of Dorimant meanes the Duke of Monmouth & his intrigue with Moll Kirke, Mrs. Needham, & Lady Harriott Wentworth.'[17] Yet by 1707 editors of Rochester were claiming *him* as the model for Dorimant, an identification strongly affirmed by John Dennis in 1722.[18] Dennis was 19 in 1676 and apparently a regular visitor to London, though not yet a resident. Have we any basis for crediting or discrediting either source? Killigrew is much closer in time, but Rochester was a friend of Etherege's and seems far likelier than Monmouth to have gone about spouting Waller.[19]

Readers of *The Ring and the Book* and viewers of Kurosawa's *Rashomon* learn one of the grim truths of historical reconstruction: witnesses disagree. Where we have abundance of testimony, we can study the contradictions. Where we are

---

[16] Tolstoy, *War and Peace*, Book XII, ch. 2.

[17] Joseph Spence, *Observations, Anecdotes, and Characters of Books and Men*, ed. James M. Osborn, 2 vols. (Oxford: Clarendon Press, 1966), ii. 638.

[18] *The Critical Works of John Dennis*, ed. Edward Niles Hooker, 2 vols. (Baltimore: Johns Hopkins Press, 1939–43), ii. 248.

[19] Contemporary annotation can be treacherous. Harold Love points out to me that there are three radically contradictory sets of MS commentary on Sir Car Scroope's 'In Defence of Satyr'—only one of which was picked up by the editors of the Yale edition of *Poems on Affairs of State*.

struggling with Dearth, we will often have no way to assess the truth of a unique piece of evidence. When John Evelyn's wife expresses delight and wonder at the feigning of virtue in Dryden's *Conquest of Granada*, we can only guess how many members of the audience agreed with her, how many found the virtue offputting, and how many just laughed at it.[20]

Even if one is basically going to rely on ready-made syntheses for one's context, one ought to do some backchecking in primary sources. A generation ago many readers of texts simply employed Basil Willey (*The Seventeenth-Century Background*, 1934) or Jerome Hamilton Buckley (*The Victorian Temper*, 1951), or Walter Houghton (*The Victorian Frame of Mind*, 1957) as the referential basis for interpretation. These are dangerously generalized contexts. A slower, harder, better way is to establish your own context from primary evidence. The bigger and more broadly derived the generalizations, the less likely they are to be true or pertinent. If I am working in 1623, then I want documentation from that decade and that particular year, not from any old time in half a century. However good your predecessors, you always want to stop and think: what else might be found? What has been scanted or overlooked? Where might I do a little trial digging?

I shall conclude this rather homiletic discourse with yet one more warning. Of necessity we rely on our predecessors. But every time we too readily accept a fact, a report, a conclusion, a summary, then we are building on rotten foundations. Wrong dates, false attributions, and a lot of plain malarky get passed on from generation to generation as scholars plunder one another's footnotes. The temptation to assume that a respected predecessor got it right is sometimes overwhelming. Good methodology demands that we ask over and over, 'How do we *know* this?' Take a tiny but gruesome example. A major reference source, the *Biographical Dictionary of Actors*, reports of the actress Mary Davis that 'on 7 November [1667] she was Ariel in *The Tempest*'.[21] The source, unstated, is *The London*

---

[20] 'The most refined romance I ever read is not to compare with it; love is made so pure, and valour so nice, that one would imagine it designed for an Utopia rather than our stage.' *The Diary and Correspondence of John Evelyn*, ed. William Bray, 4 vols. (London: H. G. Bohn, 1889–95), iv. 25.

[21] Philip H. Highfill, Jr., Kalman A. Burnim, and Edward A. Langhans, *A Biographical Dictionary of Actors, Actresses, Musicians, Dancers, Managers, and Other*

Stage. Turn to that date, and you discover that no original cast is known. The editors do, however, report some *conjectures* by John Harold Wilson, clearly so labelled and referenced. Wilson was an excellent scholar; the speculation is plausible; and his text says merely 'may have played Ariel' in November 1667. Two steps on, this has hardened into 'fact'.

Take another example. The 1674 Drury Lane is a famous theatre at which many major plays received their premières. Look in Richard Leacroft's *The Development of the English Playhouse* (a magnificent and authoritative piece of work), and you will find a lovely, detailed reconstruction—just what anyone proposing to do a performance analysis of *The Country-Wife* needs. But—and this is a gigantic But—what has the reconstruction been based on? This is a question no one really wants to ask. The unhappy truth is that while we know the site dimensions, we have virtually no other hard evidence about this particular theatre. Like virtually every other twentieth-century architectural historian, Leacroft chose to *assume* that the so-called 'Wren section' at All Souls, Oxford, is a plan of this theatre, or at least a preliminary design for it. There is no actual evidence to support such an association with Drury Lane. No one wants to admit that we are virtually clueless about so important a theatre, and this handy little assumption long ago achieved the respectability of tradition. It is convenient; it might even be true—and it is bad history. Error, once embedded, becomes virtually ineradicable. One hopes not to fall victim to it too often, and one is honour bound to try not to add to it.

Reconstructing Contexts

Historical contexts as they are available to us are *our constructs*. To pretend otherwise is dangerous nonsense. However rigorous our search for evidence, however rational and above board our principles of selection and presentation, we do the building from such traces as survive, sparse or plentiful. We decide that a context is needed, and we assemble it—unless we simply take it on trust from a predecessor. Contexts are of many kinds and not

Stage Personnel in London, 1660–1800, 16 vols. (Carbondale: Southern Illinois University Press, 1973–93), iv. 222.

readily categorizable, but the motive of the assembler is usually either to construct a particular area as a background resource (for example, Victorian actresses, Renaissance views of marriage) *or* to create a backdrop specifically designed to help us understand a particular work or author. Both sorts of context are inevitably selective and constructed, and the principles on which the compiler has worked need to be made absolutely explicit. If the subject is 'the romantic lyric', the least the investigator can do is tell us what is included under this heading, what is excluded, and why.

In deciding to build a context one needs very early on to determine where the evidence will come from. The need for a context is often evident long before one has actually tried to assemble the necessary raw material. Sometimes one finds that it is not to be had. Barring some astonishing discoveries, *Shakespeare's Holographs* will not be written. *Acting Theory in Shakespeare's Day* is not a book I expect to see on a library shelf any time soon. *Scene Design in the Seventeenth-Century British Theatre* is not a writeable book: apart from masque designs and a few oddments, the evidence is long gone. I get queries from would-be thesis writers every month, asking where evidence can be found (for example) about costume in the late seventeenth-century theatre, or where there is a handy catalogue of contemporary descriptions of 'Restoration acting'. Asking does no harm, but trying to write where there is grossly insufficient evidence will produce no good result.

Yet evidence sometimes proves more plentiful than one might imagine. Here is an example from my own current work. A couple of years ago, doing preliminary research towards a book on theatre finances, Judith Milhous and I started to wonder how much eighteenth-century English playwrights earned from their plays. This is clearly important to an understanding of playwriting as a profession, and recent interest in money and economics—by no means restricted to Marxists or theatre historians—makes it a terribly obvious question. So far as I know, it has gone unasked and unanswered save for repetition of some stray anecdotes. Evidence turns out, however, to exist in bulk. A large number of Covent Garden and Drury Lane account books survive (mostly in the British Library and the Folger), and in fact most of the crucial information was printed a generation ago in

The London Stage. Indeed there is so much information available that analysing it is a major chore. Some of what can be learnt is quite startling.[22] Why did someone not make use of the account-book evidence long ago? Search me. One should not simply assume that no evidence exists, however often inquiry produces a blank.

If you have some evidence from which to work, you need to start by asking on what principles the context is being assembled. Is the focus biographical? Institutional (a publishing house, a theatre company)? Generic? If audienced-based, then how broadly in time and class? Narrow-angle and wide-angle are quite different. Kathleen Tillotson creates what can serve as a fine background for Dickens in *Novels of the Eighteen-Forties* (1954), but I would regard an attempt to create a complete intellectual context for Robert Browning as essentially unmanageable. One must ask what influenced a writer in positive terms or served as a source (Shakespeare used a lot of Holinshed; Thackeray admired Fielding) and what he or she rejects or reacts against (Defoe loathed the theatre; Byron ridiculed Wordsworth).

The most crucial principle of context-reconstruction is that no a priori assumptions are admissible. The archaeo-historicist is strictly bound to work from particulars, not to illustrate general propositions with reference to selected evidence. The dangers of accepting blanket truths about a period are evident if we consider the work of such scholars as D. W. Robertson, Jr., Aubrey Williams, and Roy Battenhouse.[23] All three justify their enterprises in what I am calling historicist terms. The gist of their somewhat different positions is that because all medieval, Renaissance, and late seventeenth-century readers in England were believing Christians, we are not only justified in reading 'their' texts through a strong Christian/moral mindset but are

[22] Milhous and Hume, 'Playwrights' Remuneration in Eighteenth-Century London', *Harvard Library Bulletin*, forthcoming.

[23] See particularly D. W. Robertson, Jr., *A Preface to Chaucer: Studies in Medieval Perspectives* (Princeton: Princeton University Press, 1962). Aubrey L. Williams, *An Approach to Congreve* (New Haven: Yale University Press, 1979). Roy W. Battenhouse, *Shakespearean Tragedy: Its Art and its Christian Premises* (Bloomington: Indiana University Press, 1969). For some cogent objections to Battenhouse, see Harriett Hawkins, *Likenesses of Truth in Elizabethan and Restoration Drama* (Oxford: Clarendon Press, 1972).

indeed actually obliged to do so. This is not a completely foolish contention. Many twentieth-century scholars are not practising Christians; neither have they much sympathy for serious
religious practice. Scholars—males anyhow—who readily em-
pathize with the horny Pepys are often baffled by the religious
Pepys who was an enthusiastic connoisseur of sermons. The
degree to which Pepys took sermons seriously, bought them,
read them, and thought about them is seldom attended to with
much interest, sympathy, or respect—and yet it is an important
component in his psychological makeup. Robertson *et al.* are
certainly right in saying that the dismissive attitude of many
scholars towards the religious and moral beliefs of a historical
audience is a serious falsification of context. The question,
however, is whether their decidedly uniformitarian constructs
represent an improvement.

   Any text can be read through a moral lens, *The Miller's
Tale* included. That all readers in a specified period read texts
in identical ways seems a much more dubious proposition.
Chaucer's *General Prologue* and his selection of pilgrims seem
to me prima facie evidence that he presumed radical differences
in reader response from person to person back in the reign of
Richard II. Whatever the utility of the 221 volumes of the
Patrologia Latina, I am inclined to doubt that all medieval
readers or hearers of texts owned all these texts, had memorized
the crucial bits, or were disposed to apply such thinking to
'naughty tales'. We may likewise wonder whether quasi-Puritan
readings of Shakespeare make sense: had Shakespeare supposed
that he was writing to Puritans, he would probably not have
addressed them in dramatic form. We can certainly read Congreve's comedies as moral tracts but have we evidence that his
contemporaries did so? Jeremy Collier thought they *ought* to
have been moral tracts and denounced them violently in *A Short
View of the Immorality, and Prophaneness of the English Stage*
(1698). When Congreve defended himself in *Amendments of
Mr. Collier's False and Imperfect Citations* the same year, he did
not do so on the basis that they were moral tracts. Rather, he
charged that Collier was demanding something he had never
designed the plays to be. Pamphlets by several of his contemporaries take similar lines of defence. Congreve was a Christian,
and he employs 'providentialist' terminology in *The Mourning*

Bride (1697). Being a good Christian, however, did not require him (in his own eyes) to make his comedies vehicles of Christian morality.[24]

To say that 'all late seventeenth-century English readers were Christians' is more or less true, but this does not get us very far in comprehending the manifest contradictions in audience response to *The Country-Wife*. Brilliant and learned as Robertson *et al.* may have been, their insistence on *single* viewpoint makes their readings of texts unacceptable except as hypotheses representing the responses of particular groups of readers. We may readily agree that some of Congreve's readers might have seen his plays as successful tracts, or might have chosen to take them in those terms in order to justify reading them. Such evidence of actual reading as has come down to us, however, suggests that those who sought Christian edification failed to find it in Congreve. The point here is simple. A historical method that cannot comfortably accommodate radical diversity in reader response will generate procrustean enforcement of generalities. Good historicism must rest on its employment of specific facts. Whatever the inadequacies of the contexts we build, there is no excuse for founding them on a priori generalizations.

All writers and works possess a multiplicity of contexts. What, for example, are the contexts of Dryden's heroic plays (1664–75)? At a minimum one would need to account for the following: (1) Dryden's personal life from roughly age 32 to 45; (2) Dryden's career circumstances; (3) other plays and playwrights of the 1660s and early to mid-1670s, notably work by the Earl of Orrery, Sir Robert Howard, Elkanah Settle, John Crowne, Nathaniel Lee, and Thomas Otway; (4) pre-1642 plays in the current repertory, particularly those of Beaumont and Fletcher; (5) the plays of Corneille, and the early plays of Racine; (6) the King's Company (in which Dryden was a sharer), its actors, and its theatre buildings; (7) dramatic theory, including contemporary English and Continental work as well as Dryden's own; (8) current history and politics; (9) intellectual context,

---

[24] For a pair of very different but highly effective rebuttals of Williams's methodology, see Harold Love, 'Was Congreve a Christian?', *Themes in Drama*, 5 (1983), 293–309, and Derek Hughes, 'Providential Justice and English Comedy 1660–1700: A Review of the External Evidence', *Modern Language Review*, 81 (1986), 273–92.

particularly Hobbes (whose ideas tend to be spouted by Dryden's villains). A compelling case can be made for any and all of these contexts as significant influences on the creation of *Aureng-Zebe* (1675). Indeed, the erratic history of criticism of the heroic plays shows that many of the twists, turns, and contradictions stem directly from which context is privileged. Critics with good French tend to find Corneille important; students of performance are more likely to concern themselves with the acting skills of Charles Hart and Michael Mohun. The pertinence of each context is easy to show. How to weigh one in the balance against any or all of the others is a question to try the wisdom of Solomon.

Contexts generated in relation to a particular author or text or small set of texts are a very different proposition from 'period' contexts. Let us consider 'The Romantic Age'. This is hardly a mysterious concept: virtually every current anthology of British literature has a substantial unit devoted to this subject, and innumerable books and articles over the past century have used the term. Students write examination essays in which they lay out the basics: the time period is generally taken as 1798 (*Lyrical Ballads*) to c.1830 or 1832 (death of Scott) or perhaps 1837 (accession of Victoria). Wordsworth, Coleridge, Byron, Shelley, and Keats were the Big Five, and Blake was later recognized as a related if quirky phenomenon. I would not deny the significance of the common ground conjured up in some of the classic studies of Romanticism. René Wellek convincingly demonstrates the wide dissemination of 'organicism' throughout European literature and philosophy of the late eighteenth and early nineteenth centuries.[25] Morse Peckham pulls together seemingly scattered and disparate phenomena in a famous essay centred on secular conversion.[26] M. H. Abrams's *Natural Supernaturalism* (1971) creates a compelling *über*-vision of romantic transcendentalism. Fine and dandy: these notions work wonderfully to illuminate a few authors and poems. One can use Peckham's concept of negative (dark) romanticism as an inversion that 'explains' Gothic novels of the time (which I did in print myself, many years ago). But let me ask a doubting question.

[25] René Wellek, 'The Concept of "Romanticism" in Literary History', *Comparative Literature*, 1 (1949), 1–23, 147–72.
[26] Morse Peckham, 'Toward a Theory of Romanticism', *PMLA* 66 (1951), 5–23.

Did Jane Austen know that she was living in the Romantic Age? Well, of course the term itself was a late coinage. Would she have defined her *Weltanschauung* in terms of Wordsworth and Coleridge? Hardly likely she would have done anything so pretentious, let alone selected those rather dubious characters as her point of reference. The public, to be sure, tends to be slow to appreciate what later critics define as great and important. As of about 1815 the conspicuous 'Romantic' writers were Scott and Byron. Poor Jane led a rather sheltered life, but did Francis Jeffrey (who was *au courant*) conceive himself as a denizen of what we have subsequently defined and named 'The Romantic Age'?

Theorists of romanticism have certainly acknowledged the individuality of Byron, Keats, and Shelley (and their differences from Wordsworth and Coleridge). But what do we conceive romanticism to have been? It was not a publicly defined credo to which anyone could subscribe. 'Movements' are sometimes available as bandwagons (imagism, beat poetry) but this hardly seems to have been true of romanticism. Whether one respected Wordsworth and Coleridge or mocked them *c*.1815, they were not so conspicuous a part of the cultural milieu as to constitute a defining essence. Only a truly prescient critic could have imagined that they would ever be so conceived. 'Spirit of the Age' historicism has had few apologists in the last half-century, but it has left us a considerable and dubious legacy in the realm of early nineteenth-century literary study.

If we were somehow to take a core sample of intellectual outlook from 1815 or 1820, what would the picture look like? Not, I would venture to argue, much like what is so magisterially delineated in *Natural Supernaturalism*. What has happened here, I think, is that a period characterization has been extrapolated out of a few privileged texts and then read back onto the literature of the time. The reading has enormous coercive power, in part because it grows out of a set of value judgements that are difficult to challenge unless they are out in the open. Wordsworth and Coleridge became heroic/valorized figures in the course of the late 1830s and 1840s. Reading this mythic construct back onto the beginning of the century has created a monstrously distorted sense of what the world looked like to the people who actually lived then—including the 'romantic poets' themselves. Relatively little as the Big Five (and Blake) had to do with one another in their lifetimes, I like to imagine that they have taken the hint from critics and formed a club in the hereafter, meeting for drinks at an appropriate pub—The Aeolian Harp, perhaps. Only radical departure from the canon can get us out of the cul-de-sac in which spirit-of-the-age thinking has left us.

Virtually all 'period' characterizations to date have been rubbish, though I do not believe that this has to be the case. The touchstone has to be plausibility to an actual inhabitant (as opposed to a statistical mean). Very specific contexts such as I identified for Dryden are easier, safer, and simpler to justify. This does not deny the possibility of sketching 'outlook' at a particular date. One of the things wrong with most discussions of romanticism is that they are absurdly vague in chronological terms. To a hard-core primary-source historian, 1800 and 1830 are staggeringly far apart. Any cultural historian who treated 1925 and 1955 as pretty much the same thing would be ridiculed. Nothing but ignorance could justify treating the plays of 1670 and those of 1700 as though they emerged from the same context (as generations of critics did), any more than one could say that those of 1965 and 1995 did so.[27]

A defensible context needs a very specific site.[28] If it is generated in response to a specific problem ('How did the Third Dutch War affect Dryden?') it is likely to connect well to what is at issue. Conversely, one may wonder if it is *too* tidily connected. A relatively local context generated without so specific a motive is much less likely to be distorted by predisposition (for example, British attitudes towards the French Revolution in 1793). In either case, however, there is a huge difference between tightly defined context and overarching generalities. Consider, for example, A. O. Lovejoy's celebrated and long-cited essay on 'The

---

[27] David Boucher has raised pointed questions about the coherence and immediacy of 'context' in political history as W. H. Greenleaf, J. G. A. Pocock, and Quentin Skinner have attempted to use it in the recovery of authorially intended meaning. See *Texts in Context: Revisionist Methods for Studying the History of Ideas* (Dordrecht: Martinus Nijhoff, 1985), particularly Boucher's 'Assessment and Conclusion' at 255.

[28] For a useful discussion of this point, see Richard L. Levin, 'The Problem of 'Context' in Interpretation', in W. R. Elton and William B. Long (eds.), *Shakespeare and Dramatic Tradition: Essays in Honor of S. F. Johnson* (Newark: University of Delaware Press, 1989), 88–106.

Parallel of Deism and Classicism'.[29] Lovejoy claimed to be outlining the 'characteristic idea-complex' that constituted 'classicism' or 'the rationalism of the Enlightenment'. He gives nine
particulars in a numbered list, including such items as 'negative philosophy of history' and 'intellectual equalitarianism'. It
sounds highly impressive, but no particular period is specified
and allusions range over a period upwards of two centuries.
Even applied to a mere half century or so (say 1680–1730), the
construct collapses if tested against actual individuals. Dryden
believed in progress, and if Pope and Swift were intellectual
equalitarians they expressed this conviction oddly. Meaning no
disrespect to a major intellectual historian, I have to say that if
Lovejoy's brand of context represents the best historicism can
do, then we ought to go out of business. Fortunately, we can try
to learn from the errors of our predecessors—and trust that our
successors will learn from ours.

   A context is not a 'fact' but a 'hypothesis'. We construct it; we
employ it as a way of representing the past; we use it to interpret
texts, authors, and situations. Because contexts as they are
available to us are not givens, they need interrogation and
challenge. Lovejoy pulls his 'characteristic beliefs' out of a hat
with the panache of the expert magician, but this will hardly do
if the object of the scholar is to allow successors to retrace
routes, examine evidence, and (perhaps) arrive at the same
conclusions. Some form of verification must be provided—
neither a complex nor a mysterious matter. Lovejoy's construction violates two basic principles laid down here: short duration
and specific site. It is uniformitarian. It comes with no explanation of how it was arrived at, what alternatives might be found,
or what exclusions it makes—all of which violate common-
sense procedure in the establishment of plausible hypotheses. If
we want to test the construct in a simple but effective way, we
need do no more than pick half a dozen writers and philosophers from Dryden to Samuel Johnson and ask how well
Lovejoy's list describes their mentalities. The beliefs Lovejoy
identifies are widely present in European thought over a broad
span of time, but as an account of the beliefs of individuals they

---

[29] First published in *Modern Philology* in 1932 and reprinted in Lovejoy's *Essays
in the History of Ideas* (1948). For a methodological attack on this enterprise, see
my *Dryden's Criticism* (Ithaca: Cornell University Press, 1970), 158–62.

are a disastrous misrepresentation. Are they the orthodoxy of
any particular time and place? I would flatly deny it.

Validation is crucial. Both the constructed context and its
application require justification. Equally vital, however, is our
acceptance of the tentativeness of our results. *All conclusions
must be regarded as provisional.* Additional evidence or better
analysis may change our minds. Here we do find a valid parallel
to physical science. We answer our questions as best we can,
and there is no disgrace in finding our answers supplanted in
due course. Consider two examples of challenge to validity. In
1934 R. S. Crane published 'Suggestions Toward a Genealogy
of the "Man of Feeling"' in *ELH*. Thirty-five years later when I
was in graduate school the essay was still being taught virtually
as 'fact'. Not until 1977 was the subject seriously reopened. In
that year Donald Greene mounted a full-scale refutation, arguing that 'Latitudinarianism' in the early eighteenth century was
not the intellectual foundation of the cult of sensibility after
1760.[30] I shall not undertake to serve as arbiter, but at the very
least we may say that Crane's hypothesis can no longer be
treated as the last word on the subject, and should be regarded
as deeply suspect, perhaps actually discredited.

A very different kind of problem is presented by the question
'How influential was Shakespeare in the first half of the eighteenth century?' Virtually all scholars of the last forty years have
turned to the standard source of context, which is Hogan's
exhaustively detailed study of Shakespeare's performance history. Hogan draws a conclusion that has been quoted over and
over—that one in six theatrical performances in the period
1701–50 was Shakespeare.[31] This is 'true', but there are some
complexities. Hogan counts only mainpieces, ignoring the
fact that most performances after 1715 were double bills. If
one counts afterpieces—which demonstrably had an enormous
appeal for audiences—then 'one in eleven' is closer to accurate.
But what counts as a performance of 'Shakespeare'? A large
number of the performances Hogan includes were in fact of
adaptations, including some very drastic adaptations. The 1674

---

[30] Donald Greene, 'Latitudinarianism and Sensibility: The Genealogy of the
"Man of Feeling" Reconsidered', *Modern Philology*, 75 (1977), 159–83.
[31] Charles Beecher Hogan, *Shakespeare in the Theatre, 1701–1800*, 2 vols. (Oxford: Clarendon Press, 1952–7), i. 460.

operatic *Tempest* counts, and so does Otway's *Caius Marius* (which recycles the Romeo and Juliet story as a subplot). Hogan is perfectly honest about this, but it does make a big difference to the public perception of 'Shakespeare'. So does the little-known fact that the majority of playbills for genuine and un-altered plays by the Bard do not mention his name until the 1730s. How many members of the audience knew that they were seeing 'Shakespeare' is undeterminable. The context Hogan supplies is absolutely legitimate, exceptionally accurate, and dangerously misleading.

Carelessly constructed or cavalierly applied, contexts are worse than useless.[32] Both in the study of genesis and in the study of reception, however, a properly constructed context can supply crucial aid in comprehension. The basic principles of context-building do not seem terribly difficult: (1) Avoid a priori assumptions; (2) eschew single viewpoint and uniformitarian-ism; (3) stick to a specific site and a narrow time range; (4) expect to have to take change into account if covering more than a very few years; (5) cite primary documents as your evidence and explain principles of selection or exclusion; (6) always remember that any context is a constructed hypthesis; that it is subject to validation; and that both contexts and conclusions drawn in the light of them must remain provisional.

Entering a Foreign Horizon of Expectation

At this point we need to consider a practical problem made famous by Jauss but never fully confronted by him.[33] Exactly how does one 'enter' or otherwise explore a horizon of expecta-tions other than one's own? Jauss implies a movement back and forth between the two, and a process of mediation, but in actual practice how does one do this?

Past horizons no longer exist, so we have to reconstruct them. Jauss tiptoes around this fact. Indeed, he almost seems to regard

---

[32] For some examples of slovenly construction, see Richard Levin, 'Unthinkable Thoughts in the New Historicizing of English Renaissance Drama', *New Literary History*, 21 (1990), 433–47.

[33] Jauss does usefully develop his position in 'Horizon Structure and Dialogicity', in *Question and Answer: Forms of Dialogic Understanding*, trans. Michael Hays (Minneapolis: University of Minnesota Press, 1989), 197–231.

the remote horizon as a separate entity that we can encounter. Using that term very loosely, I would suggest that we may encounter a past horizon in one of three ways:

1. Read or see an original work and realize that it was written from a different outlook than ours.
2. Read a critical reconstruction by a predecessor.
3. Start to reconstruct one's own version of past context.

In the first instance the reader may fail to realize that difference in outlook must be taken into account when trying to interpret a work. I have met readers who regard *Billy Budd* as a simple denunciation of the rigidity of the navy. Readers may strongly resist the different outlook even when it is made quite explicit— as my students do when faced with *Clarissa*. The fact remains that most 'old' texts contain enough internal pointers and guidelines to permit an attentive reader to deduce the logic and values of the work. Renaissance plays benefit from all sorts of contextual notes and explanations, but I have to agree with Richard Levin when he says that he cannot think of 'any major English Renaissance drama where we would go seriously wrong in our interpretation without a special knowledge of some idea of the time'.[34] This depends, to be sure, on the relative expertise of the reader and the gap to be bridged. I should not care to go bail for my ability to read Chinese literature of *c*.1600 AD with any accuracy at all, no matter how good the translation.

If we are reading a fully developed reconstruction, it obviously does already exist and can be 'encountered'. If we are putting it together from primary evidence as we go along, then the process of experiencing the remote outlook has to be a much jerkier one as we put a piece in place; stand back to assess and think; and then ponder the selection and analysis of another piece of evidence. The question that Jauss leaves us with, however, is fairly general: does our own Horizon of Expectation contaminate or destroy our ability to absorb—and in some limited fashion adopt—a remote horizon of expectation?

An answer must start with the admission that we cannot truly 'forget' our own knowledge and outlook in order to enter a foreign one. I would argue, however, that we should not want

[34] *New Readings vs. Old Plays* (Chicago: University of Chicago Press, 1979), 166.

to: we need the sense of contrast that the juxtaposition gives us, or we would have no basis for judgement and analysis of the foreign context. Jauss suggests that one moves back and forth and gradually brings the two into at least a partially overlapping position. This strikes me as a peculiar notion. The object is not synthesis but rather the ability to function imaginatively in the remote realm while still in possession of one's twentieth-century knowledge and sensibility. In Jauss's metaphor, we can inhabit only one horizon at a time. But this is only a metaphor. Are we talking about a situation like the Duck/Rabbit in which one can see *only* one at a time? Or is a split screen a better parallel? Can we in fact keep both outlooks in mind without muddling them?

I would argue that one can *enter into an outlook*, sympathize profoundly with it, see with the eyes of the participants—just as one can go to a play and be 'transported'. But even if that transport temporarily obliterates thoughts of one's own life, one remains in one's senses. As Farquhar mockingly observes, however wrought up we may be in the misfortunes of Alexander the Great, 'the whole Audience at the same time knows that this is Mr. *Betterton*, who is strutting upon the Stage, and tearing his Lungs for a Livelihood'.[35] The remoteness of the foreign outlook can be exaggerated, and so can the difficulty of entering into it imaginatively. I would liken the situation to talking with a friend who has radically different religious and personal values. You may approve, condemn, sympathize, or feel repelled—but you can very probably learn 'to think like that'. Perhaps you can get into the other person's head; perhaps you can merely look over his or her shoulder. But you can almost always learn to predict attitudes and behaviour, which is in a way what an archaeo-historicist is attempting to do across a gap in time—rather than across a difference in individual outlook.

To a high degree, what the archaeo-historicist does is to become familiar with conventions. The Westerner who encounters Kabuki drama unprepared is in for a rough evening. One is only marginally better off if one has read up in advance, or has a knowledgeable companion explaining things *sotto voce*. At some point, however, repeated exposure creates enough familiarity that one begins to understand, at first in purely

---

[35] 'A Discourse Upon Comedy', in *The Works of George Farquhar*, ed. Shirley Strum Kenny, 2 vols. (Oxford: Clarendon Press, 1988), ii. 384.

intellectual terms and then perhaps in emotional ones. To tell the truth, I have not got very far with Kabuki. I had a somewhat similar initial experience with Chekhov many years ago, but soon learnt to feel comfortable with his conventions. 'Gaps' can seem baffling and insurmountable, but sometimes they simply evaporate. About the time I went to college I listened to some Bartók and found his music impenetrably difficult, modern, noisy, and offputting. About three years later, having shunned all opportunities to listen to more Bartók, I accidentally heard one of the quartets (not his most accessible music) and was astonished to find that in the meantime he had become tuneful and old-fashioned, almost a nineteenth-century purveyor of 'easy listening'. The difference, of course, was not in Bartók but in me. I had heard a lot of twentieth-century music by then, and had by degrees absorbed far more radical conventions. With practice, the historicist often comes not only to understand formal conventions but actively to enjoy the aesthetics of the art form, whether it is Middle English metrical romances, Elizabethan sonnets, revenge tragedies, Cavalier lyrics—or Bartók.

When the modern scholar encounters a reconstructed context, or attempts to reconstruct one, we must always be conscious of the fact that neither investigator nor context is in any sense neutral. The scholar starts with his or her contextual knowledge, past reading, likes and dislikes—and often enough, some commitment to things he or she has already said in print. The context, if already extant, was created with a particular viewpoint and sense of purpose by someone, and this purposiveness cannot safely be ignored. If the scholar is trying to build a context, then aims and motives will unquestionably affect selection, presentation, and interpretation of evidence. My own subjective experience of this process is that one assembles a lot of bits and pieces of primary evidence; attempts a trial configuration; stands back to assess its plausibility for a writer or reader in one's target area; and then tries another one. The process is very much like trying to guess what a friend, relative, or enemy will do in a given set of circumstances. One can point to the specifics of background, education, family milieu, economic constraints, or whatever, but ultimately one asks what makes sense, what 'feels right'. The incompleteness with which one can enter into anyone else's mind and circumstances is obvious, and some people do it a lot better than others. Empathy can be a great help, but lack of it need be no great barrier to comprehension of how someone will think or act. I can predict my mother-in-law's reactions to books quite accurately, lack of empathy with her viewpoint notwithstanding.[36]

The position I am offering here on entering a foreign horizon of expectations is simple. I believe that within the limits of available evidence, one can familiarize oneself with remote conventions and learn to think in an alternative mentality. One is neither abandoning one's own outlook nor blending the two. For the scholar, the process is very much one of trial and error: build a model, test it, rebuild it again and again.

Historical Reader-Response Paradigms

Until the 1970s virtually all interpretive theory was directed to author and text. The function of the reader in creating meaning remained little considered, despite the research reported by I. A. Richards in *Practical Criticism* as long ago as 1929. Audiences continued to be treated as receptors for meaning they apprehended correctly or incorrectly. The concept of the 'passive audience' has been astonishingly long-lived, even in the realm of theatre, where it is manifestly untrue.[37] One of the enormous advances to which 'theory' has contributed in the past thirty years is the realization that readers and authors are neither homogeneous nor passive. Readers differ, and any but the simplest text requires active interpretation (not merely inert reception) to determine its meaning. Many old historicists, however, have clung doggedly to what little remains of the concept of 'right reading'. Conservatives tend to regard 'reader response' as mere subjectivity and Stanley Fish as High Priest of interpretive irresponsibility. In suggesting that reader response offers us a splendid tool for historicist interpretation, I am probably alarming and offending a substantial part of my natural constituency.

---

[36] Clifford Geertz comments instructively on gap-bridging in '"From the Native's Point of View": On the Nature of Anthropological Understanding', in *Local Knowledge: Further Essays in Interpretive Anthropology*, ch. 3.

[37] For a useful discussion, see Marvin Carlson, 'Theatre Audiences and the Reading of Performance', in Postlewait and McConachie (eds.), *Interpreting the Theatrical Past*, 82–98.

We should not, however, be hasty in forswearing the use of powerful tools that can be readily adapted to our line of business.

'Reader response' is so variously used a term that some clarification is required. Wolfgang Iser tries to take the authorially designed structure of the text into consideration; Norman Holland believes that every reader forces the text to conform to his or her viewpoint; Stanley Fish believes that meaning derives from the interpretive community to which the particular reader belongs. To date, reader-response theory has tended to tell us (broadly) how readers might respond in the abstract, but says very little about determining how readers *did* respond to a given text at a particular time. The challenge to traditional communication theory is welcome: the sooner we have expunged neutral/passive receptors from our thinking, the better. But somehow we need to bridge the gap between reader response as theory and 'reception history' as one of the duller forms of documentary dogwork.

What I am trying to propose here amounts to an attempt to recapture the outlook of various subgroups of readers in the past—a kind of historicization of Stanley Fish's notion of interpretive communities. Clearly we need to carry out two very different kinds of investigation. Where evidence of the response of actual readers exists, we need to collect and analyse it. Where evidence is inadequate or totally lacking, we must do the best we can to compensate for its absence by creating plausible models of the spectrum of readers at whatever point in history we are concerned with. The period of composition and original reception is naturally of special interest, but changing reception over time can tell us a great deal about both the text and successive audiences. What is 'correct' in the light of genetic origins is largely irrelevant. This is the project that Jauss implies but does not explore, and it is a good one. Jauss argues that we can reconstruct the original audience's response to a work, but cannot experience it in the same way they did. In absolute terms this is probably correct, but it does not seem to me a serious difficulty in practice.

This *process of reconstruction* seems to me to lie at the heart of the historicist enterprise. In this realm the work of Quentin Skinner offers useful guidelines—stressing particular contexts, the reasons for an author's writing what he or she did, and attention to responses from the original audience.[38] My emphasis here on audience viewpoint (and its diversity) is intended to counterbalance what seems to me a long-standing deficiency in 'historical' interpretation. To tell the truth, historicists often deal rather ineffectively with particular texts. We discover facts; we assemble backgrounds—and then we tend to fall into the trap of operating as though the background controls or delimits the meaning of particular texts—*which it does not.* Texts have meaning encoded into them (not always clearly), but that meaning is actuated only in readers or audiences. All the learning to be found in Basil Willey's *The Seventeenth-Century Background* serves only to enforce generalized readings of the dullest, flattest, most procrustean sort—unless we are able and willing to take reader diversity into account.

If we want to do more than write footnotes and drive steamrollers over the unlucky texts we have decided to 'explain' contextually, then we need some elementary paradigms for incorporating readers' responses in our explanations. Much has been written in recent years about 'ideal', 'informed', and 'model' readers—that is, the sort of person who has the knowledge and outlook anticipated by the author, and who is therefore in a position to decode the text and get something like the result planned by the author. A historicist should be suspicious of these beasts, not so much because they are hypothetical as because they are basically authenticated with reference to the text itself. Reader response seems here to be verging on the invention of model readers who serve principally to verify the critic's 'right reading' of the text. For the historicist, the most acceptable of the widely known models is Iser's 'implied reader', who is not only validated by the text but actually constructed by the author within the text. Iser's concept is a genuinely helpful contribution to the reconstruction of authorial purpose, but more useful to the textual interpreter than to the student of reception.

Granting the paucity of reception evidence for most books prior to *c.*1750 (and in many cases, much later), many

---

[38] See particularly Quentin Skinner, 'Meaning and Understanding in the History of Ideas', *History and Theory*, 8 (1969), 3–53, and James Tully (ed.), *Meaning and Context: Quentin Skinner and his Critics* ([Cambridge:] Polity Press, 1988).

possibilities await exploration.[39] Remarkably little has been done to reconstruct the reading habits and implicit theories of particular readers, even where the evidence happens to be plentiful. John Evelyn offers a splendid case in point. A vast number of his letters about books survive (mostly unpublished); some 400 books that he marked up may be found in the British Library; and we have detailed records in his commonplace books about how he progressed from initial reaction to analysis and evaluation. He is, to be sure, a single case, and probably a highly atypical one—but such a case is surely worth investigation. A good example of a single-subject study of reading is Robert DeMaria, Jr.'s recent *Samuel Johnson and the Life of Reading* (1997). Broader studies are more difficult in both method and the collection of evidence, but impressive exemplars are starting to appear for both remote and recent periods.[40] We must, of course, remember that 'reading' is demonstrably not the same activity at all times and in all places.[41]

In an ideal world, the archaeo-historicist would like testimony from a cross-section of real readers or spectators. To have ten detailed diary comments on the first run of *The White Devil* would be extremely convenient, if hardly a cure-all. Substantive newspaper or magazine reviews would be a help, though reviews can be quirky (to say the least) and in the eighteenth and nineteenth centuries they are often formulaic, expressing little but moral and critical platitudes. What do we do if such documentation does not exist?

We should *not* simply extrapolate a hypothetical audience out

[39] One of my readers points out, quite correctly, that this is not true for the Bible, or for major classical Latin texts, for which extensive commentaries existed long before the invention of printing. On *The Song of Songs*, for example, see E. Ann Matter, *The Voice of My Beloved: The Song of Songs in Western Medieval Christianity* (Philadelphia: University of Pennsylvania Press, 1990) and Ann W. Astell, *The Song of Songs in the Middle Ages* (Ithaca: Cornell University Press, 1990). For a stimulating investigation of Renaissance engagement with the classics, see Anthony Grafton, *Commerce with the Classics: Ancient Books and the Renaissance Reader* (Ann Arbor: University of Michigan Press, 1997).

[40] See e.g. Joyce Coleman, *Public Reading and the Reading Public in Late Medieval England and France* (Cambridge: Cambridge University Press, 1996), and Joseph McAleer, *Popular Reading and Publishing in Britain 1914–1950* (Oxford: Clarendon Press, 1992).

[41] Robert Darnton elegantly demonstrates this point in 'History of Reading' (1986), repr. in Peter Burke (ed.), *New Perspectives on Historical Writing* (University Park: Pennsylvania State University Press, 1992), 140–67.

of our own (prejudiced) readings of texts. To read a few 1670s
sex comedies and conclude (with Macaulay) that only a pack of
degenerate whoremongers would have wanted to see such stuff
does not get us very far, or at least not in the right direction. The
archaeo-historicist needs to be committed to the construction of
a complex model from contextual (not purely literary) evidence.
This takes us straight into the realm of letters, diaries, school
curricula, pamphlet ephemera—any sort of evidence that might
help us guess what cross-section of people read various kinds of
books or went to plays. How they would have responded to a
particular text brings us into the province of guesswork, but we
can make it educated guesswork. We are entitled to use pro-
logues, epilogues, comments within plays, 'dear reader' passages
in novels, and the like—but always with profound scepticism,
for the rhetoric is rarely straightforward. We must also remember that the material text itself often sends out powerful signals
about how it is to be interpreted—folio, quarto, pamphlet, and
broadside produce very different impressions, as can typogra-
phy and contextual content. T. A. Birrell convincingly demonstrates the impact of different publication auspices for *Mac
Flecknoe*, and observes the importance of D. H. Lawrence's
change of title for a collection of 1914: *The Prussian Officer
and Other Stories* cannot be read the same way as *Goose Fair
and Other Stories*, and especially not at the time of its publication.[42] The semiotics of the physical artefact are only starting to
get the attention they deserve.[43]

Our sense of audience needs to come primarily from some-
place other than the text. Let me illustrate. Consider the response of readers to Heathcliff. We might deduce the possibility
of (1) male identification with him; (2) female fascination/attrac-
tion; (3) male and female rejection of him on moral or social
grounds; (4) female titillation by what is fascinating but shocking. This spectrum would probably account for a fair percentage

[42] 'The Influence of Seventeenth-Century Publishers on the Presentation of Eng-
lish Literature', in Mary-Jo Arn and Hanneke Wirtjes, with Hans Jansen (eds.),
*Historical & Editorial Studies in Medieval & Early Modern English for Johan
Gerritsen* (Groningen: Wolters-Noordhoff, 1985), 163–73.
[43] On which see D. F. McKenzie, *Bibliography and the Sociology of Texts* (Panizzi
Lectures, 1985; London: The British Library, 1986), and E. A. Levenston, *The Stuff
of Literature: Physical Aspects of Texts and their Relation to Literary Meaning*
(Albany: State University of New York Press, 1992).

of the audience, but it is not methodologically sound. Good historical practice requires that we analyse the audience as we reconstruct it from diverse sources, and *then* inquire how the various parts of that audience might be expected to interpret *Wuthering Heights* and respond to it. Coming at the audience problem from a different vantage point, we might consider the riots that greeted *The Playboy of the Western World* in 1907. Bruce McConachie acutely analyses the radical differences in viewpoint and response among identifiable parts of Synge's original audience: Irish nationalists (offended by the implication that a backward peasantry made independence impossible), Protestants and middle-class optimists who believed in personal improvement, and working-class moralists who were violently offended by mention of women's underclothes and found the play contemptuous of their class. McConachie is surely right to say that there was a different performance for each of these groups (and no doubt others), and that 'If the historian is to take seriously the notion that spectators are the co-makers of a performance . . . he or she must seek to understand all of their points of view; must discover their aesthetics in the midst of their social, political, and religious values.'[44]

We must beware of simplistic assumptions. We might, for example, very plausibly analyse Ravenscroft's *The London Cuckolds* (1681) as an expression of courtier contempt for rich old Whig merchants (embodied in the hapless Wiseacre, Doodle, and Dashwell). Whether some parts of the original audience took it that way we have no evidence to tell us. But we do know that the play was revived annually until 1751 *because it became a particular favourite of the cits*. Ravenscroft may or may not have meant to express contempt, but the tone of the play seems so farcical as to deprive it of any serious satiric impact. Does 'cit pleasure' foreclose the possibility of 'courtier contempt'? By no means, for they could certainly coexist. Then again, we must allow for the possibility that the cits who came to love it were journeymen and apprentices, not rich merchants and aldermen.

Historicists with whom I have discussed historical reader-response hypotheses have tended to find the whole process alarmingly non-factual once one gets beyond a fully documented

---

[44] McConachie, 'Towards a Postpositivist Theatre History', 481–2.

kind of reception history. So it is, but so is interpretation *per se*. If we can map the variety of outlooks and sensibilities demonstrably present in (let us say) English society of the 1740s, then we are making no great jump if we investigate actual and hypothetical responses to *Pamela* and *Joseph Andrews*.[45] If we refuse to try to distinguish the probable responses of the educated, the ill-educated, the lower class, the parvenu, and females of various sorts (*et al.*), then we are consigning ourselves to the dubious benefits of a homogeneous 'eighteenth-century reader'—or refusing to grapple with the problems of the real novel audience at all. One of the major benefits of feminism to literary study has been its proponents' insistence on defining particular points of view in readers and audiences.[46]

While I am arguing for a broader contextual approach to reconstruction of original audience, I grant that quite a lot can be done by extrapolating from texts. Eric Rothstein and Frances M. Kavenik, for example, have created a stimulating and impressive 'desire-based' model of the comedy of the 1670s and 1680s in such a way. In essence, they have deduced a set of generic models that reflect the kinds of demands the audience evidently placed upon new plays and which playwrights tried to satisfy.[47] This model is an important reminder that audiences not only interpret and misinterpret texts, but exert powerful influence on those who write them, publish them, and stage them. The myth of solitary genius notwithstanding, few people now imagine that Shakespeare wrote in a state of sunny indifference as to what the Elizabethan audience liked.

Any attempt at reconstructing audience response to texts must grapple not only with the general cultural differences of 'then versus now' but also more specifically with differences in reading-theory and practice. This field remains virtually in its infancy, but it offers great promise. The prevalence of 'typological' reading in sixteenth- and seventeenth-century England is a fact, though relatively few twentieth-century scholarly

[45] See Tom Keymer, *Richardson's Clarissa and the Eighteenth-Century Reader* (Cambridge: Cambridge University Press, 1992).

[46] See, for example, Jill Dolan, *The Feminist Spectator as Critic* (Ann Arbor: UMI Research Press, 1988).

[47] Eric Rothstein and Frances M. Kavenik, *The Designs of Carolean Comedy* (Carbondale: Southern Illinois University Press, 1988).

readers have been very comfortable with this sort of interpretation (as I am not myself). Some books on theory of reading in
various periods would be extremely welcome. I continue to find
a pair of exploratory articles by John M. Wallace impressive
and provocative.[48] Wallace mounts a powerful argument to
the effect that habits of mind cultivated by some seventeenth-
century readers led them to presume the desirability of application of texts to current circumstances, regardless of whether the
author of the text intended such application or lived decades or
centuries before the events to which application might be
made. This would make a major difference to the way texts like
Absalom and Achitophel, Dryden and Lee's *The Duke of Guise*,
and Otway's *Venice Preserv'd* would have been read (or viewed,
in the case of plays). And if authors knew that readers would
tend to view texts this way, then of course that would affect the
way they wrote. Reading-theory changed drastically between
1650 and 1750. Lacking full-dress studies of reading-theory at
almost any date, we can for the present at least turn to specific
evidence in a period at issue. Dryden, Rymer, and Addison, for
instance, imply radically different concepts of what the author
should provide and what the reader should derive. The better
attuned we are to diversity of readerly practice the better we
shall deal with the complexities of historical texts.[49]

Until inquiry into the reading-theory of centuries past gives us
powerful new tools, what is the archaeo-historicist to do? I
would suggest an elementary either/or principle. If we possess a
broad spectrum of real-life reader response, then we should use
it; if we possess only a limited set of responses, we should try to
allow for what is missing. Alternatively, if the historical record is
blank or nearly so, then our only recourse is construction of a
hypothetical model of the reader spectrum.

The best situation is ample documentation of real-life reception. Lacking that, one can start by constructing the ideal/
implied reader from the text. We probably cannot, to be sure,

---

[48] John M. Wallace, 'Dryden and History: A Problem in Allegorical Reading',
ELH 36 (1969), 265–90, and '"Examples Are Best Precepts": Readers and Meanings in Seventeenth-Century Poetry', *Critical Inquiry*, 1 (1974), 273–90.

[49] The practical and theoretical work of Steven Mailloux seems to me to offer
great potentialities in this realm. See his *Interpretive Conventions: The Reader in the
Study of American Fiction* (Ithaca: Cornell University Press, 1982), and *Rhetorical
Power* (Ithaca: Cornell University Press, 1989).

have any assurance that such a reader ever actually existed, but he or she may serve as a kind of benchmark on the genetic side. For the next step, imagining possible readers, we must start by defining the scope of the potential audience pool. (Shakespeare and Bacon must have had rather different audiences.) Within that pool, we must at a minimum allow for age, gender, class, education, politics, and religion. The pertinence of these six factors will vary drastically depending on the nature of the work at issue. Gender might top the list if we are talking about *A Woman Killed with Kindness*, politics if *A Game at Chess* is our subject. The question we must ask is essentially ideological. What kinds of mindsets will approve the work, and what kinds will disapprove? Whatever the author may have built into the text, readers or spectators will pretty much respond according to their own lights, even if they have correctly understood what the text implies. (I have students who believe that killing an unfaithful spouse is eminently reasonable, and others who regard revenge as always unjustified.) A good way of generating a model reader for test purposes is to look at generically similar works from the same period, if they exist, and perform a reverse version of the kind of analysis carried out by Rothstein and Kavenik. 'Tell me what you desire, and I will tell you what you are.'

If we possessed detailed audience surveys for the comedies of Ben Jonson we could no doubt produce elaborate breakouts into subcategories. Lacking such evidence we cannot do this, but there is really no reason to want to. A contextual reading needs to take basic possibilities into account, but will only bog down if landed in a maze of fine distinctions and multiple categories. I would argue that for the vast majority of cases we need look at no more than five possibilities: (1) actual readers, if documentation exists; (2) the ideal reader implied by the text; (3 and 4) hypothesized friendly and unfriendly readers; (5) the 'desirous' reader implied by similar works of the same time, if any. For certain complex or controversial works we might have to allow for two or three sorts of friendly or unfriendly readers. A lecher and a Christian moralist might both succeed in liking *Clarissa*, though for radically incommensurable reasons. A moralist and a feminist might both dislike Faulkner's *Sanctuary*, if not on the same grounds. We do not require an elaborate machine here; we need merely establish a basis for accommodating radically divergent readings of a work in its historical setting.[50]

Analysing Texts in Contexts

Contextual analysis of texts is generally concerned with *genesis* (why the author wrote what he or she did, and what was meant) or with *reception* (how actual readers responded, or in the absence of sufficient evidence how hypothetical readers might have). In both cases the historical scholar adopts or creates a contextual template that is then used to explain the work at issue. Recent theorists have been dubious about this process, and rightly so. The contexts of original composition and reception are unrecapturable in their original totality and complexity. The particular work is not truly separable from its contextual origins or consumption, as a writer like Michel de Certeau is at pains to establish. Whatever context is employed for interpretive purposes has to be constructed by someone, with whatever degree of incompleteness or falsification. In any case, even the original contexts control neither the creation of the work nor its reception. The problems should not be lightly dismissed; serious work on the logic and methods of contextual interpretation remains urgently needed.[51] But uneven as past endeavours have been, the possibilities remain exciting.

Genetic analysis of texts has long been both enormously common and widely suspect. Simplistic assumptions about the relation of life to work are easy to challenge, and the prejudice against the 'intentional fallacy' instigated by the famous Wimsatt–Beardsley article of 1946 was followed by the much-touted death of the author championed by Barthes and Foucault

[50] Several readers of this book in draft have felt that I am (here and elsewhere) decidedly hostile to 'reader-response criticism'. This is by no means what I wish to convey. On the contrary, I am trying to argue that reader-response theory should be valued and appropriated by the historicist. Adapted and reinvigorated, it can then be usefully employed in contextual interpretation of texts. Serious historicism *demands* the acknowledgement of individual diversity on which the best reader-response critics have insisted.

[51] For useful discussion of recent theories of the text–context relationship, see Claire Colebrook, *New Literary Histories: New Historicism and Contemporary Criticism* (Manchester: Manchester University Press, 1997), esp. chs. 1 and 5.

a quarter of a century later. Common sense triumphed to the extent that scholars have continued to associate the particulars of works of literature with the authorial circumstances in which they were composed. (A definitive attribution of 'The Ballad of Reading Gaol' to Yeats would be more than a little unsettling.)[52] We need, however, to consider the logic of genetic criticism in the face of more serious objections than the disreputability of slovenly biographical criticism.

More than twenty years ago John M. Ellis mounted a strenuous assault on the idea 'that the aim of criticism is to recreate the original circumstances of composition of a text—to ascertain why it was written and for what audience'.[53] Ellis is a critic not to be lightly dismissed. He agrees with Wellek and Warren that we cannot experience a work of literature in any other way than as readers of the twentieth century, and that we would simply impoverish *Hamlet* by restricting ourselves to the meaning it had for contemporary audiences (always supposing such meaning to be recoverable). Ellis believes that meaning inheres in texts regardless of context and is consequently in favour of 'nonhistoricist criticism'. He says flatly that 'the most fundamental logical error in biographical and intentional criticism . . . is that of referring a literary text to the limited context of its origin, which by definition removes from it any literary status.'

I am prepared to dismiss the claim to 'literary status' as an arbitrary definition. Beyond that, I would make two arguments. First, criticism has a number of legitimate aims, only *one* of which has to do with reconstructing original circumstances of composition and audience. Such genetic investigation need not be specially privileged, but since many works are significantly shaped by their origins, refusing to consider those origins seems essentially perverse. We may decide that origins are relatively unimportant, or that we are more interested in something else. But a reading of *For Whom the Bell Tolls* that resolutely ignored attitudes towards the Spanish Civil War would be odd. Secondly, I fail to see why reconstructing meaning as conceived in original

[52] One of my readers points out that Yeats did in a sense 'appropriate' the poem when he gutted it for the *Oxford Book of Modern Verse*, stripping out its 'foreign feathers'.

[53] John M. Ellis, *The Theory of Literary Criticism: A Logical Analysis* (Berkeley: University of California Press, 1974), 55. Following quotations from 122, 135-6.

circumstances should in any way impoverish the work at issue. This would be true only if we supposed that original meaning somehow invalidated all other readings. Only a diehard adherent of reading for one-true-meaning would think anything of the sort. Even a strict-constructionist believer in Hirsch's *Validity in Interpretation* would make some space for new 'significance' created by changing context. Far from impoverishing the work, reference to original contextual meaning gives us a strong point of reference against which to compare other interpretations.

A genetic analysis of a text asks 'Why was it written this way?' The concern of the investigator may be with personal, social, political, or other circumstantial constraints upon the author. Alternatively, one may look at what the author has drawn upon and alluded to. If we ask why Shakespeare wrote *Titus Andronicus*, a good place to start is the theatrical context of the early 1590s.[54] We want to know what sorts of plays were getting written and staged, what sort of control was exercised over them, what sort of remuneration an author received, and so forth. Such information cannot answer the question in anything like a definitive way, but we can get a sense of circumstances, opportunities, and constraints. Writing *The Tempest*, Shakespeare took advantage of stage machinery evidently not available to him earlier. When Dryden wrote his uncharacteristically smutty *The Kind Keeper* (1678), he was not just cynically adopting what he thought would sell. From the nature of the play and its date one might very fairly conclude that he had done just that, but in this case we are lucky enough to have a letter from Dryden in the midst of composition, explaining that he was working under the direct instructions of the king.[55] Opportunistic he may have been, but hardly a free agent. Professionals tend to write what they think they can sell. Whether you are Bulwer-Lytton writing a performance vehicle for Macready, or P. G. Wodehouse peddling stories to the *Saturday Evening Post* in its heyday, you are bound by the chains of circumstance.

[54] The scanty evidence is well presented in Jonathan Bate's excellent Arden edition (London: Routledge, 1995).

[55] 'It will be almost such another piece of businesse as [Durfey's] the fond Husband, for such the King will have it, who is parcell poet with me in the plott.' *The Letters of John Dryden*, ed. Charles E. Ward (Durham: Duke University Press, 1942), no. 5.

And one of the functions of the archaeo-historicist is to elucidate the productive and constraining forces under which writers work.

In a large majority of cases, we do not possess evidence about why the writer wrote what he or she did. Where such evidence does exist, however, we are extremely foolish if we do not see what can be made of it. Gibbon's *Memoirs* offer a striking illustration. At the time of his death in 1794 he left six separate drafts (A through F) representing different attempts to fulfil his aims, whatever they may have been. The work was published posthumously in 1796 by Lord Sheffield, who selected, emended, and elided bits from the six versions to construct a single text. A century later all six were printed, but this created as much confusion as illumination. Highly intelligent critics have tried to account for Gibbon's floundering in a variety of ways. W. B. Carnochan has applied psychoanalytic methods (anachronistic but suggestive); Patricia Meyer Spacks has approached the tangle as a problem in literary form.[56]

Gibbon manifestly wavered as to whether he was writing for publication in his lifetime or posthumously, and his discomfort about certain key areas (his relations with his father, for example) is obvious. What had never been properly done until very recently indeed was to scrutinize the drafts closely in relation to Gibbon's responses to what was happening in Europe while he wrote. Such an investigation must be both biographical and bibliographical (a combination not fashionable), and is precisely what David Womersley has now given us.[57]

Gibbon was acutely aware of news from France; he strongly agreed with his friend Burke's analysis of the French Revolution; he could not but see the implications of current events for any evaluation of his own life and work as he grappled with the problems of fashioning his own image and memorial towards the end of his life. Critics tend to distrust biography and rarely descend into the technicalities of bibliography, but in the case of

[56] W. B. Carnochan, *Gibbon's Solitude* (Stanford: Stanford University Press, 1987); Patricia Meyer Spacks, *Imagining a Self: Autobiography and Novel in Eighteenth-Century England* (Cambridge, Mass.: Harvard University Press, 1976).

[57] David Womersley, 'Gibbon's *Memoirs*: Autobiography in Time of Revolution', in *Edward Gibbon: Bicentenary Essays*, ed. id. with the assistance of John Burrow and John Pocock (Studies on Voltaire and the Eighteenth Century, 355; Oxford: Voltaire Foundation, 1997), 347–404.

Gibbon evidence about genesis is both copious and compelling. It is not the whole story, but ignoring it cannot be justified.

A very different kind of genetic/contextual analysis occurs when we ask why the work contains what it does and alludes to what it does. The writer's relationship to his or her material (whether the material is personal or quite otherwise) is a legitimate subject for historicist investigation. The reasons for Marvell's writing 'Last Instructions to a Painter', what he was trying to say, and the nature of the communication and argument involved are surely vital to making any sense of a complex poem deeply situated in particular political circumstances. *The Prelude* in any of its three major versions can stand as a poetic text, but would we really wish to divorce it from the context of its creation? Another kind of contextual problem is presented by *Ulysses*. In all three cases, different though they are, the work is as it is because of the circumstances of its genesis, not because of abstract aesthetic choices. Is the meaning of *Ulysses* somehow inscribed within the dense layers of personal and topical Irish allusion? By no means. Can we read Joyce's novel in blank ignorance of all local and biographical references? Undoubtedly we can, but doing so would leave us unable to account for a substantial part of the whole, or inclined to jump at what might be very unsound explanations of particulars. Neither the Homeric level nor the local Irish elements 'explain' the book, but they enrich it, and expounding them does not in any way debar another critic from attempting a more purely internal reading, or one that seeks completely different frames of reference.[58]

Even ultra-familiar canonical works may possess contextual meanings of fundamental importance to the comprehension of their artistic construction. Melville's *Billy Budd* is a spectacular and unsettling example. It was written between 1886 and 1891, though not published until 1924. It has been the subject of endless and rancorous debates over its position on capital punishment, but so far as I am aware, not until 1997 did anyone point out in print that Melville wrote the story while living in New York in the midst of an enormous and ongoing hullabaloo

[58] As a particularly fine example of contextual reading, I offer Michael J. Colacurcio's *The Province of Piety: Moral History in Hawthorne's Early Tales* (Cambridge, Mass.: Harvard University Press, 1984).

over capital punishment and the means of carrying it out if it were not to be abolished—as there was very powerful sentiment for doing.[59] Newspapers and magazines were full of the issue, fueled by Thomas Alva Edison's scare campaign against AC (as opposed to DC) electrical current. The first execution by electrocution was carried out in August 1890 and immediately generated violently hostile descriptions of a 'nauseating' spectacle. Bruce Franklin demonstrates quite devastatingly from the text that Melville is systematically alluding to contemporary debate while carefully keeping all direct mention of it out of his text—the story, after all, is set in 1797. However a critic may respond to the text today, or choose to read it, Franklin seems to me to prove beyond reasonable doubt that Melville composed the text while intensely conscious of a hot topic, and must have presumed awareness of contemporary debate on the part of the audience that would have read the story had it been published in 1891 when he completed it. The meaning of *Billy Budd* is by no means controlled by its genesis and context of composition, but ignorance of them severely distorts our understanding of the shape and content of the work as it has come down to us.

When we turn our attention to contextual analysis of reception, we face greater complexities. The sensible archaeohistoricist (unlike some old and new historicist predecessors) must be prepared to encompass radical diversity and disagreement on the part of actual or hypothetical audiences. But how do we get text and context to interact? Interpretation is always done by *someone*: it is not an abstract process, and it cannot happen by itself. The text of *Absalom and Achitophel* possesses some pretty clear intrinsic indications of how the interpreter should decipher and respond to it, but the actual reading must be done by a 'someone', and that person consciously or unconsciously applies his or her contexts—whether in 1681, 1800, or today. The meaning is not changed by juxtaposing text with background; the key is *whose* background. The correct question for a historical interpreter is not 'what did *Absalom and Achitophel* mean in 1681?' but rather '*what did it mean to particular readers?*' We are certainly free to ask what Dryden meant (or thought he meant) and why he wrote what he did. His life and

[59] See H. Bruce Franklin, '*Billy Budd* and Capital Punishment: A Tale of Three Centuries', *American Literature*, 69 (1997), 337–59.

other works are a legitimate part of the context. But neither his aims nor the genetic background of the work controlled the responses of contemporary readers (plenty of whom were outraged), and nor should we imagine that they ought to dictate ours. 'Meaning' is certainly built into texts (few literary works are simply invitations to free association), but meaning is actuated and comprehended only in individual readers.

The analyst of reception asks how a work was read by original or subsequent audiences. To discover the full range of potential meanings, an interpreter will often do well to explore later responses as well as those in the context of the origin. Reception changes. Looking at the criticism of the last forty years, one might conclude that *Tom Jones* is an ethical treatise and that *Clarissa* is a veritable cesspool of sex. Yet in the eighteenth century the opposite opinion was common, and the abrupt reversal of long-standing opinion after two centuries is a bit startling.[60] Or consider the menstruation references in Book XVIII of *Ulysses*. What was liberating or startling or disgusting in 1922 has long since lost its impact. The documented controversies of yore generally seem ridiculous in retrospect. They can, however, serve as more than occasion for wonder or derision. The *Pamela/Shamela* dispute of the early 1740s, quaint as it now seems, has much to tell us about why Richardson's novel became an important cultural artefact.

If we lack much in the way of documented reception, a very natural tactic is to generate a 'contextual viewpoint' from other materials of the time. This should be done only with great caution. Consider, for example, the comedies of the period 1680–1710. How can we see them through contemporary eyes? D. R. M. Wilkinson, in a learned monograph, has proposed extracting a moral code from conduct books of this period (which are numerous and explicit) and assessing the behaviour in the comedies in light of it.[61] The judgements are, naturally, exceedingly negative. We learn that the plays condemn what they show (which is odd, since they reward virtually all of their

---

[60] A *Punch* cartoon of 1891 illustrating 'Emancipation' shows a new bride and her husband at a railway bookstall, departing on their honeymoon. Bride to husband: 'Oh, Edwin dear! Here's *Tom Jones*. Papa told me I wasn't to read it till I was married! . . . Buy it for me, Edwin dear.' *A Century of Punch Cartoons*, ed. R. E. Williams (New York: Simon and Schuster, 1955), 94.

[61] D. R. M. Wilkinson, *The Comedy of Habit* (Leiden: Universitaire Pers, 1964).

erring protagonists without benefit of repentance). But were the authors and readers of conduct books regular ticket buyers at the theatres? Would we collect the pronouncements of the Revd Billy Graham and other televangelists and use them to analyse current films and television sitcoms? I doubt it. As an alternative perspective on Congreve, Farquhar, *et al.*, we might ask how people of the time looked at marriage, adultery, bastardy, and so forth. But once having generated a suitably varied set of views, we would bump up against an awkward question: how many members of the audience applied real-life standards to plays? These plays, though often projecting an aura of realism, turn out often to be far from faithful to actuality. The spectacular 'divorce' at the end of *The Beaux Stratagem* (1707), for example, is illegal and impossible. The audience appears totally to have ignored this. There are those who judge identically in life and in literature, but there are those who do not. We would be rash to assume that documented opinion in real life will be a reliable indicator of literary or theatrical judgement.

What did the author mean and how did the audience take it? These are not always separable questions. Consider the case of Dryden and Purcell's *King Arthur* (1691). Critics have variously found it a muddled adventure story, an exercise in British patriotism, and a sly allegorical satire against King William III in the aftermath of the 'Glorious' Revolution of 1688. The opera was popular, but reception is virtually undocumented. Seventeenth-century opera has been widely assumed in recent years to be a vehicle for covert political satire, and the Jacobite reading is certainly the most interesting, subtle, and exciting one. Any vagueness or internal contradictions can be put down to camouflage. The historicist, however, would like to know whether the reading can be validated. I have argued at length elsewhere that it cannot.[62] Negatives cannot be proven, but there are a number of grounds on which to be sceptical of the allegorical reading. Point 1: if we look at all extant English and Continental operas of the seventeenth century, I do not believe that we will find a single one in which there is *documented* evidence of covert satire against the government. There is a great deal of obvious allegory, all of it devoted to glorifying the

---

[62] 'The Politics of Opera in Late Seventeenth-Century London', *Cambridge Opera Journal*, 10 (1998), 15–43.

incumbent monarch. Point 2: Dryden had lost his laureateship in 1688; he needed money; he would have been taking an enormous risk if a judicious contemporary reader could presume that he was attacking the king. Point 3: Purcell derived most of his living as a member of the King's Musick. He is not known to have been a Jacobite, and he would have had to be mad to risk setting a work he thought would be taken that way. Could a disgruntled supporter of the exiled James II have found an agreeable application in the opera? Undoubtedly. Is this what the text 'means' for a reader not strongly predisposed that way? I would say pretty clearly not. What a contextual reading can do for us here is to demonstrate the multifariousness of a complex text, even in the absence of hard evidence about original audience response.

A study of the reception of *Women in Love* will require little if any hypothesis or speculation: documentation exists. An account of the reception of *Othello* prior to the late eighteenth century can consist of hardly anything but hypothesis and speculation. The play was popular. Evidence on racial views in the seventeenth century is scanty. For many Londoners running off with a blackamoor might not have seemed significantly stranger than running off with a Martian, and hence perhaps not ground for moral concern, especially as Desdemona promptly comes to a sticky end. Evidence about views of patriarchal authority, in sharp contradistinction, is plentiful, but how many members of the audience read those views into plays is anyone's guess. Certainly most do not seem to have done so in comedy. *Internally*, the play seems to imply strong sympathy for Desdemona, and the possibility of tragic stature for Othello. In this instance, I would have to say that the text may be our safest guide. We have no way to know how many members of the audience went home thinking (with Thomas Rymer) that Othello was a booby and Desdemona a fool.

A contextual reader builds templates and applies them. Just as a critical theory can fit a work well or badly, so can a historical template, whether genesis- or reception-based. The lens we create will affect what we see through it. If we place Fielding in an intensely moral-Christian context, then *Joseph Andrews* will become an awfully solemn book.[63] This reading is

[63] As it does in Martin C. Battestin's vastly influential *The Moral Basis of Fielding's Art: A Study of Joseph Andrews* (Middletown: Wesleyan University Press, 1959).

not wrong: the morality is there. But it fails to do justice to the jokes, humour, and buoyant high spirits that give the book its tone. Likewise if we construct Blake as solitary mystic genius, he can appear totally disconnected from the worlds of everyday life and politics in Napoleonic-era England. If we attend to the evidence first so cogently presented in David V. Erdman's *Blake: Prophet Against Empire* (1954), Blake abruptly becomes a totally different kind of person and writer. Assumptions about audiences can be at least equally distortive, as long-standing clichés about the coterie audience in the time of Charles II remind us. The dangers are obvious, but the potential benefits of contextual interpretation remain enticing.

Testing Results

Archaeo-Historicism is worthless if its results are not subject to testing and verification. A generation ago even literary critics sometimes gave lip-service to such an idea. Writing an introduction to R. S. Crane's collected papers, Wayne C. Booth commended Crane's scorn for 'those who invent new and improved interpretations of Gulliver's fourth Voyage with no thought for how they might be tested'.[64] Tested? *Tested!* The post-structuralist snorts. Authorially controlled single meanings are an exploded hypothesis, and good riddance, but does this really mean that any interpretation is as good as any other, Rymer's analysis of *Othello* included? This is not the place to argue about the evaluation—testing, if you will—of textual interpretations.[65] Documentary historical research is something else again, and so is textual interpretation carried out in the light of it. Archaeo-Historicism claims *truth* within the limits of available evidence, and such a claim both demands an attempt at validation on the part of the proposer and invites direct challenge.

One of the most basic principles of Archaeo-Historicism is that you can only claim what you have evidence to support.

[64] *The Idea of the Humanities*, i, p. xxi.
[65] For a trenchant discussion of plausibility and proof, see Harriett Hawkins, *The Devil's Party: Critical Counter-interpretations of Shakespearian Drama* (Oxford: Clarendon Press, 1985), esp. ch. 3, 'Conjectures and Refutations'.

Additional evidence may someday appear, but very probably it will not, and therefore we must work within the limits of what we possess. Skating onto thin ice tends to land one in cold water. History and science are different in this regard. A scientist may routinely hypothesize ahead of experimental results, hoping that confirmatory evidence can be obtained. Short of forging manuscripts, we can rarely do this.[66]

Accepting the limitations of our evidence can be incredibly frustrating. Shakespeare's biographical puzzles are a familiar instance. Looking at the facts collected in Schoenbaum's *Shakespeare: A Documentary Life*, one sees how pitifully limited and impersonal the evidence is,[67] but living with it strikes me as a better idea than writing a biography in the fashion of A. L. Rowse. Students are often advised to say 'I don't know' when stumped by an examiner, and scholars could do worse than apply the lesson to themselves. Good ones do. I once wrote Richard Leacroft to ask why he had not included a reconstruction of Dorset Garden in *The Development of the English Playhouse*. He promptly replied that omitting one of the most exciting theatres was maddening, but that he lacked the design details that would permit him to make the kind of reconstruction he was committed to. He could certainly have imagined an appropriate theatre for the site dimensions and the staging of plays and operas done there, and designed one in accordance with the limited pictorial evidence extant. But it would have been a speculation, not a reconstruction in the light of hard evidence.

Speculation is not wrong, especially not if clearly labelled as such. The question is how fundamental the speculation is to what is being claimed. If a substantial portion of the hypothesis is solidly grounded in hard evidence, then some speculative frosting is not out of place. There is no way to draw a tidy line and say 'here is the limit; do not go beyond the pale', but one can definitely go too far. Shakespeare's texts have given rise to legitimate questions about his possible bisexuality, but if I

[66] For a stimulating challenge to Heidegger, Gadamer, and Foucault for their evasion of empirical validation, see Allen Thiher, 'The Tautological Thinking of Historicism', *Texas Studies in Literature and Language*, 39 (1997), 1–26.

[67] S. Schoenbaum, *William Shakespeare: A Documentary Life* (New York: Oxford University Press, 1975).

infer from those texts that he was a transvestite molester of puppydogs I trust the reader will demand some pretty rigorous explanations of how I reached this exciting and original conclusion. One reaches the unsound long before one arrives at the outrageous.

One of the primary commitments of the historical scholar is that he or she will make every effort to avoid the propagation or transmission of error. A critic has the right to indulge in speculative and risky readings; an archaeo-historicist does not. In the realm of criticism, one may ignore or dismiss offhand a reading one finds misguided or unsound. Criticism is not an 'additive' field: ten books are not necessarily an improvement on three or four. Historical study in sharp contradistinction does claim to be additive: one builds on predecessors, tries to correct them, aims to improve on them. A critical book is lucky to remain significant for as long as a decade, and few survive twenty years. A historical book may eventually be superseded, its arguments absorbed and extended by its successors, but if it is any good at all it cannot simply be ignored and forgotten.

Shoddy handling of evidence and irresponsible conclusions do lasting damage in an additive field. Consider the issue of attributions, for example. We want to know what our authors wrote, and when we encounter something that 'seems like' the work of a prolific and incompletely documented writer of interest, the temptation to make a case on the basis of internal evidence can seem overwhelming. And is a plausible and carefully hedged attribution so great a sin? Perhaps not, but the cumulative effect can be fairly disastrous, as in the embarrassing case of the Defoe canon. The massive roster of works embodied in Moore's standard bibliography melts away most alarmingly if one starts to examine the solidity of the evidence for a vast number of those titles.[68] How many books and articles have founded their arguments about Defoe on works whose attribution is doubtful or just plain wrong?

[68] Compare John Robert Moore, *A Checklist of the Writings of Daniel Defoe* (2nd edn., Hamden, Conn.: Archon, 1971) with P. N. Furbank and W. R. Owens, *The Canonisation of Daniel Defoe* (New Haven: Yale University Press, 1988); *Defoe De-Attributions: A Critique of J. R. Moore's Checklist* (London: Hambledon Press, 1994); and *A Critical Bibliography of Daniel Defoe* (London: Pickering and Chatto, 1998). Furbank and Owens suggest that nearly half the works heretofore attributed to Defoe should not be regarded as his.

Once a factual error is in print, it is virtually ineradicable, for it will be picked up and repeated. I have done this myself. Who wrote *The Rape of Europa by Jupiter*, published anonymously in 1694? A book by Eugene Haun attributed it to William Ranson, citing Wing as the source.[69] To my shame, I did not check, but said '(by William Ranson?)' when I discussed the work in *The Development of English Drama in the Late Seventeenth Century*. I subsequently realized that when Haun consulted Wing he failed to realize that the work was unattributed, and simply looked up the column from the title until he found an author's name. ('Ran' comes right before 'Rap.') I see the attribution in print from time to time, and curse my witless contribution to its acceptance. Trivial in itself? Possibly, but every error gives rise to more errors. A historical study must stand up both at the level of its nuts-and-bolts evidence and at the level of its general conclusions. Here are two very different sorts of failure.

Louis I. Bredvold's *The Intellectual Milieu of John Dryden* (1934) remained utterly standard for more than three decades. It was taught to me in graduate school essentially as truth to be memorized. Bredvold looked about in seventeenth-century religious and philosophical pamphlets and constructed a context for Dryden's poetry that 'proved' he was a Pyrrhonist. Many critics subsequently used that conclusion in analysing Dryden's work, and under the circumstances this was not an unreasonable thing to do. In 1968, however, Phillip Harth published *Contexts of Dryden's Thought*, which so totally demolished Bredvold that the Pyrrhonist interpretation became a non-issue. Bredvold had not read as widely as he might, and on closer scrutiny the 'fit' between Dryden's poems and the context he had constructed was not so good as it could have been. In a sense, the system worked exactly as it should. Bredvold was wrong, but not foolishly so. He produced a plausible interpretation out of the evidence he assembled and in due course it was superseded by a better one.

My second example is a recent book by J. C. D. Clark, *Samuel Johnson: Literature, Religion and English Cultural Politics from*

---

[69] Eugene Haun, *But Hark! More Harmony: The Libretti of Restoration Opera in English* (Ypsilanti: Eastern Michigan University Press, 1971), 145.

the Restoration to Romanticism (1994).[70] The central thesis of
this learned and heavily documented monograph is that Johnson
was a deeply committed Jacobite who refused to take the oath
of supremacy (rejecting belief in the Pope and foreign princes)
or the oath of allegiance to the Hanoverian dynasty. Consequently, for example, we are to ascribe his leaving Pembroke
College, Oxford, to moral scruples rather than to poverty. If
true, this represents a truly radical reorientation of our understanding of a major and much studied figure. I am not a John-
sonian, have no stake whatever in the argument, and am willing
to be convinced. Having read the book, however, I feel anything
but convinced. Clark presents no new evidence, and his revisionist handling of familiar sources comes across to me as ingenious
(one might say perverse) special pleading. The picture of Johnson as Jacobite does not, ultimately, make much sense to me.
Johnson's extensive political writings *may* all be twisted to hide
his real convictions, but if he was indeed a deep-dyed Jacobite,
then we must regard him as not only direly muddled but profoundly disingenuous. We need not accept the most creditable
interpretation of a major writer, but we ought to ask how well
any interpretation hangs together. The picture that emerges from
many sources of Johnson as Anglican pragmatist accounts well
for a very high proportion of his life and work. Clark's revisionist interpretation seems pertinent to much less of the life and
work and explains almost nothing more convincingly. I may be
wrong. I may have been brainwashed by the School of Donald
Greene. But one of the reasons I find Clark so unpersuasive is
that he is so contemptuous of his predecessors. He makes no
attempt to see why they thought what they did, or to explain
why no one had an inkling of Johnson's true outlook until 1994.
Were they all fools and knaves? Clark ends up giving the impression of an attorney making an aggressive and one-sided argument for a far-fetched case.[71]

[70] For devastating commentary, see particularly Howard D. Weinbrot, 'Johnson,
Jacobitism, and the Historiography of Nostalgia', *The Age of Johnson*, 7 (1996),
163–211; 'Johnson and Jacobitism Redux: Evidence, Interpretation, and Intellectual
History', *ibid.*, 8 (1997), 89–125; 'Johnson, Jacobitism, and Swedish Charles: *The
Vanity of Human Wishes* and Scholarly Method', *ELH* 64 (1997), 945–91. Real and
alleged Jacobitism have become a hot topic in the last few years. The last 1997 issue
of *ELH* is devoted in its entirety to the subject.
[71] Clark insists on calling the Old Pretender 'James III' while describing George I

When we are presented with a new historical construct or a new contextualization of a work or writer we need to ask terribly obvious questions. Does it try to change our understanding of the subject? Is it accurate? Does it make use of the known evidence? Does it adduce new evidence? Are the analysis and conclusions persuasive? Does the overall picture that emerges explain more and make better sense than its predecessors? A literary critic can rejoice in the refreshing, the exciting, and the provocative. The archaeo-historicist has to ask *is this true?* And if not, is it at least the best we can do on present evidence? Karl Popper is dead right when he insists that new hypotheses must be subject to close scrutiny and harsh challenge.

Assessing someone else's results is always easier than turning a cold eye on one's own. Yet the best time for rigorous testing of results is *before* they get into print. Just as wonder drugs should not be rushed onto the market without extensive clinical evaluation, so historical research ought to undergo a genuine process of validation. If the author is serious about what he or she is doing, the process will start with self-scrutiny. What we need to ask is far from subtle or complicated. I would suggest four simple questions.

1. How much evidence is ignored or not explained by your hypothesis?
2. What would the two most hostile reviewers of your last book say about it?
3. To what extent do your conclusions correlate with your own predilections?
4. Does your hypothesis accord with common sense? If not, what justifies rejecting the obvious?

Few hypotheses can account fully for all evidence. All of us are liable, however, to overlook what is inconvenient. The innumerable books and articles that assert the dominance of 'sentimental comedy' after 1700 ignore not only very large numbers of new 'laughing comedies' written and staged between 1700 and 1780,

in the index as 'Georg Ludwig (1660–1727) Duke of Braunschweig-Lüneburg, Electoral Prince (from 1692) and Elector (from 1698) of Hanover, from 1714 also styled King George I of Great Britain'. This is the Jacobite viewpoint, but why is Professor Clark writing as a Jacobite?

but also the predominance of old laughing comedies in the repertory.

The suggestion about hostile reviewers is obviously an adaptation of Crane's proposal that we treat our hypotheses as though they were by someone else and attempt to refute them. I venture to add that if you are on speaking terms with your opponents—a highly desirable state of affairs—then you might do well to ask them to read your manuscript. Facts you can check, and evidence you can survey, but judging the degree of one's own predisposition is really difficult. To become the victim of one's own political or sexual or moral preferences is extraordinarily easy. I know that I have a strong predilection for economic explanations: having a friend (or an enemy) challenge this tendency can only be healthy.

My fourth test is meant neither pro forma nor as mockery of post-structuralists. I very seriously agree with J. H. Hexter's dictum that 'historians must not be careless of common sense'.[72] I will readily grant that at times the simple, obvious, and predictable will not be true. The simple explanation is not always the right explanation. We must beware, however, of such complexity of hypothesis or such a flood of detail that we befuddle ourselves with complexities of our own importation. If our hypothesis is not in accord with common sense, then we must explain what justifies rejecting the obvious. Scholars can be astonishingly resistant to admitting that a great writer behaved stupidly, incompetently, or dishonestly (though such behaviour is not uncommon). They can likewise cling to overcomplicated traditional theories with all the tenacity of Ptolemaic astronomers. There is perhaps not much glory to be achieved in proposing clear and simple answers to historical questions.

At bottom, Archaeo-Historicism is at once a simple business and a hard business. One need not be a 'Doctor of Subtleties' to ask interesting historical questions, or to propose plausible answers. The kinds of analysis involved are not rocket science, and neither are they philosophically profound. What is hard is acquiring the relevant evidence, handling it fairly, and drawing from it conclusions that are both satisfying and defensible. Where the evidence is insufficient, one must accept frustration,

[72] J. H. Hexter, *The History Primer* (New York: Basic Books, 1971), 296.

which few literary critics have learnt to do. Above all what makes Archaeo-Historicism a serious business is the commitment of the practitioner to discovering what is *true* — and acceptance of the possibility that a cherished hypothesis may be superseded or proved wrong.

3
The Limits of Archaeo-Historicism

IF YOU manufacture a 'machine', you need to demonstrate a use for it. You should also realize that there are circumstances in which it will prove unnecessary, and others in which it will fail to work. A better mousetrap may not be wanted in a house full of cats, and the best mousetrap yet conceived by human ingenuity offers little protection against woodpeckers. To justify a method, one must show that it can be used to do worthwhile things, and that it delivers sound and reliable results. To suggest employing it where it cannot work properly is about as sensible as trying to cure athlete's foot with a tonsillectomy.

Archaeo-Historicism is a method by which we attempt to reconstruct past events and past viewpoints. Sound practice demands that we ask some sceptical questions. What can Archaeo-Historicism *not* do? What does it do badly? Where is the investigator most vulnerable to error and self-deception? Three obvious objections must be confronted.

1. Not everything is susceptible to reconstruction.
2. The solidity and utility of the results vary drastically, depending in part on the nature of the evidence available.
3. Application of the method may be challenged methodologically. The 'constructedness' of contexts, the investigator's claim to relative impartiality, and the feasibility of historical explanation of causes have proved particularly controversial.

In the present chapter I attempt to expose the failures, inadequacies, and limitations of Archaeo-Historicism as a method. Putting the point more positively, I would say that I am endeavouring to establish the limits of its valid applications and conclusions. I shall start by attempting to disentangle Archaeo-Historicism from 'literary history' before moving on to consider some practical problems (lack of evidence, differences between genres) and then taking up more philosophical issues (ideology, determinism, causation).

The Failure of Literary History

> The attempts at an evolutionary history have failed. I myself have failed in *The History of Modern Criticism* to construe a convincing scheme of development. I discovered, by experience, that there is no evolution in the history of critical argument. . . . This is, at least for me, the end of an illusion, the fall of literary history.
>
> René Wellek[1]

We commence of necessity by asking what is meant by the phrase 'literary history'? Many meanings have been attached to this term, but for our immediate purposes a simple two-part definition will suffice:

1. Any study of the language and historical contexts in which literary works were produced, and/or the lives of the authors.

2. The history of the succession of literary works, conventions, genres, or techniques, almost always including an explanation of temporal changes based on an implicit or explicit causal theory.[2]

The second meaning—sequential explanation—constitutes our subject here. Literary history in this sense has been a prominent part of literary scholarship for more than a century, but in recent years it has fallen into severe disrepute. Important theorists and practitioners of literary history have publicly disavowed it as a discipline. Disrespect for it on the part of critics and critical theorists contributes to the low esteem for 'old historicism', of which it is commonly considered an integral part. I shall argue that this association is adventitious. A fresh consideration of the claims of sequential explanation will do little to bolster its sagging reputation, but I see no reason to regard this as a liability to Archaeo-Historicism, which advances no such claims.

In a celebrated essay of 1946, Wellek defined several quite

---

[1] René Wellek, *The Attack on Literature*, 77.
[2] Quoted from Harris, *Dictionary of Concepts in Literary Criticism and Theory*, 185.

different sorts of 'literary history'. These included history of books, intellectual history, history of national civilizations, sociological history, historical relativism, and literary development taken in its own terms.[3] For another twenty-five years he continued to champion literary development, though he was clearly uncomfortable at times about the separatist nature of the enterprise. As early as 1941 Wellek had asked 'Whether it is *possible* to write literary history . . . which will be both literary and a history? . . . Most histories of literature are either social histories or histories of thought as mirrored in literature, or a series of impressions and judgments on individual works of art arranged in a more or less chronological order.'[4] A double-barrelled question confronted Wellek then and us now: what kinds of sequential explanation should be attempted, and how much validity can the results possess?

That 'literary history' of a sort can be written is not in doubt. Hippolyte Taine produced one in the 1860s, and university libraries are chock-full of the things. They have become historical documents themselves. Anyone proposing to trace the evolution of literary study in Britain and America will consider *The Cambridge History of English Literature* (1907–16), the *Oxford History of English Literature* (whose publication commenced in 1945—a venture completed in 1997 after a generation of struggle to make it work), and the sort of quasi-encyclopedic 'history' now being attempted in the realm of American literature.[5] At a less pretentious level, one can turn to Baugh or Daiches.[6] But mere chronological list is not 'history', and the kinds of 'explanation' proffered in such enterprises have seemed increasingly simplistic, mechanical, and unsatisfying. Wellek said cheerfully in 1941 that 'Literary history . . . can be understood to begin with the accumulation and collection of documents, their editing and placing in a

[3] René Wellek, 'Six Types of Literary History', *English Institute Essays 1946* (New York: Columbia University Press, 1947), 107–26, esp. 113.

[4] René Wellek, 'Literary History', in Norman Foerster *et al.*, *Literary Scholarship: Its Aims and Methods* (Chapel Hill: University of North Carolina Press, 1941), 115.

[5] *The Cambridge History of American Literature*, Sacvan Bercovitch, gen. ed. (Cambridge: Cambridge University Press, 1994–). As I write, vols. i, ii, and viii are in print.

[6] *A Literary History of England*, ed. Albert C. Baugh, 4 vols. (1948; 2nd edn., New York: Appleton-Century-Crofts, 1967); David Daiches, *A Critical History of English Literature*, 2 vols. (London: Secker and Warburg, 1960).

chronological scheme.'[7] So far so good, but what next? Wellek and Warren regarded literary history as 'a view of literature which sees it primarily as a series of works arranged in chronological order and as integral parts of the historical process'.[8] What exactly is 'historical process' and what is the key that allows us to interpret the 'integral' relationship between work and context? The archaeo-historicist is prepared to tackle the genetic problem, but 'arranged' and 'chronological order' present yet more daunting ones. Presumably the literary historian does the 'arranging', but on what principles? The presumption that there is significance in chronology should not go unquestioned. Must this always be true, and if not, how do we determine when it is false? I have no difficulty accepting the sequential connection of *Pamela* and *Joseph Andrews*, but the nature of the connection between *Robinson Crusoe* and *Tristram Shandy* seems much more tenuous.

Writing more than three hundred years ago, Dryden offered a sensible distinction between '*Annals*' and '*History* properly so call'd' in his *Life of Plutarch*. Annals are 'naked History: Or the plain relation of matters of fact, according to the succession of time, devested of all other Ornaments. The springs and motives of actions are not here sought, unless they offer themselves, and are open to every Mans discernment.'[9] History proper seeks these crucial springs and motives of action and change. Easily said, not so easily done. Consider a modern formulation from J. H. Hexter, an admirably blunt-spoken and practical historian. 'History is an attempt to render a coherent, intelligible, and true account of some . . . events, intentions, and happenings.'[10] This assumes not only the availability of evidence as to *what* happened, but our access to evidence of *motive*. Even more alarming is the presumption of 'coherence': this seems uncomfortably reminiscent of the New Critics' *idée fixe* about 'unity' (which can be found in virtually any poem, play, or novel if one insists). Does history necessarily make sense? I would argue, on the contrary, that even the motives and actions of individuals are

[7] Wellek, 'Literary History', in *Literary Scholarship*, 92.
[8] Wellek and Warren, *Theory of Literature*, 30.
[9] *The Works of John Dryden*, xvii, ed. Samuel Holt Monk, A. E. Wallace Maurer, and Vinton A. Dearing (Berkeley: University of California Press, 1971), 271–2.
[10] Hexter, *The History Primer*, 47.

often hopelessly jumbled, contradictory, and illogical. If history is a sum of individual and corporate thinking and doing, then why should it be tidier than the sum of its parts?

In both historical theory and practice (literary and otherwise) one finds a powerful desire 'to discover or construct a *meaningful* continuity'.[11] The difficulty lies in determining what confers this meaning. What units or parts make up the series being studied, and what is the nature of their relationship? The cohesiveness of 'story' offers a seemingly potent way of achieving coherence. Hayden White has pointed out the startling degree to which actual historical studies have tended to be cast in quasi-literary genres, recognizable in structural outline as tragedy, comedy, tragicomedy, and the like. The reason for this (so White speculates) is the power of narrative form to bestow pattern and meaning on the events it comprises, leaving the reader a comforting impression that historical events are not meaningless, but somehow add up to a satisfying and conclusive totality.[12] A sceptic may wonder whether the 'meaning' has been drawn from the events or simply imposed on them.

If the historian tells a story, he or she must almost inevitably be tempted to give it a tidy beginning and a satisfying end. Far worse, teleology rears its ugly head. A good story is coherent and 'makes sense'. We know how it will come out, and therefore we not only concentrate on the logical steps that take us from beginning to end, but we presume that the story as we know it possesses something akin to inevitability. Granting the ineluctability of the past, we need to remember that much of what happens is odd or unpredictable or the product of fluke and trivial circumstance. If J. E. B. Stuart had not taken Lee's cavalry out of the battle of Gettysburg. . . . If Marlowe had stayed home with a hangover. . . . If Defoe had been the prosperous businessman he longed to be. . . . If Coleridge had wound up on the banks of the Susquehanna. . . .

Many historians of different stripe have been almost pathologically hostile to 'what if?' history. Croce sneered at it; E. H.

---

[11] Wesley Morris, *Toward a New Historicism* (Princeton: Princeton University Press, 1972), 6.

[12] Hayden White, *Metahistory: The Historical Imagination in Nineteenth-Century Europe* (Baltimore: Johns Hopkins University Press, 1973); 'The Value of Narrativity in the Representation of Reality', *Critical Inquiry*, 7 (1980), 5–27.

Carr dismissed it as a 'parlour game'; E. P. Thompson calls it '*Geschichtenscheissenschlopff*, unhistorical shit'.[13] Michael Oakeshott says flatly that

The question in history is never what must, or what might have taken place, but solely what the evidence obliges us to conclude did take place. . . . The Historian is never called upon to consider what might have happened had circumstances been different.[14]

I strongly disagree, especially as regards 'what might have taken place'. Deterministic assumptions about history seem to me deeply inimical to a proper understanding of how often fluke, mischance, and vagary affect the course of events large and small. Even major events in history are often by no means fated to occur, and while the historian must reckon with what actually happened, it should not be seen as inevitable. The British civil war did not have to happen, and the victory of the North in the American civil war, though economically likely, was anything but a certainty. Hitler came close to defeating the Soviet Union. John F. Kennedy might easily not have been assassinated. Much would have been different had these events not fallen out as they did.[15]

Consider some instances of unlikely actuality. Why should Charles II have restored theatre to London as a patent duopoly in 1660? Had he not imposed the patent restriction, the course of English drama and theatre would almost unquestionably have been very different. As Paulina Kewes has demonstrated, one result of the patent grant was that playwrights were routinely and immediately allowed to publish their plays as literary works—a shift that helped transform the status of playscripts into literature.[16] Charles gave patents not because he foresaw

[13] Croce, '"Necessity" in History', in *Philosophy, Poetry, History: An Anthology of Essays by Benedetto Croce*, trans. Cecil Sprigge (London: Oxford University Press, 1966), 557; Carr, *What is History?*, 90–1; E. P. Thompson, *The Poverty of Theory and Other Essays* (London: Merlin Press, 1978), 300.
[14] Oakeshott, *Experience and its Modes*, 139–40.
[15] These and other imaginable alternatives are considered in a provocative collection of essays, Niall Ferguson (ed.), *Virtual History: Alternatives and Counterfactuals* (1997; London: Papermac, 1998). Ferguson's lengthy introduction makes a strong case for facing up to the chaotic and unpredictable nature of events as they have actually occurred.
[16] See Paulina Kewes, *Authorship and Appropriation: Writing for the Stage in England, 1660–1710* (Oxford: Clarendon Press, 1998). Kewes elegantly establishes the gap between modern and 17th-c. understandings of 'playwriting' as an

any such result, but because he wanted to reward two old friends from exile, and giving them theatre companies and a joint monopoly was a very cheap way of doing so.

A second case: what if Sir Robert Walpole had been content to impose censorship on plays in the Licensing Act of 1737, and had not also insisted on putting non-patent theatres out of business? He apparently did so just to keep Covent Garden and Drury Lane from complaining about the censorship, but the result was to alter the shape of London theatre for more than a century. The restriction was not fully removed until 1843 — which led in the meantime to elephantiasis of auditoriums and degeneration of plays into spectacle and melodrama.

A third case: David Garrick's purchase of a half-interest in Drury Lane in 1747. Few if any events had as much impact on London theatre and the plays written for it in the next thirty years. Garrick had quickly become a star actor, but only his becoming co-owner and manager of Drury Lane gave him his extraordinary power and influence. For more than two hundred years, however, his purchase was treated as a matter of course, as somehow natural, right, and inevitable. In fact, Garrick's purchase was a fluke, made possible only by the dishonesty and incompetence of a former owner, Charles Fleetwood.[17] Our whole picture of mid-century drama and theatre in London is postulated on Garrick's dominance, but that dominance was anything but predictable or likely. Telling a story obliges the historian to conform to what actually happened, but that obligation ought also to compel attention to *untidiness* and *unlikelihood* where they are present.[18]

Someone attempting 'literary history' must start by making three key choices. These involve what is being focused upon,

activity. Her evidence is prefaces and fragments, and she gets astonishingly good mileage out of play catalogues like those of Langbaine—long known by scholars, but heretofore mined almost entirely in non-conceptual ways. She is ultimately able to demonstrate the existence of concepts of literary 'originality' well before the Copyright Act of 1710 from which they have long been supposed to derive. This is historicism as it should be practised, constructing a point of view that has been virtually obliterated by our post-romantic preconceptions.

[17] See Judith Milhous and Robert D. Hume, 'A Drury Lane Account Book for 1745-46', *Theatre History Studies*, 10 (1990), 67–104.

[18] Readers of my draft have commented on the similarities in what I say here to the approach of the 'revisionist' school of British historians, which I readily acknowledge.

principles of organization, and principles of explanation.[19] What
are we writing a history *of*? A sequence of writers? A sequence
of works? If writers, then how do we choose them? Do we, for
example, restrict ourselves to British playwrights of the seventeenth century? All British writers of the seventeenth century?
British and French writers of the seventeenth century? Trans-
national literary history is a rarity until one gets to the twentieth
century. If our subject is 'works', then what selects them? We
can choose to concentrate on a particular form—the sonnet, let
us say. The relatively narrow focus yields a reassuringly manageable subject in such a case. We must wonder, however, to what
extent each successive sonneteer was equally aware of and influenced by his various predecessors. We need also to ask whether
sonnets are affected only by sonnets, and in the unhappy eventu-
ality that there might be other influences, we must be prepared
to try to allow for them. We can, of course, choose to write a
history of audience reception as opposed to author-production
or work-in-itself. In one sense, reception is tidier: the evolving
audience gives us a single entity to focus on, and we can trace a
set of shifts through time. What this tells us about, however, is
more the constitution of the audience than the nature of the
literature consumed; the results may be of greater interest to
sociologists than to literary critics.

Crane makes the point that beyond 'succession in time' a
crucial issue of organization concerns 'likeness and difference
in character' (ii. 67). Dealing with single authors or works
leaves one writing 'atomistic history'. If we impose 'classifying
devices' they will generate groupings, and 'history thus becomes a record of successive manifestations of literary characteristics' (ii. 69). Common ground among authors and the
works they produce will allow us to develop characterizations
and categorizations (for example, of eighteenth-century critics
or early nineteenth-century poets). Incommensurable principles
of organization generate problems here: 'political', 'moral', and
'economic' paradigms would result in radically different pictures of the same period. Crane argues that to get beyond such
chaos we will do best to concentrate on 'the narrative history
of forms':

[19] I take this formulation from R. S. Crane, 'Critical and Historical Principles of
Literary History', *The Idea of the Humanities*, ii. 45–156.

The crucial problem . . . is the discrimination of the various artistic ends pursued by writers from time to time and the organization of these differences into significant lines of change. . . . It is not a question either of classifying works grammatically in terms of their conventional genres or of schematizing them dialectically in terms of a predetermined pattern of rational oppositions to which their differing characteristics are reduced; rather it is a question of distinguishing with adequate precision, in terms of the constructive principles operative in each, the generic and specific natures of the concrete wholes which writers, for one reason or another, chose to produce. (ii. 82)

With some qualms and reservations, I am prepared to entertain the possibility of identifying 'constructive principles' that have generated literary works, and of identifying changes in those principles (and in the resulting works) over time. We should certainly be wrong to dismiss 'formal' factors, whether in exploring the use of iambic pentameter from Chaucer to Eliot or investigating the use of diatonic harmony from the beginnings of organum to the second Viennese school. When we come to 'Principles of Explanation', however, we find ourselves embogged in difficulties.

What 'conception of causality' is sufficient to explain both particular works and change from work to work (let alone period to period)? If a play or a poem expresses the 'spirit of the age', why are particular plays and poems so different? We can construct a more complex model, allowing for both hegemonic and contra-hegemonic expression, but consider the full implications of *Geistesgeschichte*. The work expresses *Weltanschauung*? Good. Then *Hamlet*, *The White Devil*, and *The Maid's Tragedy* 'say' the same thing, and their message ought to be tidily consonant (or disconsonant) with that of *As You Like It* and *The Tempest*? This way lies drivel. The range of particularities from work to work remains staggering. That all these plays contain and express Renaissance ideas is unquestionably true, but what gives them their particularity and power is not common expression of background or resistance to it. All the parallels that we may draw among works of roughly the same date do not begin to account for their 'specific natures' (in Crane's phrase, ii. 82).[20]

---

[20] For a useful exploration of the particularity of single works and their resistance to contextual uniformitarianism, see Richard Strier's *Resistant Structures*.

Accounting for change poses even greater difficulties. Let me illustrate with a question: Can we write 'the history of the eighteenth-century novel'? Easy enough to do, if by 'history' we mean merely a chronicle of prominent examples. Literary scholars have been painfully slow to learn that the historian of literature has no business taking isolated examples in chronological order and assuming that by describing them in sequence he or she is proving something about progression. Enormous efforts have been made by brilliant and learned scholars (notably Ian Watt and Michael McKeon) to account for the 'rise' of the novel in the first half of the eighteenth century—*ex post facto* attempts to find logic, order, reason, and teleology in a chaotic jumble of particulars. Richardson certainly stimulated Fielding, and Fielding manifestly had some influence on Smollett. Many of the problems and ideas raised in novels of the time reflect current political, social, and economic issues. The key question here is whether 'the novel' exists and develops as an independent entity. If not, then it cannot possess a 'history' of its own.[21]

Basically, I am denying the feasibility of generic history as it has long been known and practised. This may seem a drastic conclusion to pull out of a rather cursory examination of a large subject. I stand by my conclusion, however. The concept of generic history violates two basic principles: *independence of context* (we must be able to study the elements by themselves) and *connectedness of the parts* (the elements must have a necessary relationship with one another). Generic history has long been with us, but so have astrology, creationism, and black magic. Anti-gravity machines flourish in science fiction, but I have yet to be offered a ride in one. Let us reconsider some elementary principles.

Works of literature are not laboratory rats. One does not beget another. We may certainly agree that the ideas about poetry shared by Pope and Prior at the beginning of the eight-

---

[21] Aspiring writers of sequential history need to be particularly wary of the 'Great Books Fallacy'—the idea that great writers are inspired only by other great writers. Minor authors are often more influential than those we now choose to privilege, and the 'story' makes better sense when they are not expunged. Dryden probably held James Howard in contempt, but he appears to have learnt a lot about split-plot tragicomedy (a genre in which he wrote play after play throughout his career) from his long-forgotten brother-in-law.

eenth century differ substantially from those shared by Words-worth and Coleridge at the beginning of the nineteenth. How we get from the one to the other is hard to say. Almost all literary history has rested on a largely unexamined biological metaphor. In exactly what sense, however, are we dealing with *evolution*? We are free to say, loosely, that genres or ideas 'evolve', but we are committing a frightful methodological error if we fail to realize that we are erecting a grand edifice upon a very cloudy metaphoric foundation.[22]

How do we explain the relationship between Swift's poems and those of Edward Young? This strikes me as an extremely iffy enterprise. We can chronicle literature with no great diffi-culty. Dryden is followed by Pope who is followed by Samuel Johnson. . . . But to say why each of them writes as he does, and *what necessary connection they have to one another*, is a fiend-ishly complicated and unsatisfactory business—unless we are prepared to invoke our Lovejoy-model steamroller and its deter-minist assumptions.

The problem in writing a history of poetry is that poems have no necessary connection to one another. Laboratory rats do, poems don't. This is precisely where our biological metaphor collapses. Pope read Dryden. How significant was Dryden's influence? Impossible to say, but we may guess that Pope would have been pretty much the major poet he was even if Dryden had taken a Treasury post in 1662 and never written another poem or play. The literary historian is not entitled to treat Dryden and Pope as necessary steps in the evolution of English poetry. They are contiguous in the annals of poetry, and the later poet definitely knew at least some of the work of the earlier one, but they are not connected in any way that makes the earlier poet a shaping influence for the later one, let alone a necessary condition.[23] A history whose basis is chronological

---

[22] Wellek and Warren assert flatly in their influential *Theory of Literature* that literary 'development' should be 'used in the sense elaborated by biology' and that a 'biological analogy' holds insofar as '*historical* evolution' 'recognizes that no mere series of changes but, instead, an aim for this series must be postulated' (267–8). The teleological assumption in 'aim' seems to me totally unacceptable.

[23] Harold Bloom might argue the 'anxiety of influence' here. Such a theory is sometimes persuasive (Milton and Wordsworth, the Romantics and Arnold), but seems about as procrustean as Freudian psychology when treated as a universal. If Dryden made Pope terribly nervous, I have not spotted the evidence.

sequence must be largely false and arbitrary—no true history if it cannot supply (1) an account of the connection between the units and (2) an explanation of change. Literary history fails the test of 'connectedness' of what it studies.

What about the problem of independence? Can we in fact separate and isolate our subject in such a way that it can be studied by itself? The answer is clearly No. If we attempt anything of the sort, we distort and falsify our subject. Because particular works are largely disjunct, the connective framework and structure of literary history must be derived from something beyond the works themselves. The usual mechanisms invoked are a quasi-platonic sense of generic form, or alternatively a fuzzy and generalized sense of the state of society and changes in the human psyche.[24] (Wordsworth and Coleridge respond to industrialization, the French Revolution, and the evolving implications of Lockean psychology—crude, but after a fashion, true.) Most literary scholars admit (and rightly so) that changes in literature are not caused by something intrinsic in literature or genre, but rather reflect a set of complex relationships to the political, psychological, cultural, economic, and sociological factors that affect authors and readers.

This admission has devastating implications. If we cannot treat our subject as an entity in itself, then attempting to write literary history that goes much beyond the realm of annals is a fundamentally misguided enterprise born of narrow vision and overspecialization. Literature is a cultural phenomenon, not a world unto itself. David Lodge states this point forcefully:

A distinctively *literary* history ought to be founded in the description of literary form, but there is no single characterization of literary form that will account for all that is literature . . . the terms of its definition must be sought beyond boundaries of the arts, in the alteration of human consciousness by developments in science, applied science, philosophy, and psychology.[25]

[24] Examples of such histories are, respectively, Michael McKeon's *The Origins of the English Novel, 1600–1740* (Baltimore: Johns Hopkins University Press, 1987) and Laura Brown, *English Dramatic Form, 1660–1760: An Essay in Generic History* (New Haven: Yale University Press, 1981). Both have been influential, but I find myself acutely uncomfortable with their theoretical assumptions.

[25] David Lodge, 'Historicism and Literary History: Mapping the Modern Period', in *Working with Structuralism* (London: Routledge and Kegan Paul, 1981), 74–5.

A full-dress literary history would have to be situated in a much broader kind of cultural history. Foucault raises stimulating possibilities, and Hayden White offers wonderfully lucid speculations on the nature of such study. But from the point of view of the archaeo-historicist, cultural history is still an alarmingly tenuous discipline, and one that takes us well beyond an immediately *literary* milieu.

Literary history is a disastrous failure because its practitioners have fallen foul of elementary methodological principles. I reiterate: to write a legitimate 'sequential-explanation history', one must be able to isolate the subject from fundamental outside factors and one must be able to demonstrate necessary connection among the elements that have been thus isolated. I do not believe that this means that *all* attempts at sequential explanation in literature are wrong. Huge differences exist in the kinds of sequences at issue. Who can 'explain' the progression from Fielding to Austen to Dickens to Joyce to Drabble? Is this a useful, let alone a manageable question? (To undertake to describe the complexity, variety, and contradictions to be found in the English novel from say 1740 to 1770 is a daunting but a more thinkable proposition. And choice of elements matters quite a lot: 'Richardson to Austen' is less easy to dismiss.) Like poems, novels tend to have little necessary connection from one to the next. They can be written in isolation, and in ignorance of major predecessors and current fashion—or they may be strongly influenced by remote ancestors. As Wellek admitted late in life, 'A work of criticism is not simply a member of a series, a link in a chain. It may stand in relation to anything in the past. The critic may reach into the remotest history. An evolutionary history of criticism must fail.'[26] The situation is significantly different in a 'closed system' such as the London theatre from 1660 to 1728. During that period no more than two theatre companies were in operation (sometimes just one) and most of the dramatists were demonstrably familiar with recent hits and current norms. There are some oddball cases (John Gay's *The What d'ye Call It* in 1715, for example), and quite a lot of generic diversity and change—but the would-be historian has far better grounds for seeing connections among

[26] *The Attack on Literature*, 143–4.

the works studied than would be the case in poetry or fiction during the same era. A playwright working in the 1670s was probably acquainted with virtually every other recently produced playwright in London; saw the new shows, successful and unsuccessful; designed parts for the same principal actors; and peddled scripts to the same managers. Small wonder if the plays exhibit a high degree of conceptual and technical similarity.

'Historicism' should not be blamed for the difficulties—nay, impossibilities—in which 'literary history' has bogged itself. We need to abandon the laboratory-rat theory of literature. Developmental analysis has no overwhelming virtue. Large-scale 'why' questions are rarely subject to single answers, let alone definitive ones. In the realm of literature they rapidly take us beyond texts, authors, and audiences, and into areas not safely approached from purely literary perspectives. Our inability to make sequential explanation work in 'literary history' does not, however, have damning implications for contextual historicism. The sort of work proposed by Jerome McGann is not subject to the same objections. McGann argues for historically situated reading of single texts, approaching them in highly particular contexts.[27] David Perkins questions 'whether such readings count as literary history'.[28] I do not claim that they should, merely that they are a useful and valid form of historicist enterprise.[29] So is the quasi-encyclopedic series of snapshots comprised in *A New History of Early English Drama*.[30] This volume contains some spectacularly good chapters (I have special admiration for Peter W. M. Blayney's 'The Publication of Playbooks'), but virtually all of them concern venues (Oxford, Cambridge, street theatre), social context (court entertainments, civic entertainments), performance conditions (touring, censorship, audience, acting style), and physical evidence (MSS, revisions). One might question whether this is indeed a 'history', and also whether it is really about 'drama'. It

[27] See particularly Jerome McGann, *The Beauty of Inflections: Literary Investigations in Historical Method and Theory* (Oxford: Oxford University Press, 1985).

[28] Perkins, *Is Literary History Possible?*, 22.

[29] I strongly agree with Wendell V. Harris's sharp distinction between *historical scholarship* and *literary history*. See 'What Is Literary "History"?' *College English*, 56 (1994), 434–51, esp. 436.

[30] Ed. John D. Cox and David Scott Kastan (New York: Columbia University Press, 1997).

neatly solves the methodological problems of 'history' by refusing to attempt not only explanation but even description of 'change'—which I do not mean as a criticism. But if I were asked for a more accurate descriptive title, it might be *Contexts of English Drama, 1500–1642*.

The failure of literary history has been glumly proclaimed by René Wellek in his old age and analysed with almost Germanic solemnity by David Perkins. Both have good things to say. One must admire Wellek's unflinching honesty in admitting that literary history is an 'illusion': he had spent his life studying, theorizing, and attempting to write it. He says bluntly that 'the vast new literature on historiography' has 'little or no relevance to the writing of a history of criticism' (I agree), and asks the crucial question: how well can criticism be isolated from other human activities in order to write a history of it?[31] I have just argued that it cannot be separated. Perkins, the author of a well-respected two-volume *History of Modern Poetry*, confesses that 'having tried to write literary history', he is now 'unconvinced (or *de*convinced) that it can be done' (11). He finds 'insurmountable contradictions in organizing, structuring, and presenting the subject' and admits that attempts 'to explain the development' of literature are 'always unsuccessful' (ix). Literary histories give us all sorts of tidy and comforting paradigms and explanations; where would we be without them? How would we make sense of our territory? Yet I must agree with Perkins that 'fantasies abound' (33), and these fantasies are simplistic maps foisted by historians on territories that they manifestly misrepresent.

If we believe . . . that the satisfactions of literary history can only be aesthetic and intellectual, a conceptual history has obvious merits and no serious disadvantages. The tight coherence of such literary histories gives aesthetic pleasure, and the concepts themselves may be interesting. But if we hold that literary history should strive for a plausible representation of the past, we make a different evaluation. Any conceptual scheme highlights only those texts that fit its concepts, sees in texts only what its concepts reflect, and inevitably falls short of the multiplicity, diversity, and ambiguity of the past.[32]

[31] Wellek, *The Attack on Literature*, 135, 137.
[32] Perkins, *Is Literary History Possible?*, 51.

Insofar as 'literary history' goes, I believe that this is both true and utterly damning. I would differ only in maintaining that *if* we abandon the conceptual straitjackets imposed by the requirements of developmental history, then at particular points in time we can attempt to represent 'the multiplicity, diversity, and ambiguity of the past'. The problem lies not in the representation of complexity, but in our imposing the biological metaphor and claiming to explain change.[33]

Archaeo-Historicism aims to reconstruct particular contexts in something like their full complexity insofar as evidence exists from which to work. Using such contexts, its practitioners endeavour to analyse and understand the genesis, circumstances of production, initial reading, and reception of literary works. Our inability to write developmental history is a fact, not a failure in the method—which need make no such claim. Developmental history can legitimately be attempted in some limited realms. Biography meets the test of connectedness and offers at least the possibility of plausible explanation. Institutional history can certainly be written—as for example of a publishing house or a theatre company. Delineation of periods can be useful if heterogeneity and conflict are fairly represented—so long as we remember that the construct is of our making and for our convenience, not historically 'true'. Basic methodological principles, however, debar the archaeo-historicist from attempting to write developmental history where the nature of the material forces it to fail our tests for connectedness and causal explanation within its own terms.

Inadequate Evidence

In recent years the concept of 'thick description' popularized by Clifford Geertz has been widely cited as the way we ought to practise historical reconstruction.[34] As an ideal in the best of all

---

[33] David H. Richter mounts a vigorous critique of Perkins's negativity about literary history in ch. 1 of *The Progress of Romance*. I find his account of the Gothic novel provocative and even plausible, but it works—if it does—at the level of a subgenre studied over a fairly limited span of time.

[34] Clifford Geertz, 'Thick Description: Toward an Interpretive Theory of Culture', in *The Interpretation of Cultures: Selected Essays* (New York: Basic Books, 1973), 3–30.

possible historical worlds, no doubt this is true. Or at least true up to the point at which the description becomes so thick in redundancy that investigator and reader alike are too overwhelmed to conduct any serious analysis. For most pre-1800 historical investigations, however, thick description is not a possibility because the evidence has not yet been found and very probably no longer exists.

The practice of Archaeo-Historicism rests centrally on the availability of evidence. Perhaps because so much literary scholarship consists of textual analysis, and because British and American literature offer very large numbers of texts to interpret, the acquisition of evidence has rarely been considered a pressing problem. Nor is it often given more than lip-service in the considerable twentieth-century accumulation of books on historiography. One might deduce that if 'evidence' cannot be ordered up by the cubic yard then it will be supplied at minimal cost by willing drudges. Those who have not prospected for new evidence often have touchingly naive pictures of how the search process works and how the evidence discovered must be processed. Like oil or uranium, historical evidence is not easy to find. If you are rich enough, you can perhaps send drudges to do your hunting—if you trust them to recognize paydirt when they hit it. If, contrariwise, you are working in a period in which Plethora is the problem, are you prepared to have a graduate assistant or a hireling make the crucial judgements as to what is important and what is not? Evidence in the raw is rarely much use: it needs to be combined, compared, and analysed before conclusions can be drawn. Trusting the skills and discrimination of novices is not a good idea.

Two fundamental problems of evidence haunt the archaeo-historicist. Simple *lack of evidence* is the more dire and the easier to see. *Inadequate or untrustworthy evidence* can be much more treacherous. *The archaeo-historicist is honour-bound to respect the limits of the available evidence.* This basic principle is easy enough to enunciate, but the practical complications constitute a major difficulty in contextual scholarship. The pressure to 'know' can be most intense when the pertinent evidence is most meagre. Some subjects can be relatively well documented from very early dates; others cannot. Dance is intrinsically even more evanescent than theatrical performance. Scenarios can help with *ballet d'action* (where they exist), and labanotation sometimes permits reconstruction of actual steps from pre-film eras, but much dance is simply gone. Astonishing amounts can nonetheless sometimes be recovered and analysed, as for example Mark Franko has done with dance at the French court, 1573–1670.[35] A subject like popular theatre in Africa suffers from many of the same evidentiary problems to an even greater degree. In a high proportion of cases verbal scripts never existed or do not survive. So far as I can judge, David Kerr has put together a remarkably convincing overview, but the evidence is woefully scanty and often misleading.[36] Much of what is known from earlier periods comes from visitors whose 'use of words such as "obscene" and "hideous" convey far more about the attitudes of the European onlookers' than about what is ostensibly being described.[37] These are especially dire problems, but even in the familiar realms of major British authors we must often confront severe difficulties.

In biography, in context of production, and in reception we are faced with gigantic gaps in the historical record until the nineteenth century, and sometimes even later. How many scholars have dug with fanatic enthusiasm to discover any tiny fragment about Shakespeare? With how much result? What we do *not* know about Shakespeare is enough to have generated many books of irresponsible speculation written to fill the vacuum. We can turn to the plays (on the risky supposition that he wrote them all by himself), but what would lead us to imagine that Shakespeare's plays are a faithful mirror of the psyche and opinions of their creator? Of how many complex and varied authors can we truly make such a claim? Scholars are accustomed to concentrate on what they have; good historical practice requires us to be blunt in admitting what we lack.

---

[35] Mark Franko, *Dance as Text: Ideologies of the Baroque Body* (Cambridge: Cambridge University Press, 1993). Franko draws on scenarios, contemporary performance theory, commentary of various sorts, and illustrations. He is able to construct a very plausible evolving aesthetic reflecting the politics and ideology of the noble class, blending archival research with critical/cultural theory.

[36] David Kerr, *African Popular Theatre from Pre-Colonial Times to the Present Day* (Oxford: James Currey, 1995).

[37] June Layson, 'Dance History Source Materials', in Janet Adshead-Lansdale and June Layson (eds.), *Dance History: An Introduction* (2nd edn., London: Routledge, 1994), ch. 2 at p. 27.

Consider the evidence concerning late seventeenth-century drama—by comparison with Shakespeare and his era, a well-documented territory. More than 400 play texts survive, the vast majority of them printed. Of roughly ninety 'lost' plays about a third turn out to be ghosts, so no more than about 15 per cent are actually unavailable, and most of those are historically insignificant.[38] We can date most of the plays to within two or three months (and many of them quite precisely), a situation very different from Shakespeare's day. Performance records, however, are drastically incomplete: we can identify no more than about 13 per cent of the performances, and a substantial number of the 'known' performances are estimated dates or conjectures. We are often unable to say how well a play succeeded, or whether it was revived after its initial run. Many casts are known, but plenty are not. Virtually no scene or costume designs survive. Anecdotal evidence gives us some sense of popularity (as do reprints), but popularity is essentially unknowable for many plays. Commentary on reception is so scrappy as to terrify any responsible scholar. One can hardly forbear using it, and yet its representativeness is undeterminable. Virtually anything we say about acting style has to be dangerously speculative. Evidence of various sorts has been added to our scanty stock over the last fifty years, but the likelihood of major improvement in documentation seems slight. Except in the realm of playtexts (and to a lesser extent, casts), we are basically in the position of someone shown forty or fifty pieces of a thousand-piece picture puzzle who is asked to opine on what it would look like when complete.

If you lack the evidence, you should face the fact. Things that can be done easily and well in later periods cannot be done properly if the primary evidence does not exist. Biography in the post-Boswellian sense of the genre can be written for very few people prior to 1800 (and not for all people even after 1900). Biography as it is now practised means getting inside the subject's mind, and for this one needs letters, diaries, private documents, and (preferably) extensive personal commentary from friends and family. Such evidence can rarely be found for anyone

[38] See Judith Milhous and Robert D. Hume, 'Lost English Plays, 1660–1700', *Harvard Library Bulletin*, 25 (1977), 5–33.

prior to 1700 (Cicero, Erasmus, and Pepys are obvious excep-
tions), and even well-documented public figures like Pope and
Swift present huge problems. Pope self-consciously promoted
his image for posterity, making his letters to close friends works
of art. Swift did less deliberate self-presentation, but his irony
and humour force the interpreter to make all kinds of allow-
ances for distortion of a sort that one does not have to cope with
in Wordsworth's letters. For neither Pope nor Swift can we have
any real confidence that we know what their sexual lives consisted of, though some of Swift's poems display strong sexual
response and his friendships with women unquestionably form
a vital part of his psychic life. With all due respect to the
achievements of Maynard Mack and Irvin Ehrenpreis, both
seem to me to fail to create convincing psychological portraits
of their subjects.[39] Barring the discovery of extensive private
diaries, I see no way it could be done.

What happens when the scholar scours the face of the earth
for new evidence and comes up with a very scanty haul? Too
often, the need for evidence breeds over-interpretation. As an
example, consider the Battestin biography of Fielding.[40] Martin
Battestin is unquestionably the foremost Fielding scholar of the
later twentieth century, and he put many years and an immense
amount of labour into the biography. In all likelihood, he has
found a high percentage of what will ever be discovered—but
documentation remains thin, and the Wilbur Cross biography
of 1918 was a fine job for its day. Very naturally wanting more
that was new and fresh, Battestin speculatively read the possibility of incest from works into life, and attributed a large
number of *Craftsman* essays (1734–9) to Fielding from purely
internal evidence.[41] I am sure that he did so in good faith, and
for all I know Henry Fielding lusted for Sarah Fielding, took her
to bed, and wrote every single essay in the *Craftsman* that

[39] Maynard Mack, *Alexander Pope: A Life* (New Haven: Yale University Press,
1985); Irvin Ehrenpreis, *Swift: The Man, his Works, and the Age*, 3 vols. (London:
Methuen, 1962–83).
[40] Martin C. Battestin with Ruthe R. Battestin, *Henry Fielding: A Life* (London:
Routledge, 1989).
[41] *New Essays by Henry Fielding: His Contributions to the Craftsman (1734–
1739) and Other Early Journalism*, ed. Martin C. Battestin, with a Stylometric
Analysis by Michael G. Farringdon (Charlottesville: University Press of Virginia,
1989).

Battestin thinks he did. The evidence, however, does not make these conclusions more than provocative speculations. They fill major gaps in our understanding of Fielding's psyche and career, but are they *true*? Either *might* be true, but one should not hang a cockroach on 'might', let alone a dog. Should a 'standard biography' rest important portions of its argument on speculation? Battestin is passably cautious about actual incest, but he does essentially treat the 'new essays' as Fielding's work. Yes, some of them have ideas and expressions that can be paralleled in Fielding, but is this proof of authorship? The computer stylistics analysis offered in evidence seems to me totally unconvincing, in part because the alternative samples are so crudely rigged. I have a bad ear, but I need no computer to tell me the difference between *Spectator* essays and *Craftsman* essays. There is much in the biography to admire, but its straining after originality on the basis of such evidence seems to me lamentable.

Both the glory of Archaeo-Historicism and its most frustrating limitations stem from its nature as an *evidential* enterprise. The investigator must discover a sufficiency of evidence, must test it insofar as testing is possible, and must analyse it rigorously. No tidy formulas will tell us what is sufficient, how to test, or what rules apply. If we fail in any of these regards, we should, however, be sharply challenged by our sceptical successors. Let us examine some particular cases, large and small.

1. Misleading facts: the popularity of Handel's *Rinaldo* in 1715. The shaky opera company at the King's Theatre, Haymarket, in 1714–15 performed Handel's opera of 1711—and nothing else—for a period of two months in the early winter. In the absence of box-office figures for the company, its financial health has been essentially undeterminable. Music historians have presumed, not unreasonably, that performance after performance of *Rinaldo* can be taken as proof of Handel's popularity with the London audience. Newly discovered lawsuit evidence, however, tells us that receipts reached the break-even point (about £150) at only one performance, and that the series as a whole averaged a dismal £92 per night—a quick route to bankruptcy. Why then did the company keep giving the opera? Illness among the singers may have made variety difficult. The company was awaiting the arrival of Nicolini, its star castrato

(who finally turned up in April), and it was basically marking time until then. Possibly George I (newly arrived in England) or the Prince of Wales was terribly fond of *Rinaldo*: there is evidence suggesting that the Prince attended *Rinaldo* seven times this winter. We cannot be sure why Handel's opera was put up again and again, losing money every time but one. The presumption of its popularity was not foolish, merely (as the new evidence proves) wrong.[42]

2. Untrustworthy evidence: the failure (or success?) of Alexander Dow's tragedy, *Sethona*. Premièred at Drury Lane on 19 February 1774, it enjoyed an excellent nine-night run. However, the generally reliable *Biographia Dramatica* informs us that

This play may properly be styled a faggot of utter improbabilities, connected by a band of the strongest Northern fustian. Overawed by Scottish influence, Mr. Garrick prevailed on himself to receive it; but though his theatre was *apparently* full several times during its nine nights' run, it brought so little cash into his treasury, that he would not have lamented its earlier condemnation. It expired on his premises, but hardly left enough behind it to defray the expences of its funeral.[43]

This appears to be powerful evidence for Garrick's having papered his house, and in the absence of other testimony we would accept it as proof that paying customers were few in number. The prompter's diary, however, says that 'This Play was receiv'd with very great Applause' (Folger Library MS), and by good luck the Drury Lane account book is extant. Its figures— reported in *The London Stage*—likewise strongly contradict the *Biographia Dramatica*. Dow's play grossed £1,983 over its run, or £220 per night at a time when house charges were only £73. The lowest receipts were £181 the sixth night, and Dow was paid £345 for his three benefits (versus an average profit to playwrights of £271 at Drury Lane between 1760 and 1776 in the latter half of Garrick's reign). That Garrick ordered the treasurer to falsify the accounts, or that he and his partner James

[42] See Judith Milhous and Robert D. Hume, 'Heidegger and the Management of the Haymarket Opera, 1713–1717', *Early Music*, forthcoming.

[43] *Biographia Dramatica* [ed. Isaac Reed], 2 vols. (London: Mess. Rivingtons *et al.*, 1782), ii. 335. This work is a revision and continuation of David Erskine Baker's *The Companion to the Play-House: or, an Historical Account of all the Dramatic Writers (and their works) that have appeared in Great Britain and Ireland* (1764). The reliability of both editions has been almost universally assumed.

Lacy paid Dow a very substantial sum of money that the play did not earn, seems well-nigh inconceivable. That Garrick might paper his house we can readily believe, but the financial facts argue that the tale in the *Biographia Dramatica* is both malicious and untrue. Its comments on Dow reek with anti-Scottish prejudice, and in this case we really must dismiss its claims, however 'reliable' it is generally found to be. In the case of *Rinaldo* our evidence was inferential (and turned out to be inadequate). Here the evidence turned out to be untrustworthy. In most cases of anecdotal evidence, there is no way to cross-check. Even when an anecdote appears late or in suspicious variant forms, scholars tend to resist all attempts to stamp out good stories. The likelihood that the elderly Dryden crushed a hopeful beginner with the verdict 'Cousin Swift, you will never be a poet' is small, but the anecdote contains a legitimate point to which biographical fact is largely irrelevant.[44] So what to do?

Some kinds of evidence are rarely impeached. (A theatre might falsify its account books, but demonstrable instances are rare.) Others need to be regarded with much greater suspicion. People do regularly fix up diaries, rewriting, suppressing, adding material—notable instances include John Evelyn and James Boswell, who in very different ways radically revamp their rough records. The scholar who presumes that Evelyn's diary may be used as an actual daily record of doings and observations (as we use Pepys) will make a godalmighty fool of him or herself.[45] Lawsuit testimony consists largely of self-serving accounts of hotly disputed events. Anyone who reads a flock of Chancery suits soon realizes the truth of the old saw about there being two sides to every story. Eyewitness reports from ostensibly neutral observers will not necessarily agree. In the autumn of 1983 I was in London, reading the newspapers every day. After a hot Parliamentary debate *The Times* headline tended to be 'Thatcher Triumphs' while the *Guardian* story would be headed 'Thatcher Humiliated'. Historical reconstruction relies on first-hand testimony, but eyes of beholders may vary on subjects other than beauty.

The scholar must be prepared to reckon with the possibility

[44] See Maurice Johnson, 'A Literary Chestnut: Dryden's "Cousin Swift"', *PMLA* 67 (1952), 1024–34.
[45] See Arthur H. Scouten, 'The Perils of Evelyn', *Restoration*, 16 (1992), 126–8.

of deliberately falsified evidence. If we do not possess holograph letters, for example, how confident can we be that transcriptions and early printed versions represent the originals fully and accurately? In many cases where the originals survive, comparison shows that handling of accidentals may be careless, but that the substance is essentially reliable. Where we cannot check, we usually hope for the best. Occasionally, however, gruesome distortion and even fabrication come to light. The letters of Vincenzo Bellini offer a wonderfully cautionary instance.[46] Bellini wrote extensively and intimately to his close friend Francesco Florimo between 1828 and 1835. These letters are and will probably always be 'our chief evidence for his life, working methods, and personality'. Like a great many nineteenth-century editors, Florimo edited, bowdlerized, and tidied up in small ways—but he went a lot further. As John Rosselli has shown, Florimo not only destroyed many letters (because they contained details of an affair with a married woman), but fabricated important new matter that radically changed events and Bellini's sentiments. Whether he actually concocted letters from whole cloth is not clear, but the possibility exists. Florimo's commentary is likewise profoundly tainted: he demonstrably 'recalls' conversations that could not have taken place. Bellini's biographers were long uneasy about both content and style of some of the letters, but almost always used them uncritically for want of any alternative. We are left with a dismal situation: we have to question much of what has ever been 'known', and we must make do with greatly reduced evidence—unless we are prepared to erect our tower of speculation upon quicksand.

The prudent archaeo-historicist must cultivate a habit of perpetual doubt and suspicion. Do we have first-hand reportage or hearsay? How close to the date of the event? Are we working from holograph, fair copy, or a printed version? What is the likelihood of doctoring? Visiting the Earl of Jersey many years ago to examine a Buckingham manuscript, I asked him about some pages that had been roughly hacked out. 'Grandmother' was his succinct reply. Modern technology allows us to read passages inked out of Johnson's prayers and meditations by

---

[46] See John Rosselli, *The Life of Bellini* (Cambridge: Cambridge University Press, 1996), esp. 6–7 and 160–2.

zealous protectors of his orthodoxy, but a more thorough-going vandal like Fanny Burney simply destroyed or cut up manuscripts of which she disapproved—thereby permanently damaging our documentation on her eminent musicologist father, Dr Burney.[47] Even where tampering or fabrication are not an issue, the scholar must be rigorous about taking the possibility of bias into account. 'Consider the source' is a good motto. One often cannot be sure of the reliability of crucial evidence, but one can at least be above-board in indicating the degree of doubt that attaches to it.

3. Perspectival distortion: the case of 'Shakespeare' in early eighteenth-century London. We move here from absent evidence or false evidence to a more complex problem that arises when we know things that our subjects did not. Consider a specific question: Why did the London audience of 1703 tolerate William Burnaby's abominable perversion of Twelfth Night? My answer would start with a counter-question: Why should we imagine that anyone was aware of the source of Love Betray'd? Viewing the matter from the twentieth century, we think of Shakespeare as 'the greatest writer who ever lived' (etc.), but in 1703 this was not the way most people saw the matter. Yes, one can find bardolatrous comments as early as the 1660s, but very few straight Shakespeare plays were in the repertory (so far as we can tell). Only four were separately reprinted between 1660 and 1700. How easily could genuine Shakespeare be read? Not very. The Fourth Folio (1685) could still be bought—a very large and expensive book in a time when public libraries did not exist. How many owners of Shakespeare folios read them? The language was obsolete, and the minimal scene division and stage directions must have been extremely offputting. A faithful reader of the folio would of course have accepted as Shakespeare's work The London Prodigall, The History of Thomas Lord Cromwell, Sir John Oldcastle, The Yorkshire Tragedy, The Puritan Widow, and The Tragedy of Locrine. Plays were rarely performed with the author's name advertised, and a lot of the 'Shakespeare' performed in early eighteenth-century London was in drastic adaptations by Dryden, Shadwell, Tate, and

---

[47] See Memoirs of Dr. Charles Burney, 1726–1769, ed. Slava Klima, Garry Bowers, and Kerry S. Grant (Lincoln: University of Nebraska Press, 1988).

others. Shakespeare was a well-regarded English classic, but someone who turned to Charles Gildon's *The Lives and Characters of the English Dramatick Poets* (1699)—the standard guide to the canon—would have found that present-day playwrights were regarded as fully the equals of their Renaissance forebears.[48]

My point is simple: their 'Shakespeare' was not our Shakespeare.[49] We are the recipients of 300 years of systematic digging for every scrap related to Shakespeare and Shakespeare reception. To reimagine Shakespeare as he must have been seen (and harder yet, *not* seen) at the beginning of the eighteenth century is fearfully difficult. We might as well be nineteenth-century Protestant missionaries confronted by pagans. An educated theatregoer of 1700 could easily have been cheerfully ignorant of Shakespeare except as a name. Margreta de Grazia says 'It is impossible to imagine the study of Shakespeare without authentic texts for his works, historical accounts defining his period, facts about his life, chartings of his artistic and psychological development, and determinations of his meaning.'[50] True. Yet this is precisely the situation in which literate and interested Londoners found themselves at the beginning of the eighteenth century—and what we now need to try to imagine. The problem here is that we possess all sorts of evidence that people in the context at issue did not. Instead of knowing far less than they and trying to fill in gaps and extrapolate from fragmentary evidence, we must confront the difficulty of imagining ignorance.

4. Predilections: what happens when the investigator is driven by his or her own predispositions? Whether the predisposition is Marxist or feminist or Freudian or Christian or patriotic, the investigator will almost unquestionably be able to find evidence and can draw conclusions in the light of it. Where relatively plentiful evidence exists other scholars may object, pointing to what has been left out of account. Where evidence is scanty, entirely lacking, or largely negative, refutation is much harder.

---

[48] A point convincingly made by Kewes, ch. 7.

[49] See Robert D. Hume, 'Before the Bard: "Shakespeare" in Early Eighteenth-Century London', *ELH* 64 (1997), 41–75.

[50] *Shakespeare Verbatim: The Reproduction of Authenticity and the 1790 Apparatus* (Oxford: Clarendon Press, 1991), 1.

Consider the issue of homosexuality. On statistical probability alone, a substantial number of writers, composers, artists, and painters must have been gay, though most of them left no paper record or even an anecdotal one. Sodomy was subject to severe penalties. It may have been widely practised, but most participants evidently took care to be discreet. Sexual preference and practice is a legitimate object of biographical investigation, and whether the scholar is personally gay or not, he or she may have to confront questions about a subject's sex life. This can be done soberly or quite otherwise.

Let me offer two exemplary instances. In his biography of John Gay, David Nokes raises the possibility that a poor and obscure linendraper's assistant helped better his position in life by becoming a catamite (my term, not Nokes's).[51] John Gay quickly became a part of the Burlington circle, which is suggestive in itself, though proof of nothing. Nokes bluntly admits that there is no preserved evidence of genital activity, but of course we would hardly expect any. Whether John Gay was homosexually inclined anyway, or saw a chance and took it, one can only guess—always supposing that the conjecture is accurate. Nokes would have been irresponsible not to raise the question. Without special patronage, John Gay's dazzling rise is not impossible, but it is improbable. Nokes's hypothesis accounts very plausibly for what is otherwise difficult to understand.

My second example is Gary C. Thomas's 'Was George Frideric Handel Gay?'[52] No anomaly confronts us here, merely a virtual blank. Handel was either massively discreet (whether gay or not) or asexual. Thomas very fairly and sensibly concludes that we cannot be certain how to answer his title question, though admitting that he is inclined to suspect homosexual inclination and possibly activity. What is striking about the essay—indeed, horrific—is its demonstration of the degree to which several generations of Handel scholars not only evaded the question but actually cooked up a lot of bogus reassurance

[51] David Nokes, *John Gay: A Profession of Friendship* (Oxford: Oxford University Press, 1995), esp. 43–50.
[52] Gary C. Thomas, '"Was George Frideric Handel Gay?" On Closet Questions and Cultural Politics', in Philip Brett, Gary Thomas, and Elizabeth Wood (eds.), *Queering the Pitch: The New Gay and Lesbian Musicology* (London: Routledge, 1994), 155–203.

about Handel's heterosexuality. This essay deserves careful reading both for its honest insistence upon staying within the (frustrating) limits of our evidence and for its devastating exposure of the way prejudice can distort scholarship.

Prejudice, to be sure, works both ways. Scholars used to cover up homosexuality; now they assiduously proclaim it, not always with sufficient evidence. (I admit to doubts that Beethoven was Black and gay.) Sally Peters's recent analysis of George Bernard Shaw serves to illustrate what I consider perversion of evidence.[53] Unlike the lives of John Gay and G. F. Handel, Shaw's life is extraordinarily well documented. His letters are voluminous; his diaries extensive; testimony from friends exists in bulk. Shaw was a celebrity for many decades, and his acquaintances included enough raffish types that we might expect some comments about his sexual proclivities if they were unusual or interesting. Lack of diary commentary about marital sex might be taken as an indication of 'white marriage' (and has been), but seems far likelier to represent a Victorian sensibility. Peters turns Shaw into a homosexual basket case, his frustrated (or possibly not frustrated) inclinations fundamentally affecting his whole life and output. She announces a focus on 'secret spheres' and 'erotic secrets', and justifies radical selectivity by saying that 'to sweep away the obscuring clutter, I have included only those facts and events . . . that are significant in telling his story' (pp. ix–x). The 'evidence' is entirely gaps, silences, and subtle (I would say strained) readings of events and words that can be more simply construed in other ways. Most of us now accept the proposition that we all have a bisexual component lurking in our psyches, and no doubt Shaw had one, too. I do not, however, see problems in Shaw's life or writing to which a hypothesis of profound homosexual inclination offers a solution. The evidence of heterosexual inclination and activity seems strong. In these circumstances, Peters's reading seems forced and gratuitous—a case of the scholar's predisposition dictating conclusions despite the plentiful evidence.

Let me conclude this discussion with a terse summation of circumstances and principles: (1) The archaeo-historicist often

---

[53] Sally Peters, *Bernard Shaw: The Ascent of the Superman* (New Haven: Yale University Press, 1996).

has to work from very scanty evidence; (2) where the evidence is non-existent or manifestly insufficient, the best thing to do is admit defeat and retreat to other territory; (3) gaps in evidence must be acknowledged, not just worked round; (4) the trustworthiness of evidence must always be assessed sceptically; (5) the conclusions drawn from evidence need to be *plausible* in common-sense ways. Juries are not always right, but there are good reasons for insisting that they be unanimous or close to unanimous. Archaeo-Historicism is not, God knows, a mathematical discipline, but if you want to draw a conclusion sharply different from one reached by predecessors, you need to ask what justifies the different result. What evidence were they lacking? Where did they go wrong? What prejudice distorted their judgement? How is their analysis faulty? If the difference in conclusions derives from speculation from very limited evidence, then this needs to be explicitly admitted. In all too many instances the evidence simply does not exist, or you cannot trust what you have got—in which case no good will come of trying to force your way to a conclusion.

Problems of Genre and Reading

Difference between periods is glaringly obvious. The aims of Archaeo-Historicism remain much the same whether the subject lies in 1600 or 1900, but the nature and amount of material available radically affect practice. What about generic difference? Can we employ the method much the same way in poetry, fiction, and drama? I shall maintain that while significant differences exist, the common ground is greater than it may at first appear.

Performance and performance milieu offer the student of drama a rich historical territory not available to those who work on literature read by individuals in private. Indeed, the theatre historian has the option of restricting him or herself to recreating the conditions and background of performance—studying heights of proscenium arches, depths of forestages, costume designs, scenery, actor biography, acting style, censorship, management and finances, and so forth. Such subjects can become ends in themselves. (A distinguished eighteenth-century theatre historian once asked me, 'How can you bear to read those awful plays?') A book on theatre architecture or costume history may in fact be a more substantial and long-lasting contribution to knowledge than a reading of plays. I would argue, however, that intensive study of performance conditions of plays one would not want to see is an arid and self-indulgent exercise.

The methodology by which theatre history can be brought to bear interpretively on plays has so far been developed only in rather rudimentary ways. The possibilities, however, are open to exploration. Here are a few examples:

1. Testimony about performance in Shakespeare's day is basically a lost cause, but one can deduce quite a lot about staging practices by analysing explicit and implicit stage directions, as Alan Dessen and David Bradley have done.[54]

2. By the late seventeenth century, casting often implies a whole performance concept for the play. The analytic potentialities of this fact were first systematically developed by Peter Holland as late as 1979.[55] Here is an example. Mr Sullen in Farquhar's *The Beaux Stratagem* (1707) is almost always now conceived as a clown and a buffoon. The part was created, however, not by Penkethman or Bullock (the company's low comedians), but rather by John Verbruggen, a heavyweight actor who played Iago against Betterton's Othello. This makes a startling difference to the impact of Sullen's mistreatment of his wife.

3. New historicists are very interested by the connection between Milton's divorce tracts and the end of *The Beaux Stratagem*. We should remember, however, that virtually all the serious marital-discord material was cut out of the play as early as the first run (perhaps after the first night). The play enjoyed

[54] Alan C. Dessen, *Elizabethan Stage Conventions and Modern Interpreters* (Cambridge: Cambridge University Press, 1984), and *Recovering Shakespeare's Theatrical Vocabulary* (Cambridge: Cambridge University Press, 1995). David Bradley, *From Text to Performance in the Elizabethan Theatre: Preparing the Play for the Stage* (Cambridge: Cambridge University Press, 1992).

[55] Peter Holland, *The Ornament of Action: Text and Performance in Restoration Comedy* (Cambridge: Cambridge University Press, 1979). For examples of cast analysis (and illustration of contrasting interpretations from different casts), see Milhous and Hume, *Producible Interpretation*, esp. 102–3, 132–6, 156–64, 214–19, 282–5.

its long stage history without the content that now makes it seem 'important', whatever the playwright's intentions may have been, and regardless of the concept of the first production. Here text presents serious issues while performance history tells us that the piece almost immediately became a romp.

4. Otway's *Venice Preserv'd* (1682) started life as anti-Whig propaganda during the Exclusion Crisis. Soon shorn of the nicky-nacky scenes, it became an eighteenth-century embodiment of libertarian sentiment, with Pierre as the hero. In the 1790s, such sentiment became unacceptable, and in an abrupt flip-flop Pierre had to be reconceived as a Republican villain, hoodwinking the noble but misguided hero, Jaffeir.[56] The case offers an instance in which reception history forces us to recognize the potential instability and indeterminacy of textual meaning. Even at the time of first performance or publication different factions may interpret a work in radically incommensurable ways, Addison's *Cato* (1713) being a famous instance.

All very well, says the student of the sonnet, but where do I get proscenium arches and prop bills—or their equivalent? Performance unquestionably makes plays a special case, but if we return to our basic paradigm (author, genetic context, genre, circumstances of original and later reception), I see every reason to suppose that Archaeo-Historicism offers a plenitude of possibilities in poetry, fiction, and intellectual prose as well as in drama. At least five realms are wide-open in all cases.

First and most obviously there is biography. This has been something of a dirty word in recent years, what with New Criticism, the intentional fallacy, the death of the author, and all that. Biography tends to be more directly relevant to poets than to playwrights or novelists, since poetry tends to be the most personally expressive form. I do not see biographical investigation as an invalid method for the critic. Trying to discover what the author attempted to say (and why) is not the same as claiming that the author's intent determines the meaning of the text.[57] Biography need not mean psycho-anything. Even where

[56] See Aline Mackenzie Taylor, *Next to Shakespeare: Otway's Venice Preserv'd and The Orphan and their History on the London Stage* (Durham: Duke University Press, 1950).

[57] Quentin Skinner has commented helpfully on this distinction, particularly in 'Motives, Intentions and the Interpretation of Texts', *New Literary History*, 3 (1972), 393–408.

personal information is woefully lacking, we can validly explore career circumstances and choices. We know, for instance, precious little about the personal life and feelings of Henry Fielding in the early 1730s, but we can discover quite a lot about why he wrote what he did, why it was staged where it was, and what kinds of economic and ideological pressures affected him.[58] The exploration of genesis does not tell us what works mean, but can often supply important explanations of what would otherwise be artistically baffling features of them. Why did Aphra Behn leap abruptly from romantic tragicomedy to the raunchy intrigues of *The Rover* (1677) and *Sir Patient Fancy* (1678)? The answer surely lies in the sex comedies that were hits in 1675 and 1676. Here the evidence is contextual, but for some writers, letters are profoundly revelatory, and not just for themselves or the reading of their work. The immense labour that has gone into collecting and annotating the correspondence of such writers as Byron, Dickens, Shaw, and Woolf has made an almost unimaginable difference to the way we conceive them and their worlds.

Second, investigation of genre offers rich possibilities in the realms of both genesis and reception. Few authors write in anything like a vacuum, and readers bring to any work a variety of conditioned expectations that may be either fulfilled or frustrated. Reconstruction of contextual reading goes far beyond genre, but genre is an excellent place to start. Any reader finds a work familiar or unfamiliar in its form, techniques, devices, and language. *Hamlet* needs to be considered in the context of revenge tragedy, just as *Astrophil and Stella* and Shakespeare's sonnets ought to be assessed in terms of the sixteenth-century English sonnet tradition. The point, interpretively, is not to limit meaning to generic norms, but to see what is conventional and what abandons or defies convention. This works equally well in sonnets, crime novels, and absurdist plays.

Third, we may explore print culture, which has a powerful impact upon both genesis and reception. The economics of publication (and, for playwrights, of theatrical production) exercise powerful pressure on writers. Biographers commonly take such pressure into account, but interpreters seldom do. The

---

[58] As I have attempted to demonstrate in *Henry Fielding and the London Theatre*.

costs of printing; the process of distribution and publicity; the rise of circulating libraries; the direct influence exerted on writers by publishers and the reading public—all these are part of what the archaeo-historicist hopes ultimately to bring to bear in the service of textual and career interpretation. For earlier periods, exploration of the impact of 'scribal culture' remains in its early stages, if not quite in its infancy.

Consider, for example, the dissemination of Shakespeare in print. The First Folio made virtually the whole corpus available in 1623, but how available, and to whom? The price was £1. William Ingram has recently suggested that the equivalent cost in buying power in the 1990s would be £1,000.[59] Such calculations are always dicey, since different goods and services go up in price at different rates. Even if we adopt £500 as a more conservative figure, however, the implications must be reckoned with. How many people bought the book, let alone read it? There was no paperback, and no library access unless one had a wealthy friend of literary bent. A fanatic might save up and splurge on a copy, but the book was simply beyond the means of most readers. How much did this situation change when Tonson published the six-volume Rowe edition in 1709? Almost all scholars have treated this as a popularization, but the price was 30 shillings, which was a week's wages for the Drury Lane prompter (in season—he did not work all year). The prompter was the highest-paid house servant, making more than many junior actors. I am not so rash as to estimate a present-day value, but I should suppose that the Rowe edition seemed about as costly as a multi-volume Oxford English Texts edition seems today. The 'cheap' reprint of 1714 (as it is commonly referred to) sold for 25 or 27 shillings, which is not a lot less. The Pope edition of 1723–5—a subscription venture—cost a dizzying six guineas. Not until the 1730s, when Walker brought out cheap single-play reprints and Tonson had to cut prices and reply in kind, did all of Shakespeare become affordable for ordinary book buyers. By no coincidence, I think, the 1730s are exactly

---

[59] William Ingram, *The Business of Playing: The Beginnings of the Adult Professional Theater in Elizabethan London* (Ithaca: Cornell University Press, 1992), 36–7. At around this time entry to an expensive theatre like the Phoenix cost a shilling (one-twentieth of the price of the First Folio), while admission to the Red Bull or the Fortune was only 2d. The present-day equivalent at Ingram's conversion figure would be £50 for a ticket to the Phoenix, £8.33 to the cheaper theatres.

when we find a basic shift in Shakespeare's reputation.[60] Until then, the books existed, but access to them was far more limited than most critics have realized.

The impact of print culture affects not only distribution but the reading experience. Venue, layout, and context affect reader response. Different publishers create different impressions. (Would you rather have your book appear with Oxford or Edwin Mellen?) A piece is not read the same way if encountered in the *TLS* rather than in *Private Eye*. The *Daily Telegraph*, the *Sun*, and the *Independent* have their own readers. A modern edition that plucks a Dryden poem from a miscellany falsifies it in significant ways: we need to know what the original book was like, how it was dedicated and introduced, who wrote the other poems, and what sort of poems they were. Venue, format, and subgenre definitely matter in fiction. Why are some writers of fiction reviewed with monotonous regularity in the *New York Times Book Review* and others sedulously ignored (Harlan Ellison, for instance)? If we want to understand original reception, we must learn to construct print-culture context.

Fourth, we can reconstruct and analyse reception. If we possess reviews, letters, diary comments, and the like, naturally we use them. If not, then we must attempt 'historical reader response' analysis, which is every bit as applicable in poetry and fiction as it is in drama—in fact, easier, because unmediated by performers. If we are reading the poetry of Pope, we must be struck by the density and range of its allusions. The 'ideal reader' comprehends all of them, but Pope can have enjoyed few such readers. How did his poems come across to the spectrum of readers he actually had? One of the ironies of scholarship is that our massively annotated editions sometimes give us tremendous advantages over original readers. Reading the highly topical and often scabrous stuff in the original volumes of *Poems on Affairs of State* (1689–1716) must have been a profoundly baffling experience for much of their contemporary audience— and radically unlike slogging through the modern Yale *POAS*, which attempts to footnote every name and arcane allusion.[61]

Politics and topicality offer one sort of historical problem.

---

[60] See Jonathan Bate, *Shakespearean Constitutions: Politics, Theatre, Criticism 1730–1830* (Oxford: Clarendon Press, 1989).

[61] A point well made by Michael McKeon in 'What Were Poems on Affairs of

Construction of social and psychological reality presents an even greater one. Just as the history of painting demands that we reckon with radically changing notions of right representation, so does fiction. What is presented, what distorted, what suppressed, and how the audience reacted to each, are of enormous importance in comprehending their understanding of poems, plays, and novels. Defoe and Fielding construct reality in enormously different ways. So do Lawrence and Joyce. 'Realism' must be treated largely as a changing convention, but much can be learnt from comparing different degrees of violation of probability or departure from consensus reality. We need to ask what the audience saw when it viewed its literature. When someone sat down with Delarivier Manley's immensely popular *Secret Memoirs . . . from the New Atalantis* in 1709, what did he or she think it *was*? Who read such a book? How was it perceived to fit the literary categories of the day? How seriously was it taken? Until we tackle such questions we have not begun to attempt serious analysis of reception.

Fifth, we can construct our own contextual reading of a work in any genre. Obviously one must specify the sort of reader or spectrum of readers being hypothesized. Insofar as possible, one attempts to imagine the actual experience of a first reading. This remains an area understudied by theorists of reading. Part of the impact of some complicated works stems from their difficulty. To encounter *Ulysses* cold in 1922 or *Gravity's Rainbow* in 1973 must have been frustrating, disconcerting, bewildering, exhilarating, and infuriating. Both adopt flagrantly deconstructive tactics and aim to tease, taunt, confuse. After several readings, however, such books start to reveal hidden connectives.[62] They are not anything like completely chaotic, whatever their impact on an innocent first-time reader.

An archaeo-historicist reading will vary greatly depending on the nature of the audience for which the interpretation is being constructed. If we are tackling *Pamela*, one reading does not fit all customers, as Fielding's derisory response reminds us. The more we think about reading, the less we should imagine that

State?', *1650–1850: Ideas, Aesthetics, and Inquiries in the Early Modern Era*, 4 (1998), 368–82.

[62] See Kathryn Hume, *Pynchon's Mythography: An Approach to Gravity's Rainbow* (Carbondale: Southern Illinois University Press, 1987).

even a mildly complex poem, play, or novel would be read in only one way, no matter how strenuously the author attempts to retain control of the meaning. Allowance must be made for both overt and covert meanings. A very plausible form of archaeo-historicist construction involves evasion of censorship where camouflage or indirection is employed to convey a message to a particular audience. Good examples are Lois Potter's account of royalist writing under Cromwell and Blair Worden's recent political reading of Sidney's *Old Arcadia*.[63]

At its best, archaeo-historicist reading can be vivid, particular, and surprising. I must grant, however, that this is the exception rather than the rule. In a high proportion of cases, the results seem bland. On reflection, this should not surprise us. Most historically situated readings are remote from the interests and sensibilities of late twentieth-century readers, and especially if they are not directed to specific meanings for particular audiences, they almost inevitably arrive at a lowest-common-denominator sort of reading. The results can be extremely useful as benchmarks against which to measure other kinds of readings, but they are rarely the most subtle, stimulating, or provocative account of the text. If the critic aims to establish a middle-of-the-road reading appropriate to a fairly wide audience, then small wonder if the results prove tame or even stodgy. I felt this acutely when writing about Fielding's plays. My aim was to supply elementary contextual readings of rather unfamiliar texts. I would not argue that these are particularly good readings, merely that they were appropriate to an essentially non-critical book in a way that more imaginative readings would not have been.

Contextual readings vary drastically with the circumstances. If the evidence exists, one should bring genesis, original contexts of all kinds, and reception to bear on the text. No set formula can tell you what parts of context are most important for a particular case. Approaching Joyce, I might well privilege genesis. For Milton, genre and intellectual history seem para-

---

[63] Lois Potter, *Secret Rites and Secret Writing: Royalist Literature, 1641–1660* (Cambridge: Cambridge University Press, 1989); Blair Worden, *The Sound of Virtue: Philip Sidney's Arcadia and Elizabethan Politics* (New Haven: Yale University Press, 1996); Annabel M. Patterson, *Censorship and Interpretation: The Conditions of Writing and Reading in Early Modern England* (1984; rev. edn. Madison: University of Wisconsin Press, [1990]).

mount. For Pope, print culture yields rich dividends. For Sterne or T. S. Eliot, reception makes a powerful tool. For Dickens, I might emphasize construction of social reality. Different choices would yield variant (but not necessarily incommensurable) results. Some choices would be only minimally productive: genesis for Shakespeare, or reception for Blake. Historically sited reading needs to be done with imagination and flexibility. To deny its 'thinness' in the absence of full contextual evidence, or its remoteness from the concerns of most present-day readers, would be idle. I maintain, however, that it is a powerful tool in all genres—and it will work even better as critics come to recognize the necessity of allowing for divergence of reader response.

The Constructedness of Contexts

The area in which the practice of Archaeo-Historicism seems most vulnerable to challenge lies in its context reconstruction. I have devoted an entire section of Chapter 2 to how such reconstruction should be carried out and validated, but I feel obliged to consider some of the issues from a different perspective here. Until David Perkins devoted a chapter to 'Historical Contextualism' in *Is Literary History Possible?*, virtually no systematic objections had been raised (at least in English, or so far as I know) to some dire methodological problems in commonly practised forms of historical interpretation. The objections have substance, and they should not be evaded.

A lot of old historicists have treated context essentially as though it were historical actuality. So learned and philosophically careful a theoretician as Wellek says flatly that 'a period is ... defined by a system of norms embedded in the historical process and irremovable from it.'[64] This is a deeply astonishing statement. In what sense does the 'system of norms' exist? Was it recognized at the time? What was the nature of the compulsion it exercised on writers of the day? What kind of access

[64] *Theory of Literature*, 278.

do we possess to 'historical process'?[65] Most periods are *ex post facto* constructions, and at best we have incomplete and imperfect access to any past time. When Perkins objects that 'the interrelations of texts and authors [and contexts, we may add] in a literary history are not "embedded in the historical process" for the historian to discover ... but are constructed by the literary historian' (67), he is unquestionably correct.

To imagine or pretend that the contexts we employ for interpretive purposes are the real thing is perfectly insane. The past is gone; we cannot conjure it up and use it as though it were a present and accessible reality. However carefully we reconstruct a context—and validate it as a legitimate representation of the past as best we can conceive it—the fact remains that it is a construction.[66] Assembling a context is at least as radical an act as textual interpretation—indeed I would say far more so, since any reader can go to the text, point to a line or a passage, and start arguing. Objecting to a context presents far greater complexities: one must identify gaps and absences, and try to comprehend what often turn out to be unstated principles of selection or assembly. Criticism is full of blandly authoritative assertions about Renaissance this or neoclassical that. 'The Victorian reader believed ...'. Who made these rules? Who justifies them? Consider the flood of mid-twentieth-century books and articles babbling about 'The Age of Reason' and ask yourself how well such stuff explains *A Tale of a Tub*. If this were really historicism, the less of it the better.

Any historical scholar must start by acknowledging the *radical selectivity* of what we do. This can rarely be avoided. Either much of the evidence no longer exists or so much exists that we can only deal with what we hope is a representative selection. We choose subjects, and we construct manageable-sized contexts for them. We can never be certain to what degree contextual influence determines the nature of a work of art. ('That context shapes texts is an assumption ... and cannot itself be

---

[65] 'Norms' can of course be imposed, as in the Soviet Union under Stalin. The result is sometimes conformity, sometimes rebellion, even in the case of an individual (e.g. Shostakovich). 'Compulsion' can certainly be studied in such circumstances, as can 'resistance'. But the norms of (say) 'the English Romantic period' seem to me a radically different proposition.

[66] So, to be sure, is the present, as study of 'the social construction of reality' has made evident in recent years.

proved', says Perkins—124.) Likewise we must admit another of Perkins's axioms: 'the context of any text is unsearchably extensive and can never be fully described or known' (125). Just how damaging are such admissions to the archaeo-historical enterprise?

Let us consider some of the fashions in which contextual scholars may blind themselves. Exclusion and simple ignorance can have much the same effect. A history of drama, for example, virtually always studies new plays in sequence. I did so myself in an account of late seventeenth-century drama. Yet a high proportion of the repertory consisted of old plays, not new plays—pre-1642 drama, and a steady accretion of 'stock plays' that had succeeded well enough to merit revival. If current repertory constitutes context for a dramatist in 1670 or 1690, then a large majority of the plays would not be new ones. I might defend my excluding old plays on the grounds that performance records are even more hopelessly skimpy for revivals than for premières. After 1705, however, we have essentially complete performance records—but historians of drama have exhibited no enthusiasm for trying to cope with the complexities of the actual repertory instead of just the relative trickle of new plays.

Here is a parallel case. Virtually all students of the eighteenth-century novel have treated the evolution of English fiction as something that happened in glorious isolation. Yet fiction was getting written on the Continent. The influence of particular sources has been studied (Cervantes, Rousseau), but surely the cross-pollination and fertilization was profound, complex, and important? Unquestionably it was—but also maddeningly untidy and difficult to trace, even for someone with the requisite language skills.

What is the right context? If you are coming to Wordsworth from Gray, Collins, Smart, Churchill, Cowper, Ossian, Chatterton, and Crabbe, then the 1798 *Lyrical Ballads* seems as revolutionary as textbooks still make it sound. If, however, you do what Robert Mayo did, and read extensively in magazines that published verse in the 1790s, then all of a sudden Wordsworth seems a great deal less of an innovator.[67] In retrospect, one might

---

[67] Robert Mayo, 'The Contemporaneity of the *Lyrical Ballads*', *PMLA* 69 (1954), 486–522.

have guessed this: context that does not come from within the decade at issue is unlikely to be anything but misleading.

Selection dictated by a priori assumptions will naturally give you the result you expect. As an example, take Bernard N. Schilling's *Dryden and the Conservative Myth: A Reading of 'Absalom and Achitophel'* (1961). This is not a terrible book, but essentially Schilling starts with a concept of Dryden's political and philosophical positions and then creates a setting for his conception. A similar sort of background—radically selective and incomplete—is established by Anne T. Barbeau in *The Intellectual Design of John Dryden's Heroic Plays* (1970), where basically she draws on Filmer and Hobbes. Yes, Dryden can be read in this setting, but it is a thin and simplistic representation of a complicated intellectual background.

Circularity and imposition generate falsification. Perkins's attack on Gilbert and Gubar's *The Madwoman in the Attic* is devastating:

The book merely alludes to . . . social and cultural factors in passing. No serious attempt is made to investigate them. . . . The context is constructed very selectively. . . . The major effort of the book . . . is to infer the psychic reactions of women writers from the social and literary context. We must ask, then, how Gilbert and Gubar can ascertain what took place in the minds of women. . . . [They] rely on what seems logically probable to them and in doing so, they project their own feelings onto past writers. . . . They freely quote contemporaries, such as Anne Sexton and Adrienne Rich, to illuminate the states of mind of nineteenth-century woman writers. . . . The contextualizing is, in a sense, bogus. The ideas by which the literary works are explained and interpreted are not derived from the contexts or the texts so much as they are imposed upon them. They are formed from other sources, in other experiences (for example, the experience of reading Harold Bloom), and applied to construct the contexts and read the texts. (136–8)

Whatever the critical virtues of *The Madwoman in the Attic* may be, I must agree that it is woefully inadequate as an exemplar of historical contextualization.

A contextual interpreter must never forget three crucial principles: (1) we construct the context, and we must justify it as a legitimate representation of the extant evidence; (2) the context must be built from primary evidence taken from the immediate period of what is being studied; (3) we cannot assume that context controls (let alone generates) text. R. S. Crane rightly denounces 'the illicit assumption that we can deduce particularized actuality from general probability'.[68] At best, we may argue the likelihood (for example) that *The Wasteland* (Ezra Pound's title) is an expression of the psychic aftermath of World War I. Would we draw the same conclusion about *He do the police in different voices* (Eliot's title)?

I have asked how damaging 'constructedness' of context is to the archaeo-historical enterprise. David Perkins takes an extremely dark view of the matter, implying that there can be no satisfactory way to proceed because 'we cannot concede that all constructions are equally valid' and 'we cannot completely agree on criteria as to which to prefer' (147). As the reader of Chapter 2 might expect, I disagree. Formidable practical problems do exist, but if we do not make excessive claims for what we are trying to do, I see no unanswerable objections to the enterprise. When we reconstruct contexts we are building the best hypothesis we can. They are no more than a working convenience, always subject to correction, improvement, or refutation. Likewise we must admit that contextual interpretation (whether concerned with genesis or reception) will almost never yield more than probability. Yes, we construct the contexts we use, and they are every bit as subject to misrepresentation and error as the interpretations we employ them to facilitate. Much the same could be said about the way physics and biology are practised—but hypotheses *can* be challenged, tested, and improved, whether contextual or interpretive.

The Problem of Subjectivity

The initially unpromising epistemological conditions of history are entirely owing to the fact that the claims to knowledge with which it emerges can never be subject to perceptual confirmation. . . . So it is really not to be expected that history could satisfy criteria of factuality, reference, objectivity, and truth.

Leon J. Goldstein[69]

[68] 'Critical and Historical Principles of Literary History', in *The Idea of the Humanities*, ii. 97.
[69] Goldstein, *Historical Knowing*, p. xiii.

Two generations ago Johan Huizinga could proclaim that 'the utterly sincere need to understand the past as well as possible without any admixture of one's own is the only thing that can make a work history'.[70] The objectivity of the historian must now be regarded as an exploded fallacy. Peter Munz speaks for a whole generation of historiographers when he reminds us that we are not 'engaged in a purely empirical enterprise' that consists of 'transcribing events'.[71] 'Facts' may be neutral in themselves, but their selection and interpretation cannot be so. 'Facts . . . must appear innocent of human intention', says Lorraine Daston, but 'when enlisted in the service of a claim or a conjecture . . . they become evidence'.[72]

We choose subjects and we select material. Any text or document we decide to use has partiality built into it. Munz observes tartly that 'there is no genuinely raw material at all. Everything that has come down to us is cooked by somebody for some purpose' (177). He also points out that

Anybody who has the slightest experience of working with historical documents . . . knows that these so-called raw materials cannot be understood unless the historian has some prior knowledge of the kind of society . . . to which they belong. The historian is therefore not a scholar who starts with raw material but a scholar who has some knowledge prior to the raw material. A charter, chronicle, an election return . . . or treaty is quite unintelligible without a vague preconception of the situation that gave rise to it. (157)

Absolutely true: anyone without quite a lot of orientation in a subject will simply be lost and helpless when plunged into a sea of documents. The historian must possess prior knowledge in order to function at all. Such contamination makes a mockery of 'objectivity' if we suppose that the investigator ought to be without any predisposition.

Realistically, we now know and admit that we begin with our own interests, values, and concerns, and that these exert a

[70] Johan Huizinga, 'The Task of Cultural History', in *Men and Ideas*, trans. James S. Holmes and Hans van Marle (New York: Meridian, 1959), 49.

[71] *The Shapes of Time: A New Look at the Philosophy of History* (Middletown, Conn.: Wesleyan University Press, 1977), 2–3.

[72] Lorraine Daston, 'Marvelous Facts and Miraculous Evidence in Early Modern Europe', in James Chandler, Arnold I. Davidson, and Harry Harootunian (eds.), *Questions of Evidence: Proof, Practice, and Persuasion across the Disciplines* (Chicago: University of Chicago Press, 1994), 243–74 at 243 and 244.

powerful influence on what we study, the questions we ask, and the explanations we find convincing. As Erich Auerbach said long ago, 'my own experience . . . is responsible for the choice of problems, the starting points, the reasoning and the intention expressed in my writings'.[73] How seriously does this admission damage or limit Archaeo-Historicism as a scholarly enterprise? Or let us put the question in less abstract and formal terms. If there is no objectivity, am I free to twist facts and pervert texts to my heart's content? And if not, why not?

Whether we should abandon 'objectivism' and positivism cannot be debated: they have long been a dead issue. Personally, I have never met a scholar who believed that 'facts' add up to anything by themselves, or that we can move inductively from particulars collected at random to broad theories somehow generated by meaning or order inherent in the facts. We would have to go back at least forty years to find such thinking in historiography. The abandonment of claims to objectivity is an accomplished fact, but does it simply deposit us in the quicksands of subjectivity and render all historical investigation a hollow mockery? Numerous historiographers have grappled with this problem, perhaps most interestingly, from my point of view, Pierre Bourdieu and Paul Ricoeur.

Bourdieu makes an elaborate argument, the gist of which, as I have understood him, is that objective/subjective should not be considered an absolute dichotomy, and that some parts of research method and practice are more personal and individual than others.[74] Ricoeur approaches the problems very differently in his essay on 'Objectivity and Subjectivity in History'.[75] He suggests that there are many 'levels of objectivity' in the matter of history, but that an important part of the historian's work involves 'subjectivity of reflection'. Drawing on Raymond Aron's distinction between good and bad subjectivity, Ricoeur argues that we must repudiate that 'fascination for a false

---

[73] Erich Auerbach, *Literary Language and its Public in Late Latin Antiquity and in the Middle Ages* (1958), trans. Ralph Manheim (Bollingen Series LXXIV; New York: Pantheon, 1965), 22.

[74] Pierre Bourdieu, *Outline of a Theory of Practice*, trans. Richard Nice (Cambridge Studies in Social Anthropology, 16; Cambridge: Cambridge University Press, 1977). Orig. French, 1972.

[75] Paul Ricoeur, *History and Truth*, trans. Charles A. Kelbley (Evanston: Northwestern University Press, 1965), 21, 22, 40.

objectivity' which would create 'a history in which there would no longer be men and human values but only structures, forces, and institutions'.

Subjectivity is inescapable in both history and science.[76] I would argue, however, that philosophical subjectivity and personal bias are not altogether the same thing. New Historicists have performed a valuable service by insisting that we should be conscious of our own ideological slants and agendas when conducting historical investigation and textual interpretation. The question then becomes what we do when we have confronted our own partialities and biases. Gadamer tells us that all scholars are subject to their own prejudices. Do we accept them as inevitable? Resist them as best we can? Rejoice in them? Striving for an objectivity we can never achieve may be deemed quixotic or misguided. Cultural materialists and some New Historicists argue that our research and teaching can ultimately be validated only by our own ideological commitments. They tend to sneer at all pretences to objectivity and to glory in our ability to unmask the authority structures of the past—without perhaps sufficiently acknowledging the particularity and quirkiness of their own agendas. To unmask and criticize the cultural assumptions and prejudices of the past is unquestionably both a valid and a useful enterprise. It is not, however, the object of the archaeo-historicist as I am trying to define it here.

The dangers of blithely riding our own hobby-horses should not be lightly dismissed. Thirty years ago David Hackett Fischer warned historians against 'scholarship of a kind which amounts to propaganda', reminding us of such examples as James Harvey Robinson (author of *The New History*, 1912) and the host of Eastern European historians who laboured conscientiously in the cause of world socialism.[77] My own very left-wing political convictions notwithstanding, I have major qualms about the wisdom of reading twentieth-century political, social, or sexual agendas into historical subjects. The emphasis on 'power' in New Historicist analysis is a very Marxist preoccupation. Per-

---

[76] For stimulating (and radically different) recent perspectives on subjectivity, see W. J. van der Dussen and Lionel Rubinoff (eds.), *Objectivity, Method and Point of View: Essays in the Philosophy of History* (Leiden: E. J. Brill, 1991), and Thomas Docherty, *Alterities: Criticism, History, Representation* (Oxford: Clarendon Press, 1996).

[77] *Historians' Fallacies*, 313–14.

sonally, I tend to share it. Yet I am uncomfortably aware that few seventeenth- and eighteenth-century writers would have accepted it as a valid way of characterizing their world (Hobbes notwithstanding)—or at least they would have pointed to other issues in government and religion as crucial defining forces. We are certainly entitled to use the benefits of hindsight, analysing economic history in terms of sophisticated later models, or applying Freud to *Hamlet*. An archaeo-historicist, however, will be slow to impose *ex post facto* categories and models in place of those recognized by the original inhabitants—or will at least insist on juxtaposing the two sets.

If our primary commitment is to the recreation of the viewpoints of the people and period we are studying, then witting or unwitting imposition of our own outlook constitutes a fundamental failure in methodology. If we are unable to limit the degree to which our subjectivity imposes our values on our subjects, then historical reconstruction is a fallacious and self-delusory enterprise.

The crux, I would suggest, lies in refusing to confuse practical difficulties with philosophical absolutes. Replying to 'Derrida and those who think like him', Christopher Butler grants that '"Objectivity" may indeed be a relativistic matter', but denies that this is true 'to the crippling extent that they would have us believe'.[78] The issue for the archaeo-historicist is whether subjectivity is an absolute or a variable. If subjectivity can be limited, controlled, challenged, compensated for—then it may certainly be a problem, but need not be a fatal one. Any physician will tell you that total antisepsis is impossible, but that sterile conditions vastly improve the survival rate in surgery. Likewise the historian bent on replicable results cannot attain to objectivity, but needs to make every effort to limit and control subjectivity and distortion.

Let us consider the issue from another angle. If M. Derrida were hauled before a court to be tried for some moderately repugnant crime, would he be totally indifferent to the identity and character of the judge? I think not. The phrase 'hanging judge' comes to mind. All judges are human, subjective, and

---

[78] Christopher Butler, *Interpretation, Deconstruction, and Ideology: An Introduction to some Current Issues in Literary Theory* (Oxford: Clarendon Press, 1984), 88.

biased—exactly like literary critics or historical scholars. Virtually all observers of courts, however, would agree that judges differ quite drastically in the degree to which they control their prejudices or allow them untrammelled sway in the courtroom. M. Derrida is a more profound philosopher than I, but I suspect that he would share my preference for a judge who made a strenuous effort to listen seriously to arguments on both sides and to weigh the evidence with all the impartiality he or she could summon, prejudices notwithstanding. The position of the historical scholar seems to me extremely similar. Likewise that of the teacher grading papers. Are all teachers prejudiced? Yes. Are some teachers unfair? Yes. Are all teachers equally unfair? No.

Denial of 'objectivity' in historical scholarship is only common sense. The inescapability of some degree of subjectivity is beyond question. Neither of these admissions, however, forces us to conclude that subjectivity is an absolute, or that we cannot make ourselves conscious of its influence, or that we are totally unable to control its effects. A judge sitting on a case in which he or she feels strong prejudice may recuse him or herself, or may preside in highly prejudicial ways. In a great many instances, however, judges do succeed in conducting fair trials, regardless of their own predispositions. In scholarship as in law we see wide variation. Since 'empathy' tends to be a vital part of historical reconstruction, one must expect some difficulties in sober assessment. LaCapra points rightly to E. P. Thompson's *The Making of the English Working Class* (1963) as a prime example of thick description and effective narration 'agitated by strong empathy, approaching identification'.[79] Too much identification or hostility can produce lopsided, distorted accounts of a subject. Should chilly indifference towards one's subject be our ideal? Only, I should think, if tepidity is the spice of history. Passionate interest in a subject need not be a disqualification for judicious analysis of it. Some parents love blindly; others love as much, but with painfully clear sight. 'Historian, know thyself' is probably as good a starting point as any for the serious investigation of history.

[79] LaCapra, *Soundings in Critical Theory*, 197.

Determinism and Causation

Does historicist interpretation assume that context controls genesis and meaning? I have denied this, but many critics have made the charge and it requires further consideration. Another common allegation can be summarized in a second question: Does historicism fail because it cannot supply causal explanations? This too requires direct rebuttal.

The idea that students of historical context posit the deterministic power of original circumstances has long been a commonplace. Wesley Morris expresses it in terms of a standard dichotomy when he writes that the 'literary historian . . . must be ready to affirm that the individual work is irrevocably embedded in . . . context' whereas the 'critic must argue that the individual work stands free of its historical context if he is to avoid the determinism of the literary historian's position'.[80] One need not be a lunatic devotee of the myth of solitary genius to find deterministic positions oppressive and indeed foolish.

Let us consider the issue not in abstract philosophical terms but by posing a question. If George Bernard Shaw had died of diphtheria in 1890 at the age of 34, would his plays have been written anyway? On the whole, I am of opinion that they would not. His absence from the English theatrical scene over the next five decades would have opened up space for other writers, but the likelihood that someone else would have written *Mrs. Warren's Profession*, *Heartbreak House*, and *Saint Joan* seems slight. Shaw was without doubt a man of his time (and a man in opposition to much in his time). His plays benefit greatly from contextual interpretation: they are crammed with topical issues of all sorts. Shaw's passionate commitment to social reform cannot be regarded as timeless. To imagine that he was merely a 'product of his age' would, however, be simply bizarre: if so, why was there only one of him? The impact of context on Shaw was enormous, but not even a fanatic historicist would claim that circumstances outweigh individuality in generating his plays. This would not

---

[80] Morris, *Toward a New Historicism*, 15.

be arguably true until one gets to extremely imitative and derivative writers—strictly hacks. Even at the level of Grub Street the author's individuality is often writ clearly on artistically and intellectually undistinguished works.

Some New Historicist and cultural materialist writers have indeed verged on obliterating authors' individuality.[81] (So, of course, have some other post-structuralists.) This strikes me as more a misguided attempt to insist on the crushing force of cultural hegemony than as a necessary axiom in contextual historicism. *Influence is not the same thing as control.* Writers are not captive mouthpieces of periods as defined in *Geistesgeschichte*, or even of competing ideologies within a period. Some works seem to me profoundly embedded in the historical conditions of their setting and genesis (*Ulysses*, or Thomas Mann's *Doktor Faustus*, for example), while others seem to float much freer (*Hamlet*, the odes of Keats). Yet even the most historically sited works can and should be read in other ways, and would be sadly diminished if we failed to do so. The archaeo-historicist is committed to assessing varying degrees of influence, but absolutely *not* to asserting contextual control of authors, works, or meanings.

The problem of causal explanation in history is more complex, but in my judgement does not represent a serious challenge to the legitimacy of Archaeo-Historicism as a method. The assumption that causal explanation is central to the historical enterprise goes back a long way. Thucydides works from this premiss. Causation moves human affairs; it must be taken into account when explaining what people did; the historian is obliged to assess causal factors when attempting to explain past events.[82] Historiographers are fond of such questions as 'Why did the American civil war occur?' and 'What caused the Great Depression?' Contributory causes are easy enough to identify in

---

[81] The degree to which New Historicism imposes deterministic assumptions has been sharply debated. Edward Pechter voices the charge in general terms ('The New Historicism and its Discontents: Politicizing Renaissance Drama', *PMLA* 102 (1987), 292–303), and M. H. Abrams challenges individual critics in 'On Political Readings of *Lyrical Ballads*' (M. H. Abrams, *Doing Things with Texts: Essays in Criticism and Critical Theory*, ed. Michael Fischer (New York: Norton, 1989), 364–91). Alan Liu strenuously denies 'determinism' ('The Power of Formalism', esp. 770).

[82] See Benson's analysis in *Toward the Scientific Study of History*, 88–9.

large number; identifying a necessary cause or combination of causes is something else again.[83] I have no desire to become entangled in a long-standing and basically pointless wrangle. For the archaeo-historicist, reconstruction of viewpoint looms far larger than causal explanation.

Croce insisted that *what happened* and *why it happened* are essentially different matters. Given a reasonable amount of evidence, we can reconstruct events, decisions, clashes, and specifics of situations. If we are asked for explanation of why something happened, then we must enquire what sort of explanation would be acceptable. The historian can *rationalize* virtually anything, with or without evidence. Here are four events of various sorts:

1. The character of Donne's poetry changed in major ways during his life.
2. The King's Company collapsed in spring 1682 and merged with the Duke's.
3. Wordsworth went dry fairly early as a poet.
4. The Labour party lost an election it expected to win in 1992.

I could supply a plausible causal explanation for each of these facts. Actually, I could easily provide two or three quite different explanations, each with a reasonable degree of plausibility. Traditional historiographic theory, however, demands that to validate one I must be able to invalidate others, or at least show that the others are consonant and subordinate.

Claiming to 'explain' complex events seems to me little more than a display of the historian's hubris. The evidence is generally limited, and the forces involved may well not all be known to us. I could not honestly say that I understand the *causes* of all events in my own life, or that I could give causal explanations of important events in the academic departments I have been a member of. Or rather, I could give them, but other participants would give radically different explanations. If we cannot pretend to supply verifiable causal explanations of relatively simple recent events of which we have first-hand knowledge and considerable documentation, then why should

---

[83] See S. H. Rigby, 'Historical Causation: Is One Thing more Important than Another?', *History*, 80 (1995), 227–42, for a forceful denial of the possibility of establishing 'the priority of causes' with any confidence.

we imagine we can do it for events of past centuries, let alone for vastly complex and large-scale events?

Back to the problem of what constitutes satisfactory explanation. If we demand demonstration of general laws in the fashion of Hempel, then historical explanation pretty well collapses altogether. I continue to find William Dray's classic rebuttal helpful: we can conduct 'causal analysis' without appeal to 'causal law'.[84] 'Rational explanation' as he calls it can be carried out *'from the evidence'*. The historian can show why known events seem to make sense or why they seem surprising. If the vital object in historical reconstruction is empathetic understanding, we are not debarred from asking 'why' questions or attempting to supply working hypotheses to answer them—but we do not have to make 'why' questions central if we lack the wherewithal to tackle them properly. Again and again historiographers have agonized over the question 'Is causal explanation possible?' My answer is forthright and equivocal: sometimes, to some extent.[85]

Foucault's notorious refusal to indulge in causal explanation has much to commend it. This is not to say that we should deny the influence of causation on human affairs, or resolutely exclude it from our attempts at historical reconstruction. I would suggest, however, that much of the furore over causal explanation stems from the desire to write narrative history in which change is duly accounted for. A question such as 'Why did Neoclassicism give way to Romanticism?' is only marginally better than 'How many angels could dance on the head of a pin?' The Neoclassicism–Romanticism question is invalid for two good reasons. First, it asks for causal explanation of a sort possible only with woolly generalities, and they are not susceptible of validation. Second, the dichotomy is posed in concepts artificially and selectively constructed long after the 'periods' at issue. They are essentially fantasies, and we merely befuddle ourselves if we suppose that they were created by historical causation.

Proposing a causal explanation makes perfectly good sense if

---

[84] Dray, *Laws and Explanation in History*, 114, 118, 129, 156.

[85] For a lucid argument claiming the possibility of (limited) causal explanation, see Clayton Roberts, *The Logic of Historical Explanation* (University Park: Pennsylvania State University Press, 1996), esp. ch. 11.

the evidence seems to support it. Making causal explanation the lynchpin on which all historical practice must depend strikes me as completely lunatic. Obsessive and counter-productive concern with causality seems to me ultimately to stem from eighteenth- and nineteenth-century theorists who believed that 'history' was a record of progress towards a goal. Kant believed that historical events represent movement towards rationality, and that *plan* and progress are revealed by the historian. Hegel held that history is rational. Marx believed that historical events have natural causes and that economics provide a fundamental motivating force. If, however, one has no bedrock conviction as to the larger ends of history, and if one does not subscribe to a particular theory of explanation (e.g. Marxist), then one is signally lacking the theodicy (as it were) on which large-scale historical causal explanations must rest. If life consists of hunger, lust, avarice, love, ambition, and ignorant armies clashing by night, perhaps we are unwise to imagine that we can discern explicable logic in larger developments. I return therefore to the fundamental point with which I concluded my preface. The archaeo-historicist can offer causal explanations wherever the evidence seems to warrant offering such hypotheses, but this is not the central point of the enterprise. Why things happen is often not very knowable, and a lot of things seem to occur in chaotic, unpredictable, and essentially random ways. What we *can* do is reconstruct events and viewpoint to the extent that the surviving traces permit.

4

Historicism and Theory

> Theory . . . is inescapable.
> R. S. Crane[1]

ARCHAEO-HISTORICISM as I have attempted to outline it in this book offers us a method by which we may (1) attempt to reconstruct past events and settings in relation to literature and culture and (2) employ constructed contexts to let us carry out historically sited readings of texts. My project could be described as an attempt to theorize old historicism. I would prefer to say that I am trying to focus, justify, and methodize a kind of historical scholarship long common but usually carried out without much methodological self-scrutiny.[2]

The severe phobia that continues to afflict many 'old historicists' when confronted with 'theory' has seriously impeded not only analysis of the implicit theory involved but also any attempt to connect to other methods or to apply contemporary theory within the purview of 'historicism'. A greater degree of methodological self-consciousness seems highly desirable, for as John Maynard Keynes has said, those who dislike theory or claim to do without are simply in the grip of an older theory. I have endeavoured to define the aims of Archaeo-Historicism, to supply a systematic account of it as a process of inquiry, and to admit to the limits of the method while replying to a variety of charges that could be brought against it. At this point I wish to broaden the perspective and inquire into the relationship between historical scholarship and other methods. Are they

---

[1] *The Languages of Criticism and the Structure of Poetry* (Toronto: University of Toronto Press, 1953), p. xiii.

[2] In this respect 'New Historicism' has been disappointing, whatever its virtues in practice. Greenblatt's celebrated assertion that it is 'no doctrine at all' is refreshing but leaves questions of objectives and methods alarmingly vague. The best survey I have encountered of the implicit theory to be found in New Historicism (and its relationship to the thinking of such writers as Foucault, Bourdieu, de Certeau, and Raymond Williams) is Claire Colebrook's *New Literary Histories*.

antagonistic? Potentially cooperative? Mutually irrelevant? Where might we find overlap? conflict? synergies? What larger principles of method need to be understood?

Method versus Theory

This discussion needs to open with a brief exposition of an elementary but vital distinction. 'Method' and 'theory' belong to radically different parts of the process of scholarly investigation. Confounding them can only produce methodological catastrophe. Five crucial elements can be identified as the constitutive parts of a scholarly investigation:

1. The investigator
2. The subject to be investigated
3. A method by which the subject will be approached
4. Questions that serve to focus inquiry and analysis
5. Hypotheses developed and tested as answers to the questions.

'Method' dictates the 'plan or system of inquiry' and contributes substantially to the kinds of questions asked. 'Theory' must remain outside the design of the investigation. Theories of various sorts represent potential solutions—that is, answers to questions—and can be appealed to *if pertinent* when the investigator reaches the stage of trying to develop tentative answers. If theory is allowed to dictate approach and questions—that is, to serve as a method—then the result is not an *inquiry* but rather a *demonstration*. No legitimate method of inquiry can be allowed to contain the answers to its own questions. Circularity may delight the self-fulfilling prophet, but it totally destroys the point of serious intellectual investigation.

When the investigator chooses a method, he or she is looking for a settled procedure, for a logical and systematic way of carrying out a project. The method must be appropriate to the subject chosen. If no evidence exists, the enterprise cannot work at all (the reception history of *Beowulf* prior to 1700), though the worst case is inadequate evidence severely abused (Shakespeare psychobiography). Granting that every investigation must allow for the particularities of subject matter, the scholar wants at least a rudimentary sense of logical procedure. To create a research methodology from scratch for every new investigation would be incredibly inefficient. One wishes, rather, to start with a basic model and adapt it to circumstances as appropriate. Only in this way do we draw fully on the experience of our predecessors.

The choice of both subject and method can be rationalized up to a point, but ultimately they do reflect individual disposition and intuition. As in science, the instinct of the investigator plays a vital part in choice. As I have tried to suggest in Chapter 2, however, the most critical part of carrying out any investigation comes with the formulation of questions. They may be your starting point: predecessors may have clashed or been stumped, leaving explicitly formulated problems to be tackled. Or you may read the predecessor's conclusions and find them unacceptable on grounds of evidence or analysis. In many cases, however, you must generate your own sense of 'problem'. Method may suggest some kinds of questions. Grappling with the primary evidence may lead to puzzles or contradictions that demand disentangling and analysis. What one must absolutely *not* do is to pose questions that can be tidily answered by appealing to a theory from which the question is pulled. 'Why did Hamlet delay?' is an obvious question, and if you wish to suggest particular psychological hang-ups with reference to Freudian theory as an answer, this is not unreasonable. But if your initial question is 'What are the manifestations of Hamlet's Oedipus complex?' you are merely setting up a tidy little circle.

'Method' offers us a systematized plan of inquiry. 'Theory' is commonly used in at least three meanings pertinent to this discussion: (1) a guess or conjecture, a hypothesis put forward as a possible explanation and a basis for further argument or experiment; (2) a proposed explanation whose status is still conjectural, in contrast to better-established propositions now regarded as true; (3) a coherent group of propositions used as a principle of explanation for a class of phenomena. I prefer to use 'hypothesis' in place of the first meaning. The second meaning, widely current in science and social science, is well illustrated by Darwin's theory of evolution, which progressed from conjectural/provisional status to 'well-established'. The third meaning is common in literary and cultural studies today. What is generally meant is 'a philosophical, psychological, or social construct that can be applied to explain complex problems, either historical or current'. The theory might be Freudian or Lacanian psychology, Marxist economics, essentialist feminism, or Northrop Frye's system of modes. *The crux lies in our recognizing that 'theory' belongs in the realm of answers, not questions*—which is *not* the way it is commonly conceived in literary circles today.

Literary studies have not benefited from thirty years of extreme cloudiness about what our methods are. Half a century ago, one could point with some confidence to passably clear-cut models. New Criticism was in full flower. *Scrutiny* offered an alternative. Johns Hopkins preached 'History of Ideas', the University of Pennsylvania touted 'literary history', and the University of Chicago inculcated neo-Aristotelian analysis. Today no such ready distinctions exist. Up to a point, this is good: we do not need rigid notions of method (which generate factional sniping). But if 'method' becomes so cloudy that we start to think of our preferred theories as methods, then we have got our horse well and truly behind our cart. We need to know what we are trying to accomplish before we commit ourselves to solutions.

Rigidity being pointless, I happily embrace multiplicity in methods, and see no problem in tolerating untidiness and overlap among them. Many more definitions are possible by way of combination or particularity, but I have friends who define themselves in at least eight ways: (1) as reader of texts—New Criticism lives, and its practitioners adopt the jargon *du jour*; (2) as historical scholar—whether biographical, generic, history of ideas, history of aesthetics; (3) as deconstructive reader; (4) as bibliographic scholar; (5) as reader-response critic, audience analyst, or historian of response; (6) as literary historian in the sense of tracing development; (7) as reader from present-day perspectives—Marxist, psychological, gay, feminist, or whatever; (8) as analyst of culture—treating literature within broader purviews that might involve history, art, music, sociology, popular culture, and the like. All these strike me as potentially interesting, valid, and important. All can be done crudely or badly. Obviously I have major reservations about literary history.

To have some idea of what we are doing and how to do it, we

need to know how we define ourselves in methodological terms. All too often these days people either do not bother, or they apply a term that does not establish method clearly. Consider the oft-heard statement 'I am a feminist'. What exactly does this imply? I would take the statement as a probable indicator of preference in research subjects, and very likely of preference in the kinds of questions asked. It does not, however, define either method or theory (though in practice it often implies a predilection for reading from present-day perspectives). A feminist might perfectly well practise any of the eight general methods I have just listed (and many do). A feminist who had committed passionately to a particular brand of feminist theory might be just as closed-minded as a dedicated Christian-moralist reader, but given the wide variety of conflicting feminist theories on the market we have no reason to suppose such prior commitment to one set of answers. 'I am a feminist' tells us very little about either method or theory. 'Feminism' is not a method. Contrariwise, 'I am a myth critic' might be intended and taken as a statement of method, but I question whether it should be accepted as such. The speaker indicates his or her preference in solutions, but how are subjects and questions arrived at? Where does the sense of purpose come from?

Most investigators commit themselves to a method (consciously or de facto), and the method helps lead them to suitable subjects. One may look for a subject fitted to one's preferred method, or one may become fascinated by a subject and adopt a method suited to it. In either case, 'method' should help lead you to Questions. 'Theory' should help supply *possible* Answers. If theory generates the questions, then you may be reasonably sure of tidy answers—and a high probability of self-confirming results.

Inquiry versus A Priori Analysis

The marks of the good scholar are many, but surely one of the most important is . . . a habitual distrust of the a priori.

R. S. Crane[3]

---

[3] 'Criticism as Inquiry; or, The Perils of the "High Priori Road"', in *The Idea of the Humanities*, ii. 29.

Let us turn to an even more basic question: what does literary criticism or scholarship try to accomplish? I would reply that the critic or scholar attempts to solve problems or answer questions, hoping thereby to add to or improve our understanding of our subject. At the outset of the enterprise one must have a genuine problem, to which more than one answer is arguably admissible. Puzzling over the problem, the investigator sets out on a process of *inquiry*—leading, one hopes, to discovery of pertinent evidence and formulation of a hypothesis that can be tested and offered as the best answer currently available. If this process is to produce useful results, then investigation must be undertaken in a spirit of open-minded exploration. The investigator cannot pretend to start in a state of impartial blankness, but if he or she is not prepared to entertain alternative hypotheses, then, as Crane observes, the results of the ostensible investigation can be no more than 'mere application of pre-established dogmas' (ii. 37). The comments that follow owe much to two important essays by Crane.[4] I do not agree with everything he says in them, but the basic position he tries to establish seems to me methodologically fundamental to serious work in historical scholarship.

Crane was hardly an innocent. He was not demanding that sort of 'old historicism' whose 'object was a knowledge that, once ascertained, was supposed to be independent of its methods of inquiry' (in Howard Felperin's phrase).[5] The investigator is unquestionably contaminated by biases, education, predisposition, and conditioning of various sorts. The crucial issue here is whether he or she is carrying out a genuine inquiry, prepared to accept whatever answers the accumulated evidence points to. If not, he or she may be conducting the historical-scholarly version of a kangaroo court.

Looking about for a potentially good subject, the investigator cannot be without personal predilections, and is seldom oblivious to recent work in the field, current trends, and fads. If he or she has intellectual or ideological commitments, they may quite legitimately exercise significant influence. (Bibliographers

[4] Crane, 'Criticism as Inquiry' and 'On Hypotheses in "Historical Criticism": Apropos of Certain Contemporary Medievalists', *The Idea of the Humanities*, ii. 236–60.
[5] Felperin, *Uses of the Canon*, 104.

seldom tackle genre issues.) In principle, one may start with a subject and seek an appropriate method, though in practice a lot of people commit to a method and go hunting for a suitable subject. Once you have familiarized yourself with the field as it stands, you must ask (a) how you might discover additional facts, if any might be had, and (b) where you might turn for supra-factual patterns (or, in other words, for applicable theory that may help explain the phenomena at issue). The archaeo-historicist will rarely appeal to present-day hypotheses (though doing so is a valid comparative and analytic tactic). Exponents of other methods will routinely do so for all sorts of reasons. The 'theory' appealed to may be W. W. Greg on copytext, Paul de Man on deconstruction, Eve Kosofsky Sedgwick on queer studies, or Stanley Fish on reader response. But in what spirit and with what assumptions do you make the appeal? If they are invoked as creators of potentially applicable hypotheses—as tools we may choose to employ, fine. If they are invoked as Authority, not so fine.

Reading student papers or manuscripts submitted to learned journals (and sometimes the journals themselves) I am deeply disconcerted to find an author starting out 'Judith Butler says . . .' or 'Fredric Jameson says . . .' and treating the *obiter dicta* thus quoted as a fundamentalist regards Scripture. I have respect for both these critics, and for many others so cited, but have they been elected to the status of minor deities? What upsets me is to find that they are being employed as though their writings are *true*. Back in the seventeenth and eighteenth centuries, literary critics appealed to 'authority' this way, and they have been roundly ridiculed for doing so. Indeed, criticism of earlier centuries that relies on invocation of Authority has an exceedingly bad name, and deserves it. How ironic then to find the habit spreading like wildfire among late twentieth-century iconoclasts.

'Theory' is held in high regard these days, and we have every reason to be grateful for its assistance in revamping and improving our methods. Only a fool would want to go back to the literary-critical world of 1960. Before we get too carried away, however, let us remind ourselves what we are talking about—that is, what is being venerated. When Judith Butler or Fredric Jameson (or whoever) writes a book, it is, ultimately, a book. No doubt a smart, interesting, provocative, and potentially useful contribution to knowledge, but does it really represent 'the last word'? A reading of a text, a historical reconstruction, and a book of 'theory' are all *conjectures*. They should be viewed as untested hypotheses put forward as possible explanations and as bases for argument and further analysis. People laugh when Aristotle is cited as 'be all and end all'. Most critics now mock the use of Freud as 'truth'. Why should we imagine that prominent figures of the present day should be immune to revaluation and amendment, or even outright debunking? What makes Judith Butler more 'true' than Aristotle? We do the work of any critic or scholar a terrible disservice if we treat it as 'established' when it has not yet stood the tests of time and counter-argument. We build on rotten foundations if we accept anything unquestioningly, let alone work that is still very much in the process of validation. Neither primary evidence nor theory should be imported and used uncritically.

At the outset of any genuine inquiry, the investigator must attempt to determine what evidence exists, how it can be tested or validated, and how far it should be trusted. Here is a simple instance. When I set out in 1969 to write a developmental analysis of late seventeenth-century English drama, I naturally (if foolishly) accepted the première dates in *The London Stage*. My source was recent (1965) and authoritative. About two years into the project I began to realize (with a slightly sick feeling) that the dates were a lot iffier than I had imagined. This was not a technicality. If Dryden's *Secret-Love* (1667) precedes James Howard's *All Mistaken*, then the form of Dryden's play is decidedly original. If (as I eventually concluded) Howard's play was staged in 1665, then Dryden's play becomes quite imitative. I soon found all sorts of specific problems with the performance calendar, as well as a much larger one. For about one-third of all new plays between 1660 and 1700 we have no early performance date at all; première must be estimated from publication (which is often not precisely known either). The editors of *The London Stage* based their placement of some 125 plays on the unexamined hypothesis that there was a standard lapse of about a month between performance and publication. This is basically true in the 1690s, but not earlier. Study of the statistical norm in cases for which both première and publication are known shows that in the 1660s the lapse was often upwards of a year. It drifted down to six months in the early 1670s, and to about three months by the time of the Popish Plot, after which it went up again and became erratic. Standard delay before publication gives one only a statistical norm, but in nearly fifty cases the *London Stage* date was seriously out of line with probability.[6] I cannot guarantee that the re-estimated dates are right, but the cumulative effect of the error imposed by acceptance of my source would have been severe.

Different kinds of evidence suffer from different sorts of potential error or unreliability. Even the most unregenerate New Critic would be a fool not to take a hard look at the reliability of the text he or she is explicating, and not to ponder the implications of the 'Statement of Textual Policy' that most users of standard editions do not bother to read. How many critics of Shakespeare take proper account of the origins of much of the scene division and many of the stage directions to be found in any modern edition? Yes, they are sometimes printed in brackets or reduced to the footnotes, but I have seen a lot of references to the 'heath' in *King Lear*—a term that originated with Nahum Tate and was engrafted upon Shakespeare's text by Nicholas Rowe in 1709.[7] Whether the investigator is relying on texts or anecdotes or generic categories or historical context or statistics of whatever sort, some sceptical testing is well advised. Something that looks fine to the casual eye (and has gone unchallenged for decades) can crumble disconcertingly when someone tests it. Neither primary evidence nor present-day hypotheses should be employed unless subjected to severe inter-rogation. To use a piece of evidence just because respected predecessors have used it can only be considered reckless and irresponsible. No investigator can be expected to conduct exhaustive tests on everything employed. A serious scholar, however, performs what the financial world calls 'due diligence', which means enough systematic spot-checking that blatant problems should come to light.

The investigator must exercise due diligence in checking

---

[6] See Judith Milhous and Robert D. Hume, 'Dating Play Premières from Publica-tion Data, 1660–1700', *Harvard Library Bulletin*, 22 (1974), 374–405.

[7] See James Ogden, 'Lear's Blasted Heath', *Durham University Journal*, 80 (1987), 19–26.

evidence and assessing any theory to which appeal is made. He or she is also obligated by the rules of serious inquiry to proceed (as Crane phrases the point) 'by way of working hypotheses' rather than by 'ruling hypothesis' (ii. 29–30). Allegiance is owed to independent judgement, which means that the investigator is debarred from taking over a 'first principle' from a predecessor or a present-day science and treating it as if it were true. Crane observes that 'specialization' (say as textual critic, biographer, or contextual reader) 'predetermines only the kind of problems the scholar will normally prefer to deal with; it leaves completely open the question of what particular hypotheses he will find most useful in solving them; and it involves him in no theoretical opposition to other "approaches" of the same sort'. To commit to a system of *explanation*, however, is a very different matter:

To say . . . that some one is a Freudian or archetypal or 'myth' critic or a Marxist literary historian is to define his 'approach' in a very different way: in terms not of a preferred set of problems but of a preferred principle of explanation—the special order of causes or theory about these which he will habitually invoke, to the exclusion of others, in formulating and justifying his conclusions. Such specialization is much more narrowly determinative of results than the other kind, for as long as the scholar remains loyal to his favorite explanatory principle, he will be disposed to frame all his particular hypotheses in harmony with it; his 'approach' to that extent is a closed one (the convinced Freudian interpreter may eventually lose his faith, but until he does we can almost always predict the sort of thing he will say). (ii. 248)

To put the point bluntly, if you commit to a system of explanation you become a fanatic and cease to be an inquirer. Or as Crane observes, prior commitment to theory is 'incompatible with inquiry' (ii. 35).

Crane develops the logic of this position in an elaboration of Kant's distinction between 'determinant' and 'reflective' judgements:

A 'determinant' judgment, according to Kant, is one in which the universal (the rule, the principle, the law, whatever it may be) is given and the particulars to be explained are then subsumed under it. A 'reflective' judgment, on the other hand, is one in which only the particulars to be explained are given and the explanation has to be found by critical inquiry—by making many guesses and trying to rule out all those that do not fit. (ii. 258)

This is a version of the ancient distinction between deduction and induction. To be justified in applying a 'law' one must be certain (a) that it is true and (b) that it fits the case at issue. A determinant judgement presumes that the law cannot be falsified or even improved. It imposes an absolute. Does the realm of literary and historical scholarship lend itself to absolutes? I would argue that it does not. No theory purporting to account for human activities can legitimately claim all-inclusiveness. Our knowledge of the past must by definition remain incomplete, but we can never be certain what additional information may be brought to light. We must always acknowledge the possibility of greater complexity in fact or motive than the theory invoked has allowed for. Consequently all 'knowledge' or conclusions produced in criticism or historical scholarship must be for ever regarded as provisional. Determinant judgements are not admissible in the realm of historical explanation.

Many scholars representing many methods might be held up as deplorable examples of transgression against what I shall enunciate as Crane's Law: *a priori commitment to a principle of explanation destroys the basis for intellectual inquiry.* Critics and scholars are by no means debarred from strong preferences among theories. The wise scholar, however, will be polygamous rather than monogamous in espousing theory. One is free to love them as long as one is fully prepared to leave them when occasion requires. Personally, I prefer to be an inquiring scholar rather than a True Believer and proselyte.

Let me conclude with a single example of the kind of thinking against which I am arguing. In a famous passage in his *Criticism and Ideology* Terry Eagleton says that

Historical materialism stands or falls by the claim that it is not only not an ideology, but that it contains a scientific theory of the genesis, structure and decline of ideologies. It situates itself, in short, outside the terrain of competing 'long perspectives' in order to theorise the conditions of their very possibility.[8]

In other words, historical materialism claims—in Kantian terms—to be the sort of 'law' that can stand as the basis of determinative judgements. How might such a claim be

---

[8] *Criticism and Ideology: A Study in Marxist Literary Theory* (London: NLB, 1976), 16–17.

validated? What sets this particular *theory* (for such I maintain it to be) outside the terrain of competing long perspectives? A scholar might for personal reasons prefer historical materialism as an explanatory system, or choose to privilege it—but on what basis can it claim to be *true*? Marx—at least in some circles—is a more respectable Idol than the Bible or Freud or Chairman Mao, but if historical and literary scholarship are to be more than pretentious games, then their practitioners must forswear Idols.

Syncretism and Borrowing

> Literary criticism is not, and never has been, a single discipline . . . but rather a collection of distinct and more or less incommensurable 'frameworks' or 'languages'.
>
> R. S. Crane[9]

When we commit to a method, or select one for a particular inquiry, ought we to stay strictly within its limits? Do we lose focus and muddle ourselves if we try to adopt principles of investigation from other methods? Or are we trapping ourselves in an artificial restriction if we demand methodological exclusivity?

Syncretism—attempted reconciliation or union of different principles, practices, or parties—has been variously hailed as a panacea and denounced as a false ideal. A generation ago Stanley Edgar Hyman called for the synthesis of an 'ideal critic' from the component bits of Edmund Wilson, Yvor Winters, T. S. Eliot, Maud Bodkin, Christopher Caudwell, John Livingston Lowes, G. Wilson Knight, I. A. Richards, William Empson, Cleanth Brooks, and numerous other critics—all that was 'irrelevant, worthless, or private to them' to be discarded.[10] R. P. Blackmur more modestly recommended 'marriage' between Aristotle and Coleridge.[11] At much the same period the

---

[9] *The Languages of Criticism*, 13.

[10] Stanley Edgar Hyman, *The Armed Vision: A Study in the Methods of Modern Literary Criticism* (New York: Knopf, 1948), 395–407.

[11] R. P. Blackmur, 'The Lion and the Honeycomb', *Hudson Review*, 3 (1951), 487–507.

Chicago Critics fiercely denounced syncretism as a methodo-logical sin.[12] The central premiss of Crane's *The Languages of Criticism* is that 'criticism' comprises a variety of enterprises that seek different objectives and employ different concepts (languages), whose 'results' consequently cannot be judged tidily against one another.

Both positions represent extremes. Pluralism is now widely accepted: few practising critics believe that Christian exegesis and materialist feminism can be 'reconciled' (whatever that might mean). Tolerance may be cheerful or grudging, but there is a fair amount of it. Pluralism, however, is by no means the same as eclecticism. The practising critic or scholar must ask whether he or she is best off trying to do one sort of thing at a time—or whether this simply breeds balkanization, factional-ism, and non-communication.

Can one do a Freudian-Marxist-bibliographic-sociological-textual analysis of historical reader response of Laurence Sterne? No doubt one can, but the results would surely be chaotic—a dog's breakfast of ill-assorted critical flavours. At the other extreme, however, I would question the wisdom of a biblio-graphic scholar who sedulously ignored biography and recep-tion. One need look only at the textual history of *Clarissa* to understand why some flexibility makes sense: Richardson re-wrote on the basis of his readers' responses. Should a Marxist ignore contextual meanings? Not unless he or she sees texts as ahistorical (which is bad Marxism). You do not want to be trapped in the straitjacket of a single method; no more do you want to be falling between stools.

So what makes sense? Neither rigid methodological separat-ism nor syncretism offers a satisfactory modus operandi. With-out wanting to be dogmatic, I shall offer three principles for navigating these rather treacherous waters:

1. Avoid syncretism in method. Design your investigation within the limits of a clearly-defined method.

2. Compare your results with those of other methods. What does your method force you to omit or distort?

3. Cultivate eclecticism in systems of explanation. Eclecticism

---

[12] R. S. Crane (ed.), *Critics and Criticism: Ancient and Modern* (Chicago: Univer-sity of Chicago Press, 1952), esp. Crane's Introduction, 1–24.

produces blurred sense of purpose in the realm of method, but is highly desirable when you are seeking hypotheses to test.

I am trying to suggest here that in designing an inquiry one needs to have a strongly defined sense of method as the basis for formulating one's sense of objectives. Trying to do too many things at once will just diffuse the force and clarity of the investigation. One very much wants, however, to compare one's tentative results with those obtained by other means of inquiry. Not to do so gives you no standard of comparison and judgement. A Marxist reading of *Paradise Lost* can only benefit from comparison against feminist and deconstructive readings—or indeed a historicist one. Are they (in Crane's terms) incommensurable? And if so, can the comparison lead to anything but contradiction and misunderstanding? I would argue that this is one of those cases in which the value of Reading A does not necessarily falsify Readings B and C. The point here is not to attempt to invalidate other readings, but to test the extent to which Reading A accounts for the subject under consideration. As Crane observes, the 'adequacy of any procedure in practical criticism' can be judged only 'by considering the concepts and the methods of reasoning which it presupposes and asking ourselves what important aspects, if any, of the objects we are examining they force us to leave out of account'.[13] A precise focus is highly desirable in establishing investigative procedure, but a refusal to consider alternative results becomes a huge liability when one reaches the stage of tentative conclusions. When the investigator moves beyond specifics to attempt broader explanation of whatever is at issue, refusal to entertain a wide variety of potential hypotheses can be disastrously reductive. A historian determined to 'explain' the English civil war in terms of class conflict (Christopher Hill) may add something to our comprehension of the forces in conflict, but needs to ask whether 'class' is the primary cause or merely a contributory one. In a similar way, almost any thematic reading of

---

[13] Crane, *Languages of Criticism*, 140. Crane invokes an essentially heuristic or instrumentalist position in which the value of a reading resides in the extent of its explanatory power. Popper suggests in *The Logic of Scientific Discovery* (persuasively, to my mind) that such power is particularly evident when a theory offers convincing answers to problems that had not yet been formulated when it was propounded.

a play will reduce it to a set of formulae that strip most of the life out of it.

I have suggested that eclecticism creates confusion in method but tends to prove fruitful in the realm of explanatory hypotheses. At this juncture I wish to shift from abstract generality to a pair of extremely specific instances of conceptual borrowing or importation in which a scholar ostensibly dealing with historical interpretation employs theory or viewpoint from a radically different setting.

Case 1: Garrick's Acting as Paradigm Shift. Few theories have been as regularly and enthusiastically plundered by humanists as the notion of revolutionary change outlined by Thomas Kuhn.[14] Many examples might be offered, but here is one from a widely respected book on the history of the theory of acting. Joseph R. Roach gives a summary account of Garrick's first appearance in London:

> It was immediately apparent to all factions, pro and con, that the kind of acting he offered up at his debut in 1741 broke decisively with the past. . . . As the principal surviving exponent of the superannuated system, James Quin saw that the two styles were mutually exclusive: 'If this young fellow is right', he remarked at Garrick's debut, 'then we have all been wrong.' . . . We are fortunate in having the eye-witness account of Richard Cumberland, who saw Garrick as Lothario in Rowe's *Fair Penitent* opposite the Horatio of Quin. . . . When Garrick 'bounded' onstage: 'heavens, what a transition! — it seemed as if a whole century had been swept over in the transition of a single scene'. . . .[15]

Roach analyses the situation as follows:

> I propose that this response records a theatrical version of what historians of science would term a revolutionary paradigm shift. In its purest form, such a shift of belief and practice comes about with the clarity and instantaneous completeness of a Gestalt switch . . . the terms of understanding and appreciation have irrevocably altered; one system of assumptions has been supplanted by a competing view based on radically altered presuppositions and expectations. Quin's inherited vocabulary of rhetorical gesture, founded on ancient physiological theory, has

[14] Thomas S. Kuhn, *The Structure of Scientific Revolutions*, International Encyclopedia of Unified Science (1962; 2nd edn., Chicago: University of Chicago Press, 1970).

[15] Joseph R. Roach, *The Player's Passion: Studies in the Science of Acting* (1985; repr. Ann Arbor: University of Michigan Press, 1993), 56–7.

ceased to convey meaning; *actio* and *pronuntiatio* are on their way to join the epicycles of Ptolemaic astronomy in the boneyard of dead ideas.

This is exciting, satisfying: modernity sweeps away the rubbish of the dead past. I do, however, have a question. How much of this is true?

At the level of elementary good practice in historical research, we may note some problems of evidence. Garrick unquestionably created a tremendous stir in the season of 1741–42. The comment attributed to Quin may be a fair summary of his response to Garrick, but it seems unlikely to have been made at Garrick's 'debut' in October 1741, since Quin was in Ireland from 8 June 1741 to 9 February 1742.[16] Roach quotes the comment from a trashy anthology of 1949 that does not cite any source. Perhaps an authoritative source exists, but so far as I have been able to discover the earliest appearance of the anecdote is in Thomas Davies's *Life of David Garrick* (1780).[17] Davies is a reputable anecdotalist and he was in London in the 1740s—an adult with theatrical connections. Nonetheless, anecdotes thirty-nine years after the fact are often polished up a bit and Davies is not an unbiased reporter. The Garrick–Quin performance of *The Fair Penitent* makes a marvellous encapsulation of the contrast, but I would note first that it occurred not in 1741 but in the season of 1746–47; second that Richard Cumberland was exactly 14 at the time; and third that he published this account in 1806 in old age after many years' association with Garrick.

I would not for a moment doubt that in the 1740s Quin (who was 53 in 1746) seemed old-fashioned in contrast to Garrick (who was 29). However worryingly remote in time, the anecdotes very likely do reflect a genuine contrast. Roach does not mention, however, that Quin continued to be a major attraction in London until his retirement in 1751. Another pair of facts suppressed in the interest of neatness are that Garrick thought enough of Quin to try to persuade him to become his partner in management and acting at Drury Lane in 1747 and attempted to hire him in 1750–51. Did Garrick regard Quin as a hopeless old relic of an obsolete past?

---

[16] *Biographical Dictionary*, xii. 232.
[17] Thomas Davies, *Memoirs of the Life of David Garrick*, ed. Stephen Jones, 2 vols. (1808; repr. New York: Blom, 1969), i. 45.

Broadening our consideration a bit, we need to ask what Garrick's arrival on the London stage actually changed. Did other actors (Quin excepted, presumably) promptly abandon all their training and experience and start acting in the 'new' style? If so, this revolution seems to have escaped the notice of the contemporary audience. A vast number of adulatory comments about Garrick's acting can be found, but they tell us not that he revolutionized acting in London but rather that he was unique. Did 'rhetorical' acting get swept away like Ptolemaic astronomy? The evidence suggests nothing of the sort. One might, for example, look to the manuals of speech and gesture so popular in eighteenth-century Europe: the traditional style continued to be set forth in such works for decades.[18] If one wants evidence from theatrical practice, I would suggest looking beyond Garrick to the 'next' great actor in London—John Philip Kemble, who made his London debut in 1783 at the age of 26. He was a stately, rhetorical actor whose style was radically unlike that of Garrick. (Curiously enough, Kemble does not even appear in Roach's index.) Garrick was a stunningly original and effective actor, but the evidence for his precipitating a sudden and drastic change in acting as it was done in London is virtually non-existent. The evidence against his exercising major influence on his immediate successor is overwhelming.

We come finally to the question of Thomas Kuhn. As I understand his concept of paradigm shift, an 'essential characteristic' of a work causing such change must be that its 'achievement' is 'sufficiently unprecedented to attract an enduring group of adherents away from competing modes of scientific activity'. Paradigms 'provide models from which spring particular coherent traditions of scientific research'. Kuhn offers as examples Aristotle's *Physica*, Ptolemy's *Almagest*, Newton's *Principia* and *Opticks*, Franklin's *Electricity*, Lavoisier's *Chemistry*, and Lyell's *Geology*.[19] Kuhn believes that thinking in a natural science tends to be governed by a paradigm for long periods, terminated and redirected by abrupt and drastic theoretical and practical change. We need to ask, therefore, (a) whether acting theory and style can legitimately be described in the conceptual terms

[18] See Dene Barnett, *The Art of Gesture: The Practices and Principles of 18th-Century Acting* (Heidelberg: Carl Winter Universitätsverlag, 1987).
[19] *The Structure of Scientific Revolutions*, 10.

of this model, and (b) whether Garrick's acting (and theory, insofar as he adopted and promulgated one) brought about an 'enduring' change in practice by giving rise to a 'coherent tradition'.

The answer to the second question is clearly No. Garrick was not particularly theoretical; his protégés did not work closely in his image; no School of Garrick ever emerged; the acting styles of the 1790s do not seem to reflect profound influence by Garrick. He was a titan, but apparently inimitable. The first question is more debatable, though again my answer is No. A particular acting style may be widely practised in a given period, but acting does not necessarily stem from conscious application of theory, and there is no reason several radically different acting styles cannot be practised at the same time even in the same city. An acting style may seem odd, or off-putting, or old-fashioned — but it is not *wrong* in the way that a discredited hypothesis is in biology. Where 'taste' is the ultimate arbiter, the nature of change will be quite different. We have no reason to imagine that acting style in a period reflects a dominant concept in the way that Copernicus or Darwin affected whole generations of successors.

Kuhn has been widely if loosely referred to in literary scholarship. This comes as no surprise, given humanists' inferiority complex — though Kuhn remains controversial even in the realm of science. Jejeune and pretentious application of Kuhn does not in itself invalidate Kuhn's work as a theory to which we may appeal, but its applicability in a realm for which it was never designed must be queried. René Wellek offers a trenchant critique of such utilization of Kuhn. He admits the superficial attractions of treating various schools of criticism as stemming from incommensurable paradigms, thus accounting 'for the present heightened difficulties of communication, for the Tower of Babel' that now afflicts us.[20] The application fails, however, because 'there are no such complete revolutions in the history of criticism as Kuhn stipulates for the history of science'. Wellek points to linguistics as another field where Kuhn has been applied unsatisfactorily: linguistics has not gone through 'such complete revolutions' and remains 'a cumulative science in spite

---

[20] Wellek, *The Attack on Literature*, 144–5.

of shifts of emphasis and changing interests'. Imposing the concept of paradigm shift on a field that does not work this way creates a highly undesirable illusion that useful discussion is impossible. The reason is of course that if disagreement reflects allegiance to different paradigms, then by definition the positions are irreconcilable.

Applying Kuhn's theory to humanistic subjects strikes me as profoundly misguided. The reasons for caution seem obvious. What may (or may not) describe 'progress' in a territory where verification can be largely a matter of observation and experiment seems unlikely to apply well to an utterly different sort of intellectual terrain. The problems that make nonsense of 'scientific' history (where scientific proofs are lacking) should at the least give us serious doubts about the wisdom of importing hypotheses conceived for science. We may grant in principle that any such borrowing or importation might be justified in a particular case, but the likelihood of convincing justification seems low. To apply Kuhn's concept of paradigm shift—or any other 'outside' theory—without a rigorous justification of the importation is unacceptable methodology. It conveys the illusion of profundity and currency, but all it really accomplishes is to confuse our thinking about the nature of our subject.

Case 2: Steele's Eulogy for Betterton. When Thomas Betterton died in April 1710, he was generally considered the greatest actor of his time. He was buried in Westminster Abbey, and in *Tatler* 167 Richard Steele wrote an extended eulogy in which he comments at some length on Betterton's acting in general and on his Othello in particular. In a recent cultural-studies analysis of 'theatrical, musical, and ritual performance along the Atlantic rim' Roach devotes a whole chapter to this bit of history.[21] He says that he proposes 'to demonstrate' that 'the amplitude of Steele's threnody and the celebrity of the actor whose career it memorializes . . . disclose their unavowed complicity in the catastrophic histories of the circum-Atlantic rim' (74–5)—in other words their guilt (and that of their audience) over the slave trade.

By 1710 these histories were conjoined by intensified networks of production and consumption, a juncture epitomized by the London choc-

---

[21] Joseph Roach, *Cities of the Dead: Circum-Atlantic Performance* (New York: Columbia University Press, 1996), ch. 3, esp. 74–5.

olate and coffee houses in which the papers of Steele and Addison were read and discussed by patrons who refreshed themselves with stimulating beverages extracted from the labor of West Indian slaves. Sales of slaves were conducted in the coffee and chocolate houses, advertisements for which *The Tatler* carried. (75)

Roach believes that performance is a site that allows repressed problems to emerge, in disguised form, thus providing an escape valve for society. Hence, if we look hard at representations of Blacks on the English stage in the eighteenth century, we shall find traces of white guilt. By his reckoning Steele chose Othello as his example of Betterton's acting (consciously or unconsciously) because it signified a moral dilemma he could not cope with directly.

Roach does not claim that Steele or anyone else at the time understood this: his interpretation is offered strictly as a feat of *ex post facto* mind-reading. As a demonstration of late twentieth-century American middle-class WASP Liberal guilt about racism, it is a plausible construction, elegantly written and well sprinkled with learned allusions ancient and modern. But is this true? And even supposing that it could in some fashion be 'proved', what then?

Let us start by highlighting a key statement. *Sales of slaves were conducted in the coffee and chocolate houses, advertisements for which* The Tatler *carried.* This is a damning, one may say a horrific statement. I confess to being deeply taken aback when I read it. Reprints of the *Tatler* (including the 3-volume Bond edition published by Oxford in 1987) omit the advertisements. Reading Roach's statement, one might naturally conclude that for two centuries scholars have ignored awful truths about slave auctions in London *c*.1710 and have joined a conspiracy of silence about them. Slave auctions certainly do not enter into the picture of coffee-house life conveyed in our textbooks—or even our learned journal articles. Well might Richard Steele, bleeding heart that he unquestionably was, feel terrible about his complicity in local propagation of slavery.

Shocked by my own complicity in racism (etc.), I hastened to the library to look at microfilms of the original *Tatler* issues. I did not find them overflowing with advertisements for sales of slaves. Rewards offered for the return of escaped slaves are not terribly uncommon in papers of the time, but that is at least a bit

different. Returning to *Cities of the Dead* I found that though
it has an extensive bibliography and a vast number of par-
enthetical references, Roach supplies no specific citations to
document a very serious charge. The omission hardly requires
comment. Responsible scholars welcome verification by their
successors, and endeavour to facilitate it. A letter to Professor
Roach requesting references elicited a prompt and courteous
reply citing a single instance—which I already knew from a
1984 book by Peter Fryer which documents *one* instance of the
sale of *a* slave in the time period at issue: 'Asian slaves were
sometimes advertised for sale. Steele's and Addison's *Tatler*, in
1709[/10], carried an advertisement offering "a Black Indian
Boy, 12 Years of Age, fit to wait on a Gentleman, to be disposed
of at Denis's Coffee-house in Finch-Lane near the Royal Exchange"'.[22] There may be others, or even advertisements for
actual auctions of multiple bodies, but I have done a fair amount
of skimming without turning them up. A startling indictment
has been made without any citation of evidence, and I seriously
question how much evidence exists. The *Tatler* advertisement
just quoted is certainly very ugly indeed, but it is one instance
out of several hundred issues of Addison and Steele's periodicals.
Whether Steele ever noticed this particular advertisement is
undeterminable.

   Roach adduces no direct evidence to prove Steele's sense of
'guilt'. He comments at length on Steele's meditation in the
cloisters of Westminster Abbey, emphasizing with a very ahistorical term 'Steele's liberal belief that differences among "Men"
are "meerly Scenical"' (84). Steele makes quite explicit that the
'differences' he has in mind concern rank and class, but perhaps
he is merely suppressing his guilt about racial matters. Why we
should presume that the commentary on Othello is an unconscious betrayal of such guilt, however, I do not see. Steele does
not emphasize racial issues. Othello was one of Betterton's
famous roles, and it would have been familiar to many of Steele's
readers. In the last few years of his life Betterton had played
relatively few parts, and most of them were either ignoble (Fal-
staff, Thersites, Congreve's Old Batchelor), inappropriate for an

---

[22] Peter Fryer, *Staying Power: The History of Black People in Britain* (London:
Pluto Press, 1984), 78. The reference is to *Tatler* no. 132, 9–11 Feb. 1709[/10].
Exactly what is meant by 'Indian' is impossible to say.

elderly man (Hamlet, Congreve's Valentine), or in minor plays by Edmund Smith, Mrs Manley, and John Dennis. Othello is an obvious and satisfactory choice for reasons having nothing to do with race.

I will cheerfully grant that Steele *might* have been writing under the cultural nexus Roach elaborates. I do not see how such an interpretation could be proven, or why it should be considered historically likely. From our point of view Steele should certainly have felt guilty about the slave trade and ought to have felt moral discomfort in contemplating any representation of Black people. This is, however, a twentieth-century point of view, and I have a strong suspicion that Steele would be taken aback by it if we could confront him with it. Henry Steele Commager points out that whole generations of 'good, humane, Christian men and women' not only accepted slavery 'but considered it a blessing'.[23] This may now seem abominable; we may argue that they were rationalizing, must have felt subconsciously guilty, and so forth. The fact remains that from a historicist perspective peoples of the past must be regarded as entitled to points of view that we may now find outrageous or despicable. Did the classical Athenians 'know' that sex with teenage boys was a crime against humanity? By Roach's logic they must have.

I raise the example of Steele and racial guilt because it illustrates with brutal clarity two vital principles of good historical practice. First, the scholar must be keenly aware of the dangers of what I shall call *conceptual imposition*. We are free to read as we please, but when we impute motives (especially hidden motives) to people in the past, we need to show that we are not just reading our own predilections onto our subjects. Second, any vital assertion of fact, but most especially a startling and original one, must be fully and precisely documented. Roach asserts that 'sales of slaves' (plural in both cases) were conducted in coffee houses and advertised in the *Tatler*. This is by no means common knowledge, and neither is it merely an incidental observation in passing. A reader is entitled to expect a reasonable degree of accuracy from a university press publication, and might well quote this book in the belief that its 'facts'

[23] Henry Steele Commager, *The Search for a Usable Past and Other Essays in Historiography* (New York: Knopf, 1967), 315.

can be trusted. The lack of documentation of a crucial—and shocking—part of the case can only be regarded as unsound and unscholarly.

Five Kinds of Reading

> The end of theory, for criticism, is application . . . the reading and literary *explication* of literary texts.
>
> R. S. Crane[24]

> There is no critical language . . . that cannot be made to yield valuable observations and insights when it is applied, with skill and discretion, to individual works.
>
> R. S. Crane[25]

How does Archaeo-Historicism relate to other kinds of criticism and scholarship currently practised? To move from compositorial foibles and costume bills to Derrida and Foucault is quite a jump. The seeming remoteness and antagonism between historicist and post-structuralist enterprises is magnified by our awareness of the degree to which historicism can concern itself with factual and contextual scholarship that never comes near a literary text. We must remember, however, that for the student of literature historicism is ultimately *a way of reading*. Other modes of reading are often preferable, but historicism offers us a method of reading texts that should be one of several options.

In the course of the last generation 'reading' has turned into a far more complicated enterprise than it was previously conceived to be. One can break it down in a bewildering variety of ways for analytic purposes, and I make no special claims for the five definitions I am about to offer. My aim is simply to distinguish among markedly different sorts of textual interpretation. All have virtues, limitations, and pitfalls. All offer potentially valuable results, but we need to understand as clearly as possible what each tries to do and why their results are often so radically contradictory.

To talk about 'reading' we need to start with some discrimina-

---

[24] 'History versus Criticism', in *The Idea of the Humanities*, ii. 23.
[25] *Languages of Criticism*, 108.

tions. Four dichotomies loom large in establishing sense of purpose. Are we primarily concerned with text or reader? Are we concerned with original readers or present-day readers? Do we assume that the author controls the meaning—or not? Do we assume that an individual reader controls the reading process, or do we assume control by some governing principle? Radically different sorts of readings stem from different answers.

No development in literary interpretation over the past generation has been healthier than serious acknowledgement of the importance of readers in construing meaning. What was once (in theory, anyhow) a relatively simple matter of decoding authorial meanings that had been embedded in texts turns out to be far more complicated. Can we cling to a baseline meaning? Consider an uncharacteristically subdued query enunciated some time ago by Roland Barthes:

Nobody has ever denied or will ever deny that the language of the text has a literal meaning, of which philology will, if necessary, inform us; what we need to know is whether or not one has the right to read in this literal language other meanings which do not contradict it.[26]

'Philological' meaning has since been denied, and innumerable interpreters have not only read beyond the 'literal language' but have insisted upon their right to 'contradict it'. Personally, I am prepared to defend the concept of an authorial 'baseline' meaning for most texts, but the idea that we should automatically privilege such a meaning is one whose time is long past.

In a different mood, Barthes proclaims that 'Once the Author is removed, the claim to decipher a text becomes quite futile.'[27] Barthes takes a showily extreme position here: many texts clearly imply the constitutive author. What we are really talking about is choice: we can privilege author, or text-in-itself, or original audience, or a later audience, or our own viewpoint, or a governing principle selected by ourselves. What long seemed a straightforward matter of communication theory (author creates text, which must be correctly deciphered by reader) has become dizzyingly pluralistic.

[26] Roland Barthes, *Criticism and Truth* (1966), trans. Katrine Pilcher Keuneman (Minneapolis: University of Minnesota Press, 1987), 39.
[27] Roland Barthes, 'The Death of the Author', in *Image Music Text*, trans. Stephen Heath (New York: Hill and Wang, 1977), 147.

Our immediate question is how compatible or incommensurable various forms of reading turn out to be. Barthes has a point when he suggests that 'the birth of the reader has to be at the cost of the death of the author'.[28] For the purposes of any particular interpretation the reader either is or is not bound to respect the limits of meaning conceived by the author (insofar as that meaning can be understood). Refusal to respect authorial bounds outrages conservatives, but such strict constructionism seems to me merely to impoverish reading while empowering would-be Reading Police. I find that in practice I am perfectly capable of construing Dryden's *Marriage A-la-Mode* contextually and then, if I choose, turning around and conceiving a Marxist or deconstructionist production. The matter comes down to a simple question: what rules do you choose to play by? I have seen infuriated ticket buyers walk out in the middle of an updated *Pirates of Penzance* at Stratford, Ontario, and from Jonathan Miller's 'Mafia' *Rigoletto* —both of which I thought absolutely brilliant. As a historicist, I would not care to be told that Verdi was expressing his subconscious angst over Italian criminal fraternities, but I should hate to lose the interpretive potency of the updating. One of the most thrilling theatrical experiences of my life was a 1983 English National Opera *Rienzi* updated to the 1930s with Albert Speer-style architecture and obvious allusions to Mussolini, Hitler, and Stalin. The ballet was replaced by children doing calisthenics of the sort Hitler enjoyed watching. Is this what Wagner had in mind? Obviously not, and any pretence that it was what he 'really' had in mind would be absurd. Does lack of authorial warrant make the production concept wrong? Absolutely not, unless one is clinging to the sorry remnants of 'right reading'.

In attempting to understand the five widely disparate varieties of reading that I am setting forth here, one needs to realize that they relate quite differently to the three basic objectives of reading. These objectives are elucidation of textual or authorial *meaning*; expounding *significance* for either original or later readers; and broader *explanation* of motive or impact. (For the first two I am obviously drawing on E. D. Hirsch's meaning/

[28] As phrased by Bjørnar Olsen, 'Roland Barthes: From Sign to Text', in Christopher Tilley (ed.), *Reading Material Culture: Structuralism, Hermeneutics and Post-Structuralism* (Oxford: Blackwell, 1990), 163–205 at 181.

significance distinction.) When one looks strictly to 'meaning' one is functioning more or less as Hirsch advises in *Validity in Interpretation*: one attempts to derive an interpretation from the text itself, but also to ensure that it is consonant with what is known about author and original context. Marxist, pro-Stuart, and devil's-party readings of *Paradise Lost* are out of bounds here. 'Significance', in sharp contradistinction, can take reader-response issues into account: the crux is how the reader responds to the textual meaning and uses it, contextualizes it. The third objective takes us outside textual meaning and response and into the realms of attempting to understand why something was written as it was, or explaining its impact with reference to context or theory beyond the text/reader interaction. I am trying to make a distinction here between 'significance' and some broader issues of 'comprehension' in a larger, perhaps theoretical, setting. With this background of potential aims in mind, let us examine five very different kinds of reading.

1. *Textual Reading*. By this I mean no more than what has commonly been called New Criticism, 'close reading', or *explication de texte*. Cleanth Brooks's *The Well Wrought Urn* (1947) offers a classic instance of something like 'pure' New Criticism, which has rarely been practised that way, early or late. A strict textualist might prefer to carry out readings author-blind in the fashion of I. A. Richards's experiments as reported in *Practical Criticism* (1929). In principle, where the focus of attention and the logic of the argument are derived from the text at issue, then we definitely have text-centred criticism. Most practitioners, however, import a fair number of biographical or contextual particulars. Pretending that we know nothing of Donne (and have never heard of the *OED*) might produce interestingly pig-headed readings of his *Songs and Sonets*, but probably not especially good ones.

I am not and have never been a New Critic, but I must regard widespread scorn for the enterprise as seriously misguided. The crude biographical criticism and literary history widely practised before the 1950s needed to be supplanted, and serious interrogation of texts brought about enormous improvements in our comprehension of both major and minor literary works.

Without wishing to ignore authors or readers, we should *want* to pay serious attention to poems, plays, and novels. Do they not, ultimately, constitute the point of the whole enterprise? I still remember vividly how excited I was on first reading *Seven Types of Ambiguity*, though I came to it a full generation after Empson wrote it. New Criticism retains more than historical importance: students who do not learn serious close reading will be disasters when they embark on more complex enterprises, virtually all of which presuppose the capacity to carry out sophisticated *explication de texte*. One may choose to read against a text, but one cannot do this competently if one cannot read the thing properly in the first place. Reject the authorial meaning by all means, but be clear on what you are rejecting.

A New Critic may choose to stick closely to the text or may expand the focus of investigation to include author and immediately related texts. At its best—say, Earl Wasserman on the poetry of Pope—the results can be wonderfully vivid and can stunningly illuminate the whole corpus of the author. One does this sort of reading because one wants to know what the author has to say, wants to share his or her vision of the world. As Charles Altieri says, this is

reading authors as I think most of them intended to be read—that is, as agents constructing a version of experience with a claim to influence the ways generations of readers would view themselves and their world. . . . In my view, we do not want dialogue with texts; we want to encounter the full force of what the author imagined, in the terms the author chose to present it.[29]

One could take this as an argument for historicist reading, but Altieri is taking the position that important texts have something to say across historical boundaries.

2. *Deconstructive Reading.* New Critics have notoriously valued ambiguity and sought 'unity'; deconstructive critics have valued ambiguity and sought contradiction. The dust has not yet settled from more than thirty years of confusion, factionalism, and infighting since Derrida delivered his celebrated paper at Johns Hopkins in 1966. Only gradually have the close connections between New Criticism and deconstruction become

---

[29] Charles Altieri, 'An Idea and Ideal of a Literary Canon', *Critical Inquiry*, 10 (1983), 37–60 at 57.

fully apparent. I must confess to having little enthusiasm for the ponderous and pretentious games of M. Derrida and his ingenious disciples. I willingly doff my chapeau, however, when I contemplate the practical possibilities that they have opened up for us. No doubt they scorn the relatively straightforward and popular form of close reading that is now evolving out of the philosophical and linguistic mists of the One True Theory. Leaving aside *il n'y a pas de hors-texte* versus *il n'y a pas hors de texte*, *différance*, and so forth, I think we shall find that they have created an astonishingly powerful conceptual tool.

In a sense, New Criticism and deconstruction constitute flip sides of the same coin. Both operate from super-close verbal scrutiny of texts. But where the New Critic looks for what the text *says*, the deconstructionist looks for gaps, contradictions, suppressions, and *omissions*. Derrida tells us that deconstruction is a double form of reading in which the 'conscious, voluntary, intentional' meaning 'that the writer institutes' is set against 'other senses of the words used as part of the system of language'.[30] I would argue that the sensible deconstructionist reader is entitled to look beyond linguistic contradiction or ambiguity, and to identify and challenge larger-scale conceptual omissions and discontinuities. What is actually involved here is a process with which we are all familiar in everyday life. We listen to someone say something and we *construe* it (that is, make sense of the speaker's meaning as best we can). Then, unless we are very innocent indeed, we *deconstruct* it (that is, analyse the statement for omissions and internal contradictions, conscious or unconscious).[31] The one process aims at determining what the speaker or writer has attempted to say; the other aims to find what he or she has obfuscated, left out, or suppressed. We do both every time we talk with a spouse, a friend, a rival, a colleague, or a department head.

Deconstruction is often practised as a purely text-based enterprise, but this seems to me a mistake. As I prefer to understand it, deconstruction has a great deal to tell us about the mind and

[30] Jacques Derrida, *Of Grammatology*, trans. Gayatri Chakravorty Spivak (Baltimore: Johns Hopkins University Press, 1976), 158.
[31] For the construe/deconstruct dichotomy I am indebted to M. H. Abrams, 'Construing and Deconstructing' (1986), repr. in Abrams, *Doing Things with Texts*, 297–332.

motives of the contriver of the text, and when I light upon
unresolvable contradictions my interest tends to be more in
what they imply about the author than in what they tell me
about the text itself. When deconstructive reading is practised
in largely verbal terms I tend to find it lacking in point. A New
Critic can always demonstrate Unity (which seems equally
pointless). A deconstructionist can always demonstrate Difference within Unity. The method often seems to me most useful
and effective when applied in the realms of race, gender, and
politics. A powerful illustration of the method is Terry Castle's
Clarissa's Ciphers (1982)—a book I found highly persuasive
when I read the manuscript for the publisher seventeen years
ago, and still do. Another book I much admire is Barbara
Johnson's *A World of Difference* (1987), which applies deconstructive technique to highly charged subjects with profoundly
stimulating results.

    3. *Historicist Reading*. Here the investigator concerns him or
herself with either the genesis of the work or the reception of the
work in its original context. Since this method has been extensively commented upon in the course of this book, I shall keep
the present discussion very brief. J. R. de J. Jackson, in one of
the few serious accounts of 'historical criticism' ever written,
says that 'Historical criticism . . . tries to read past works of
literature in the way in which they were read when they were
new.'[32] (Attention to later reception is also admissible, if much
less common.) The historicist reader may focus on either genetic
circumstances or reception, but in either case will be concerned
primarily with the application of context, whether biographical,
generic, political, social, economic, or whatever.

    The nature of the connection between text and context re-
mains a knotty problem. Jackson distinguishes the 'aim of the
historian' from that of the 'historical critic' by saying that the
historian is 'to reveal the course and nature of events in the past
. . . by examining the evidence provided by documents' whereas
the historical critic 'is to discover the meaning of documents in
the light of past events'. This is a bit pat. Jackson seems to
presume that we can 'read' historical documents reliably, and

---

[32] J. R. de J. Jackson, *Historical Criticism and the Meaning of Texts* (London:
Routledge, 1989), 3. Following quotation from 73–4.

that the resulting understanding can be applied to the interpretation of literary works. Margreta de Grazia observes that
though the distinction between literary 'work' and historical
'document' 'appears quite obvious', it is in fact 'approaching
collapse'.[33] 'A work has an author, a document does not. . . . A
work is fictional, a document factual.' As a reader of PRO
manuscripts soon learns, these turn out to be tenuous distinctions. Historical documents definitely require critical scrutiny
and interpretation. Such difficulties notwithstanding, the historicist reader endeavours to reconstruct the responses of actual or
hypothesized readers in a specified context.

4. *Applicative Reading*. By this phrase I mean interpretation
of the text with regard to the context and concerns of the
present-day reader, not the text itself or the original reader.
Trying to make works of the past 'relevant' to the student of
today has been one of the less happy sales tactics of American
universities of late, and prejudice against it runs high in old
historicist circles. The reader has the right to cry 'Perversion!'
and terminate the discussion immediately for fear of possible
infection. We should remember, however, (a) that all reading is
inevitably 'tainted' with subjective and ahistorical concerns, and
(b) that a work without relevance to the present-day reader is a
work willingly read only by antiquarians. If pre-1970 literature
is to retain any but a conscripted student readership, those
readers will probably not be primarily attracted by historicist
concerns. Indeed, historicist scholarship (like all scholarship)
must always be applicative to some extent, for it reflects the
interests and values of those who carry it out. The question is
one of degree.

Do we have a right to twist works to our own ends? Certainly
we do, so long as we openly admit what we are doing. The
Marxist who falls upon Pope and the feminist who dismembers
Wycherley are embarked upon enterprises valid in their own
terms. The results will probably appal the historicist—but if
they do, we must wonder if the historicist has been genteelly
hiding from something. A reader need not abjure his or her own

[33] Margreta de Grazia, 'What is a Work? What is a Document?' in W. Speed Hill
(ed.), *New Ways of Looking at Old Texts* (Medieval and Renaissance Texts and
Studies, 107; Binghamton: Renaissance English Text Society, 1993), 199–207.

agendas. At the conclusion of an early and influential account of
New Historicism, Jean E. Howard denies 'suggesting that it is
desirable to look at the past with the willful intention of seeing
one's own prejudices and concerns'.[34] Alan Liu picks up the
gauntlet and says outright that such 'willful intention' *is* desirable.[35] As a historicist scholar, my sympathies are with Howard;
as a reader and teacher I am quite prepared to learn from wilful
departure from original context.

Maureen Quilligan observes that 'in all strong modern
theories of interpretation, the assumption necessarily is that
the text does not, at the surface level, want said what the
critic finds in it to say'.[36] Depending on the rules by which one
chooses to play, this may be considered doing violence to texts
or alternatively a way of making them speak to a new audience.
Applicative reading can be found all around us and does not
need extensive illustration, but let me point to a small array of
examples I find particularly interesting.

Some of Claude Rawson's essays are among my favourite
applicative criticism—for example ''Tis Only Infinite Below:
Swift, with Reflections on Yeats, Wallace Stevens and R. D.
Laing', and 'The World of Wild and Ubu'.[37] Rawson's work is
always historically well-informed, but it takes its design and
impetus from ahistorical centres. Reading Rawson, one is
privy to intellectual exploration, not historical reconstruction.
A similar comment might be made about Felicity A. Nussbaum's
*Torrid Zones: Maternity, Sexuality, and Empire in Eighteenth-
Century English Narratives* (1995), which ranges across the
whole century and offers readings of texts from Defoe and
Richardson to Cleland, Frances Sheridan, and Phebe Gibbes.
Nussbaum adopts a post-colonial perspective. This is not how
these writers understood themselves, but the rereadings are
brilliantly provocative. I would not call Nussbaum 'uncom-
mitted' (she has manifest feminist allegiances), but the nature of

[34] Jean E. Howard, 'The New Historicism in Renaissance Studies', *English Literary Renaissance*, 16 (1986), 13–43 at 43.
[35] 'The Power of Formalism', 753.
[36] Maureen Quilligan, *Milton's Spenser: The Politics of Reading* (Ithaca: Cornell
University Press, 1983), 29.
[37] Reprinted respectively in C. J. Rawson, *Gulliver and the Gentle Reader: Studies in Swift and our Time* (London: Routledge, 1973), 60–83, and *Henry Fielding
and the Augustan Ideal under Stress* (London: Routledge, 1972), 171–227.

the commitment differs sharply from that we find in books like Jonathan Dollimore's *Radical Tragedy* or Alan Sinfield's *Faultlines*.[38] I admire these books, but both authors read much more coercively than Nussbaum. Sinfield is commendably blunt about the aggressive (one might slyly say imperialist) nature of his enterprise. Dollimore, writing earlier and from a less thoroughly theorized position, does not make the applicative basis of his interpretation nearly so clear. I must agree with Graham Bradshaw's complaint that Dollimore 'carries on the old bad Tillyardian habit of giving particular characters and speeches a supradramatic significance . . . identified with what the play or the dramatist "really" thinks'. Dollimore attributes to Shakespeare 'an intention that happily corresponds' with his own '"materialist perspective"'.[39] I think some of Dollimore's readings quite wonderful, but the implication that these are historicist interpretations and represent authorial meaning seems to me highly objectionable.[40]

5. *A Priori Reading.* I include 'a priori reading' (essentially a subset of applicative reading) as a separate variety because it rests on a philosophically distinct base. By this phrase I mean interpretation conducted on the assumption that a particular system of explanation is *true*, or at least specially privileged. Any system of meaning that the critic happens to believe in may serve: Christianity, Marxist economics, Lacanian or Freudian psychology, numerology, or Russian formalism. Even a modest empirical description of practice such as Aristotle's *Poetics* may find itself elevated into the status of Dogma, as numerous eighteenth-century critics have demonstrated to their discredit (and our acute boredom). Ernest Jones's *Hamlet and Oedipus* is

[38] Jonathan Dollimore, *Radical Tragedy: Religion, Ideology and Power in the Drama of Shakespeare and his Contemporaries* (2nd edn., Hemel Hempstead: Harvester Wheatsheaf, 1989). Alan Sinfield, *Faultlines: Cultural Materialism and the Politics of Dissident Reading* (Berkeley: University of Calfornia Press, 1992).

[39] *Misrepresentations: Shakespeare and the Materialists* (Ithaca: Cornell University Press, 1993), 9.

[40] The distinction I am making here between various sorts of reading as construing or deconstructing versus 'applicative' reading is obviously related to Umberto Eco's stress on 'the difference between interpreting and using a text'. In the former case, Eco insists, the reader must 'respect' the author's 'cultural and linguistic background'. See *The Role of the Reader: Explorations in the Semiotics of Texts* (Bloomington: Indiana University Press, 1979), 'Intentio lectoris: The State of the Art', *Differentia*, 2 (1988), 147–68, and *Interpretation and Overinterpretation*, ed. Collini, chs. 1–3.

a classic piece of a priori reading—and in fact a very good one, since the problem tackled is genuinely baffling and the proposed solution is a producible interpretation, as the Laurence Olivier film demonstrates.

Marxists and cultural feminists are among the most frequent and aggressive a priori readers. From the archaeo-historicist's point of view, their dogmatism can be irritating, especially when a witty and sophisticated post-structuralist like Terry Eagleton, who knows—and sometimes admits—that nothing can be 'true', chooses to maintain that the Marxist position is not merely a choice.[41] Unsurprisingly, the readings tend to be coercive, imposing the critics' categories on their material—as Georg Lukács seems to me to do. Even a stubbornly sceptical historicist must admit, however, that many Marxists and feminists write with a passion and commitment that gives their work a life and force often far beyond the tepidity of more 'judicious' academic writing. I confess to finding Fredric Jameson's *The Political Unconscious* (1981) so turgid as to be virtually unreadable (however committed), but a book like Lynda Hart's *Fatal Women: Lesbian Sexuality and the Mark of Aggression* (1994) strikes me as tremendously stimulating, even where I want to argue with it.

All five enterprises may usefully be applied to a given text. What emerges may be as different as portraits by Rubens and Picasso, a Stieglitz photograph, a police mug shot, and an X-ray. Each possesses its own truth and power. Texts vary enormously in precision of meaning, in sense of implied audience, in contextual referentiality. Umberto Eco (among others) distinguishes usefully between relatively 'open' texts and 'closed' ones. Closed texts are designed to generate a precise response from a sharply defined group of readers. Open texts delimit their meaning (and implied audience) much less restrictively.[42]

As a particular instance of a problematical text on which we can exercise various forms of reading in a comparative way, let us consider the ending of Dryden's *Amphitryon* (1690). The play draws heavily on Plautus and Molière. Jupiter imperson-

---

[41] In fairness, I should point out that Eagleton has modified his critical philosophy considerably over the past two decades. See *The Illusions of Postmodernism* (Oxford: Blackwell, 1997).

[42] See particularly Eco's *The Role of the Reader*.

ates the absent Amphitryon in order to sleep with the virtuous Alcmena, whom he impregnates with Hercules. Plautus's title character accedes to Jupiter's prerogative with good grace, observing 'I guess I've no complaint if I have to share my possessions with the great god Jupiter', and the cuckold goes off to tell his wife the good news about Hercules. Molière's Amphitryon, by contrast, gets very hot indeed when he finds himself cuckolded. Jupiter appears amidst thunder and lightning to lay down the law, and Amphitryon remains silent, leaving his servant Sosia to mouth some comfortable platitudes. Alcmena is not on stage. Molière emphasizes confrontation with an authority that cannot be flouted, and resignation to the inevitable seems his protagonist's likeliest response (though a director has some latitude). In Dryden's finale Jupiter issues a pronunciamento with Amphitryon and Alcmena listening, announces the forthcoming birth of Hercules, and vanishes. How do the victimized couple respond? They say nothing; Dryden has Sosia express regret that he has not been similarly honoured, but nothing we have seen of Dryden's Amphitryon suggests he will settle cheerfully for counting his blessings. During the scene, do Amphitryon and Alcmena look at each other or just stare at Jupiter? Do they turn to each other as Jupiter leaves? Does Amphitryon clasp Alcmena to him? Or do they stand apart, hostile and alienated? The director can stage a reconciliation, with the couple accepting their fate and making the best of it (a bleak form of Plautus's happy ending). Alternatively they can be left physically apart as the play ends, stunned, unhappy, unable to cope with the shambles Jupiter has made of their lives and marriage. Sending husband and wife off in different directions underlines a profoundly gloomy message about the effects of Jupiter's philandering.[43]

A strictly textual reading of the play can end only in doubt and paradox—and an appeal to directorial choice. Dryden's text and stage directions simply do not supply a meaning for the most crucial scene in the play. For a Marxist or a feminist critic, the play holds bitter lessons about the abuse of power, and in particular about the victimization of women. For a

---

[43] Judith Milhous and I have analysed the play in detail in ch. 7 of *Producible Interpretation*.

deconstructionist the play provides evidence of Dryden's entrapment, ambivalence, and enforced silence. If this is Dryden's comment on the sexual mores of Charles II and his courtiers (by no means a foolish reading), then it reflects devastating disillusionment on the part of a writer who had spent most of his adult life as mythographer and propagandist for that king. A historicist reader would concern him or herself with sources and genre. Dryden disguised a sour parable in a borrowed plot of unexceptionable respectability (sex notwithstanding). Context shows how he decked it out in the festive trappings of the magic and machinery farce boom of the 1680s, drawing freely on plays by Aphra Behn, Thomas Jevon, William Mountfort, and others. The various readings are radically different, but by no means mutually exclusive. In this instance I find the feminist and deconstructionist readings more interesting and important than the historicist reading, useful though the latter is in explaining some of the features of Dryden's conglomeration. Here as in many cases historicism cannot 'disprove' deconstruction any more than deconstruction can disprove historicism. They give us different ways of looking at complex objects. Both are useful; both are incomplete. Indeed, all readings of complex texts are inevitably incomplete.

To reject any of the five basic modes of reading I have sketched here seems misguided. A patient sometimes needs pills, sometimes physical therapy, sometimes surgery, sometimes psychoanalysis—or some combination thereof. No doubt some surgeons are knife-happy and some psychologists crazy, but both groups have a legitimate function in the medical establishment. The implications for criticism seem clear.

Archaeo-Historicism as a Method

> The greatest obstacle to the progress of science . . . is found in this—that men despair and think things impossible.
>
> Francis Bacon[44]

I have argued in this little book that Archaeo-Historicism can do things that are well worth doing. I have also tried to suggest

[44] *Novum Organum*, Aphorism 92.

that by sharpening our sense of its aims and procedures we can hope to carry out historical interpretation more rigorously and skilfully, and with better results than have been achieved under somewhat haphazard methodologies. Fellow practitioners may disagree with me about all sorts of particular points while still, I hope, finding the overall line of argument profitable. The case as I have expounded it here must be regarded as provisional and exploratory. I shall be disappointed if my successors cannot substantially improve on this attempt to set forth the principles that underlie what I am calling archaeo-historical investigation. By way of conclusion I wish to say some things about the method and why it seems to me to meet some serious tests of worth and validity.

Why practise Archaeo-Historicism? Plenty of current forms of criticism are flashier and involve a great deal less donkey-work. I have sat in the Public Record Office at the end of a dusty month in which I have discovered nothing useful and wondered whether writing sonnets or deconstructive criticism might not be a better and pleasanter use of my time. About the best one can say for serious historicist scholarship is that it will always be slow, hard, and frustrating. Evidence does not grow on trees, and when found, it must be tested—and often enough discarded as insufficient or unreliable. This very difficulty, however, constitutes part of the attraction: if you play by serious rules, rigorously applied, then success is much the sweeter.

I would point to three particular attractions to Archaeo-Historicism as a method. First, it works on a bottom-up basis, not top-down. You start by struggling with primary evidence, looking for patterns as they would have been understood by the original writers and audiences. You are not simply on the lookout for convenient sites on which to exercise your own predilections or to impose a ready-made interpretation. The touchstone is always whether you have successfully reconstructed the outlook of your subject, and if further evidence demolishes your hypothesis, then it must be discarded. Second, Archaeo-Historicism functions to a substantial degree as an *additive* discipline: you build on your predecessors, and successors will build on your work. I regularly use secondary sources that are thirty, fifty, and even a hundred years old. They retain their value, and I hope some of my books and articles will too.

If you find an exciting new document and publish it, your analysis may be surpassed or absorbed into later analyses, but the *facts* you have added to our store will remain forever useful. As a young scholar-critic starting out thirty years ago I published a flock of interpretations of texts. I soon realized that just as I had bickered with my predecessors, so my successors would bicker with me—or simply ignore my interpretation altogether. I found this depressing: I was adding precious little to a common store of knowledge. Even successful and widely noticed interpretations soon vanish under the rising tide of new ones. To what end? I asked myself. A third reason I take particular satisfaction in practising Archaeo-Historicism stems from the wide choice it gives the practitioner in explanatory theory. As a student I felt the attractions of being (as it were) a card-carrying member of a party, but as time has gone on I have come to prefer standing aloof, judging for myself, choosing the terms in which I will put a historical explanation. Archaeo-Historicism offers a strongly defined sense of purpose but leaves the investigator exceptionally free to design the inquiry as the nature of the known evidence suggests and to appeal to virtually any kind of theory in the course of constructing explanations and comparisons.

I most emphatically do not suggest that everyone should practise Archaeo-Historicism. The PRO is not big enough. And truth to tell, many other ways of approaching older literature work as well or better in satisfying present-day readers. I believe that undergraduate students should be exposed to the results of historicist inquiry and interpretation, but by no means would I argue that historical reading should be a primary part of their curriculum. Archival research takes time, experience, and access to primary documents. Learning close reading, deconstruction, and various forms of applicative reading is far likelier to benefit a student, who may then in the fullness of time want to explore contextual meanings beyond the level of textbook explanations and footnotes.

Archaeo-Historicism allows us to carry out two interlinked activities: (1) we reconstruct historical contexts, and (2) we can then employ those contexts to help us read texts in something like their original circumstances. I believe that one of the reasons historicism has failed to make its own case effectively in recent years is that its practitioners have succumbed to the temptation to play safe by sticking to background facts. Excellent and important work may be done this way, but the whole enterprise loses its point if we forget that *the ultimate goal of the historicist is to shed light on texts from original contexts.* We may do all sorts of other things en route to that end, but this is, ultimately, the *point.* I am particularly conscious of the problem because proponents of *Theaterwissenschaft* (emphasizing factual and archival research) have chosen to regard the aesthetic considerations of dramatic literature as a wholly separate (and uninteresting) matter. Context must ultimately connect to text.

Critics can be surprisingly resistant to the claims of fact where they seem to impinge on aesthetic matters. Here is a personal example. Some fifteen years ago Judith Milhous and I published an article based on newly discovered financial projections made in 1720 for the Royal Academy of Music.[45] We pointed out that the directors were profoundly unrealistic, and that the company's collapse (which occurred in 1728, despite massive subsidy) was made inevitable by these miscalculations. So far as I can see, these are simply matters of financial fact. We received a surprising amount of anonymous hate mail (suggesting that we were pigs incapable of appreciating the beauties of Handel's music), and eminent musicologists have vented dismissive and uncomfortable harrumphings about the matter in their footnotes. This seems extraordinarily silly. Handel was not (so far as we know) responsible for the financial miscalculations, and even if he had been, that would not in any way detract from the glories of his music. The beauty of his operas does not, however, alter the fact that the company was doomed to early bankruptcy—an event which had a considerable impact on Handel's career and helped reorient him towards oratorios. We sometimes need reminders that poems, plays, and novels (like operas) are written, disseminated, and responded to in the real world, and are subject to quotidian pressures. Issuing such reminders is one of the functions of the archaeo-historicist.

When choosing a method, a scholar needs to be acutely aware

---

[45] 'New Light on Handel and the Royal Academy of Music in 1720', *Theatre Journal*, 35 (1983), 149–67.

of its uses, potential abuses, and limits. Justification of any method must rest on its claims to satisfy four essential criteria:

1. Clear sense of purpose
2. An operating procedure neither self-delusory nor circular
3. Admission of its limits
4. A validation process that will demolish false results.

I have argued that Archaeo-Historicism stands up well on all four points. I stress in particular the degree to which its results rest on the existence of hard evidence and the testability of that evidence. A method that does not have built into it serious provision for validation and invalidation of its results can be no more than an elaborate game played for the self-glorification of the participants. Because of gaps and limitations in evidence we often cannot be certain whether an archaeo-historicist interpretation is correct or not, and we may never know. One of the virtues of the method, however, is that one strives to be right and is always in danger of being proved wrong.

Here is a small example. Several years ago Yale purchased at auction a manuscript list of 186 plays bought by David Garrick. He acquired five copies of most of the titles, and the sale catalogue suggested that they were for the Drury Lane theatre library. Judith Milhous and I published the list with annotation and analysis, sorely puzzled as to why the theatre would need copies of works most of which it must already have owned. We consulted eminent Garrick authorities, but came up with no better hypothesis to explain Garrick's purchase.[46] Long after putting our article in print we stumbled on evidence proving beyond reasonable doubt that Garrick bought the plays to send to a theatre in Calcutta.[47] We were simply *wrong*. To be in error is embarrassing, depressing, annoying—but very much part of a kind of scholarship in which one strives to be right and must always be perpetually in danger of failing. If anything goes, why bother? Archaeo-Historicism holds its practitioner to exceptionally rigid standards of success and failure.

The results of any method, Archaeo-Historicism included,

---

[46] Judith Milhous and Robert D. Hume, 'The Drury Lane Theatre Library in 1768', *Yale University Library Gazette*, 68 (1994), 116–34.

[47] *The Private Correspondence of David Garrick*, ed. James Boaden, 2 vols. (London: Henry Colburn and Richard Bentley, 1831), i. 295–6.

need not only to be validated in their own terms but also to be compared with those of other methods. If results do not either conjoin or contrast in productive ways, we have to wonder how far we are getting in the reconstruction of our elephant. I would argue further that more can be learnt from practitioners of other methods than most scholars and critics generally care to admit. The relatively limited practical interaction between historicism and 'theory' is a misfortune for all parties. Some noted theoreticians (Riffaterre and Greenblatt spring to mind) can and do tackle texts in convincing ways. Remarkably little theory, however, has trickled down to the level of the classroom—except *as* theory, and this I take as an indictment.

From the standpoint of the practising critic or historian, the most useful theory will be relatively short, clear, simple, and readily *applicable*. A wondrously complex critical machine may be an aesthetic joy in itself (and a fine plaything for the inventor and attendant disciples), but *does it work*? We need not just a trial flight made under ideal conditions, but proof that the thing will fly reliably under all sorts of circumstances and in the hands of many pilots. Say what you will about Brooks and Warren, classic New Criticism could be used to good effect on most texts, and could be readily learnt by almost anyone. In an increasingly crowded and overpublished field we seem now to value difficulty and inaccessibility in new methods. Worse, we are not systematically checking the results of one approach against those of another. Theorists are ill-advised to ignore facts and context; historicists are equally ill-advised to stick their heads in the sand and pretend that nothing has been learnt about 'meaning', audience, and interpretation in the last thirty years.

The degree of hostility and intimidation sometimes exhibited by persons professing old historicism when confronted by theory is both comic and strange. The Ostrich Contingent advise reading nothing after Northrop Frye and hope theory will go away. Those who dutifully 'keep up' tend to feel that loads of de—— almost choke the way, and curse the gobble-dejargon in which much of it is written. Any new method inevitably makes its way with exaggeration of claims and the bashing of predecessors, and all methods get used crudely or foolishly. But deconstruction, semiotics, phenomenology, feminism, queer studies, *et al.*, will do historicists no harm and may sometimes do them a great deal of good.

We do not have to accept all methods and theories as immediately relevant to us, or even as possibilities to be seriously entertained. The more epistemologically arcane parts of phenomenology strike me as a fine game, but of precious little use to the practising eighteenth-century theatre historian. They are about as pertinent to my work as the theory of quarks is to the building of bridges for motorways. This is not to deny the wonders of sub-particle atomic physics, but for the engineer trying to build reliable bridges, Newtonian physics will probably suffice. Or perhaps I simply do not yet see the application: I am willing to be convinced. Deconstruction and reader response, however, have implications concerning indeterminate and unstable meanings that are of tremendous importance for historical scholarship. We have the more reason to pay serious attention to non-contextual modes of reading because this is an area in which literary historicism remains decidedly weak. Historicists have long been vulnerable to charges that we fail to engage texts convincingly, or that we treat them in determinist and Procrustean ways—charges not without substance. Literary historicists have been timid and negligent, failing to stake claims that needed to be made, and failing to revamp and update methodologies of reading that represent the thinking of at least a generation back. We cannot afford to abandon textual interpretation and retreat behind the Maginot Line of the Public Record Office. If historicism matters, it must deal successfully with texts. An obvious way of improving our methods of reading is to adapt to our own needs the critical tools developed by practitioners of other methods. The danger for historicists is not 'theory' but lack of theory.

Archaeo-Historicism works. We *can*—where we have evidence—construct contexts that permit rigorous analysis of genesis and original reception. Context *can* be used to generate plausible meanings within a historical setting. The legitimation of historicist research must rest, in pragmatic terms, on the solidity and plausibility of its results. In theoretical terms, historicism stands on the premiss that the world is more than text. Part of the resistance to theory among historicists stems, naturally enough, from hostility to epistemological assumptions that necessarily imply the triviality or impossibility of valid historical research. Historicism cannot be legitimized if we start within the confines of essentially phenomenological assumptions.[48] We have, however, no reason to accept such assumptions. Indeed, I am prepared to argue, contra phenomenology, that one of the greatest virtues of Archaeo-Historicism is that it deals with *fact* of a sort that invites verification. Instead of a world in which 'you cannot know' and 'anything goes if you say so', we need productive debate about the interpretation of evidence, and the possibility of proof or disproof. Wherever our inquiries may take us, we want to begin with a clear sense of purpose, the method we shall employ, and the rules by which we judge our results.

The archaeo-historicist works out of a commitment to finding, analysing, and honouring *fact*, even though the result can rarely be more than a provisional hypothesis offered in explanation of the questions posed. The factual basis confers a solidity on the enterprise that is sorely lacking in hermeticist inquiries. Without facts, we know nothing, we can do nothing, we can understand nothing. I conclude with a strong misquotation from the American sage Yogi Berra: 'If you ain't got facts, you ain't got nuthin.'

---

[48] A point well made by David Simpson, 'Literary Criticism and the Return to "History"', *Critical Inquiry*, 14 (1988), 721–47. Simpson gives a lucid account of the philosophical difficulties, but concludes that 'analytic' history *is* possible, 'fact' *can* be appealed to, and 'stringent skepticism about the nature of historical claims can perfectly well coexist with an absolute commitment to historical methods' (747).

Bibliography

This list contains books and articles quoted or mentioned in the text and also some other items that I have found particularly helpful or provocative in thinking about the issues involved. A very large number of practical and theoretical works might have been included, and another author might have made radically different choices. I tender my apologies to any predecessor of whom I am ignorant or who has been unintentionally slighted.

ABRAMS, M. H., 'Construing and Deconstructing' (1986), 297–332, and 'On Political Readings of *Lyrical Ballads*', 364–91, in id., *Doing Things with Texts: Essays in Criticism and Critical Theory*, ed. Michael Fischer (New York: Norton, 1989).

— — *Natural Supernaturalism: Tradition and Revolution in Romantic Literature* (New York: Norton, 1971).

ADORNO, Theodor W., *Against Epistemology: A Metacritique* (1956), trans. Willis Domingo (Cambridge, Mass.: MIT Press, 1983).

ADSHEAD-LANSDALE, Janet, and LAYSON, June (eds.), *Dance History: An Introduction* (2nd edn., London: Routledge, 1994).

ALAM, Fakrul, 'The Newer Criticism: New Directions in American Literary History', *South Carolina Review*, 21 (1988), 65–8.

ALTIERI, Charles, 'An Idea and Ideal of a Literary Canon', *Critical Inquiry*, 10 (1983), 37–60.

ANKERSMIT, F. R., 'Historicism: An Attempt at Synthesis', *History and Theory*, 34 (1995), 143–61. 'Comment' by Georg G. Iggers, ibid. 162–7. 'Reply' by Ankersmit, 168–73.

— — and KELLNER, Hans (eds.), *A New Philosophy of History* (Chicago: University of Chicago Press, 1995).

ARNOTT, James Fullarton, and ROBINSON, John William, *English Theatrical Literature 1559–1900: A Bibliography* (London: Society for Theatre Research, 1970).

ASTELL, Ann W., *The Song of Songs in the Middle Ages* (Ithaca: Cornell University Press, 1990).

ATKINSON, R. F., *Knowledge and Explanation in History: An Introduction to the Philosophy of History* (Ithaca: Cornell University Press, 1978).

— — 'Methodology: History and its Philosophy', in van der Dussen and Rubinoff (eds.), *Objectivity, Method and Point of View*, 12–21.

ATTRIDGE, Derek, BENNINGTON, Geoff, and YOUNG, Robert (eds.), *Post-Structuralism and the Question of History* (Cambridge: Cambridge University Press, 1987).

AUERBACH, Erich, *Literary Language and its Public in Late Latin Antiquity and in the Middle Ages* (1958), trans. Ralph Manheim (Bollingen Series LXXIV; New York: Pantheon, 1965).

BARBEAU, Anne T., *The Intellectual Design of John Dryden's Heroic Plays* (New Haven: Yale University Press, 1970).

BARNETT, Dene, *The Art of Gesture: The Practices and Principles of 18th-Century Acting* (Heidelberg: Carl Winter Universitätsverlag, 1987).

BARTHES, Roland, *Criticism and Truth* (1966), trans. Katrine Pilcher Keuneman (Minneapolis: University of Minnesota Press, 1987).

— — *Image Music Text*, trans. Stephen Heath (New York: Hill and Wang, 1977).

BATE, Jonathan, *Shakespearean Constitutions: Politics, Theatre, Criticism 1730–1830* (Oxford: Clarendon Press, 1989).

BATTENHOUSE, Roy W., *Shakespearean Tragedy: Its Art and its Christian Premises* (Bloomington: Indiana University Press, 1969).

— — (ed.), *Shakespeare's Christian Dimension: An Anthology of Commentary* (Bloomington: Indiana University Press, 1994).

BATTESTIN, Martin C., *The Moral Basis of Fielding's Art: A Study of Joseph Andrews* (Middletown: Wesleyan University Press, 1959).

— — (ed.), *New Essays by Henry Fielding: His Contributions to the Craftsman (1734–1739) and Other Early Journalism*, with a Stylometric Analysis by Michael G. Farringdon (Charlottesville: University Press of Virginia, 1989).

— — with BATTESTIN, Ruthe R., *Henry Fielding: A Life* (London: Routledge, 1989).

BAUGH, Albert C. (ed.), *A Literary History of England*, 4 vols. (New York: Appleton-Century-Crofts, 1948). The second edition (1967) does not change the history conceptually.

BEARDS, Andrew, 'Reversing Historical Skepticism: Bernard Lonergan on the Writing of History', *History and Theory*, 33 (1994), 198–219.

BEASLEY, Jerry C., *Novels of the 1740s* (Athens: University of Georgia Press, 1982).

BEER, Samuel H., 'Causal Explanation and Imaginative Re-enactment', *History and Theory*, 3 (1963), 6–29.

BELSEY, Catherine, 'Richard Levin and In-different Reading', *New Literary History*, 21 (1990), 449–56.

BENJAMIN, Walter, 'Literary History and Literary Scholarship', *Critical Texts*, 7 (1990), 3–9.

BENNETT, Tony, 'Texts in History: The Determinations of Readings and their Texts', in Attridge *et al.* (eds.), *Post-Structuralism and the Question of History*, 63–81.

BENSON, Lee, *Toward the Scientific Study of History* (Philadelphia: J. B. Lippincott, 1972).

BERCOVITCH, Sacvan, 'America as Canon and Context: Literary History in a Time of Dissensus', *American Literature*, 58 (1986), 99–107.

BERGONZI, Bernard, *Exploding English: Criticism, Theory, Culture* (Oxford: Clarendon Press, 1990).

BERLIN, Isaiah, 'The Concept of Scientific History' (1960), repr. in *Concepts and Categories: Philosophical Essays by Isaiah Berlin*, ed. Henry Hardy (New York: Viking, 1979), 103–42.

BEVINGTON, David, 'Two Households, Both Alike in Dignity: The Uneasy Alliance between New Historicists and Feminists', *English Literary Renaissance*, 25 (1995), 307–19.

— — 'Varieties of Historicism: "Beyond the Infinite and Boundless Reach"', *Modern Philology*, 93 (1995), 73–88.

BEVIR, Mark, 'Objectivity in History', *History and Theory*, 33 (1994), 328–44.

BIERSACK, Aletta, 'Local Knowledge, Local History: Geertz and Beyond', in Hunt (ed.), *The New Cultural History*, 72–96.

BIRDSALL, Virginia Ogden, *Wild Civility: The English Comic Spirit on the Restoration Stage* (Bloomington: Indiana University Press, 1970).

BIRRELL, T. A., 'The Influence of Seventeenth-Century Publishers on the Presentation of English Literature', in Mary-Jo Arn and Hanneke Wirtjes, with Hans Jansen (eds.), *Historical & Editorial Studies in Medieval & Early Modern English for Johan Gerritsen* (Groningen: Wolters-Noordhoff, 1985), 163–73.

BLACKMUR, R. P., 'The Lion and the Honeycomb', *Hudson Review*, 3 (1951), 487–507.

BLAYNEY, Peter W. M., 'The Publication of Playbooks', in Cox and Kastan (eds.), *A New History of Early English Drama*, 383–422.

BLEICH, David, *Subjective Criticism* (Baltimore: Johns Hopkins University Press, 1978).

BLOCH, Marc, *The Historian's Craft*, trans. Peter Putnam with an introduction by Joseph R. Strayer (orig. French edn. 1949; New York: Knopf, 1953).

BLOOM, Harold, *The Anxiety of Influence: A Theory of Poetry* (New York: Oxford University Press, 1973).

BOADEN, James (ed.), *The Private Correspondence of David Garrick*, 2 vols. (London: Henry Colburn and Richard Bentley, 1831).

BOUCHER, David, *Texts in Context: Revisionist Methods for Studying the History of Ideas* (Martinus Nijhoff Philosophical Library, 12; Dordrecht: Martinus Nijhoff, 1985).

BOURDIEU, Pierre, *Outline of a Theory of Practice*, trans. Richard Nice (Cambridge Studies in Social Anthropology, 16; Cambridge: Cambridge University Press, 1977).
— — *Distinction: A Social Critique of the Judgment of Taste*, trans. Richard Nice (Cambridge, Mass.: Harvard University Press, 1984).
BOWERS, Fredson, *Elizabethan Revenge Tragedy, 1587–1642* (Princeton: Princeton University Press, 1940).
BRADLEY, David, *From Text to Performance in the Elizabethan Theatre: Preparing the Play for the Stage* (Cambridge: Cambridge University Press, 1992).
BRADSHAW, Graham, *Misrepresentations: Shakespeare and the Materialists* (Ithaca: Cornell University Press, 1993).
BREDVOLD, Louis I., *The Intellectual Milieu of John Dryden* (Ann Arbor: University of Michigan Press, 1934).
BROOKS, Cleanth, Jr., 'Literary History vs. Criticism', *Kenyon Review*, 2 (1940), 403–12.
— — *The Well Wrought Urn: Studies in the Structure of Poetry* (New York: Reynal and Hitchcock, [1947]).
BROOKS, Peter, 'Aesthetics and Ideology: What Happened to Poetics?', *Critical Inquiry*, 20 (1994), 509–23.
BROWN, Laura, *English Dramatic Form, 1660–1760: An Essay in Generic History* (New Haven: Yale University Press, 1981).
BROWN, Marshall, 'Contemplating the Theory of Literary History', *PMLA* 107 (1992), 13–25.
BUCHANAN, David, *The Treasure of Auchinleck: The Story of the Boswell Papers* (New York: McGraw-Hill, 1974).
BUCKLEY, Jerome Hamilton, *The Victorian Temper: A Study in Literary Culture* (Cambridge, Mass.: Harvard University Press, 1951).
BURNEY, Charles, *Memoirs of Dr. Charles Burney, 1726–1769*, ed. Slava Klima, Garry Bowers, and Kerry S. Grant (Lincoln: University of Nebraska Press, 1988).
BUTLER, Christopher, *Interpretation, Deconstruction, and Ideology: An Introduction to some Current Issues in Literary Theory* (Oxford: Clarendon Press, 1984).
BUTLER, Marilyn, 'Against Tradition: The Case for a Particularized Historical Method', McGann (ed.), *Historical Studies and Literary Criticism*, 25–47.
CALLARI, Antonio, and RUCCIO, David F. (eds.), *Postmodern Materialism and the Future of Marxist Theory: Essays in the Althusserian Tradition* (Hanover: Wesleyan University Press, 1996).
The Cambridge History of American Literature, Sacvan Bercovitch, gen. ed., i, ii, viii (Cambridge: Cambridge University Press, 1994–).
CARLSON, Marvin, 'Theatre Audiences and the Reading of Performance',

in Postlewait and McConachie (eds.), *Interpreting the Theatrical Past*, 82–98.

CARNOCHAN, W. B., *Gibbon's Solitude* (Stanford: Stanford University Press, 1987).

CARR, David, *Time, Narrative, and History* (Bloomington: Indiana University Press, 1986).

CARR, Edward Hallett, *What is History?* (London: Macmillan, 1961).

CASTLE, Terry, *Clarissa's Ciphers: Meaning and Disruption in Richardson's 'Clarissa'* (Ithaca: Cornell University Press, 1982).

CHAMBERS, E. K., *The Mediaeval Stage*, 2 vols. (Oxford: Clarendon Press, 1903).

CHANDLER, James, DAVISON, Arnold I., and HAROOTUNIAN, Harry (eds.), *Questions of Evidence: Proof, Practice, and Persuasion across the Disciplines* (Chicago: University of Chicago Press, 1994).

CLARK, J. C. D., *Samuel Johnson: Literature, Religion and English Cultural Politics from the Restoration to Romanticism* (Cambridge: Cambridge University Press, 1994).

COHEN, Morris R., 'Causation and its Application to History', *Journal of the History of Ideas*, 3 (1942), 12–29.

COHEN, Ralph, *The Art of Discrimination: Thomson's 'The Seasons' and the Language of Criticism* (Berkeley: University of California Press, 1964).

COLACURCIO, Michael J., *The Province of Piety: Moral History in Hawthorne's Early Tales* (Cambridge, Mass.: Harvard University Press, 1984).

COLEBROOK, Claire, *New Literary Histories: New Historicism and Contemporary Criticism* (Manchester: Manchester University Press, 1997).

COLEMAN, Joyce, *Public Reading and the Reading Public in Late Medieval England and France* (Cambridge: Cambridge University Press, 1996).

COLLINGWOOD, R. G., *The Idea of History*, rev. edn., ed. with introduction by Jan van der Dussen (Oxford: Clarendon Press, 1993).

COLLINS, Stephen L., 'Where's the History in the New Literary Historicism? The Case of the English Renaissance', *Annals of Scholarship*, 6 (1989), 231–47.

COMMAGER, Henry Steele, *The Search for a Usable Past and Other Essays in Historiography* (New York: Knopf, 1967).

COOK, Albert, *History/Writing* (Cambridge: Cambridge University Press, 1988).

COTTOM, Daniel, *Ravishing Tradition: Cultural Forces and Literary History* (Ithaca: Cornell University Press, 1996).

COUSINS, Mark, 'The Practice of Historical Investigation', in Attridge *et al.* (eds.), *Post-Structuralism and the Question of History*, 126–36.

COX, Jeffrey N., and REYNOLDS, Larry J. (eds.), *New Historical Literary Study: Essays on Reproducing Texts, Representing History* (Princeton: Princeton University Press, 1993).

COX, John D., and KASTAN, David Scott (eds.), *A New History of Early English Drama* (New York: Columbia University Press, 1997).

CRANE, R. S. (ed.), *Critics and Criticism: Ancient and Modern* (Chicago: University of Chicago Press, 1952).

— — *The Languages of Criticism and the Structure of Poetry* (Toronto: University of Toronto Press, 1953).

— — *The Idea of the Humanities and Other Essays Critical and Historical*, 2 vols. (Chicago: University of Chicago Press, 1967), particularly 'History versus Criticism in the Study of Literature' (ii. 3–24); 'Criticism as Inquiry; or, The Perils of the "High Priori Road"' (ii. 25–44); 'Critical and Historical Principles of Literary History' (ii. 45–156); 'On Hypotheses in "Historical Criticism": Apropos of Certain Contemporary Medievalists' (ii. 236–60).

CROCE, Benedetto, *Philosophy, Poetry, History: An Anthology of Essays by Benedetto Croce*, trans. and introduced by Cecil Sprigge (London: Oxford University Press, 1966).

CULLER, Jonathan, 'Beyond Interpretation: The Prospects of Contemporary Criticism', *Comparative Literature*, 28 (1976), 244–56.

— — *On Deconstruction* (London: Routledge & Kegan Paul, 1983).

DAICHES, David, *A Critical History of English Literature*, 2 vols. (London: Secker and Warburg, 1960).

DANTO, Arthur C., *Narration and Knowledge* (New York: Columbia University Press, 1985).

— — 'The Decline and Fall of the Analytical Philosophy of History', in Ankersmit and Kellner (eds.), *A New Philosophy of History*, 70–85.

DARNTON, Robert, 'History of Reading' (1986), in Peter Burke (ed.), *New Perspectives on Historical Writing* (University Park: Pennsylvania State University Press, 1992), 140–67.

DASTON, Lorraine, 'Marvelous Facts and Miraculous Evidence in Early Modern Europe', in Chandler *et al.* (eds.), *Questions of Evidence: Proof, Practice, and Persuasion across the Disciplines*, 243–74.

DAVIES, Thomas, *Memoirs of the Life of David Garrick* (1780), ed. Stephen Jones, 2 vols. (1808; repr. New York: Blom, 1969).

DE CERTEAU, Michel, *The Writing of History*, trans. Tom Conley (New York: Columbia University Press, 1988).

DE GRAZIA, Margreta, *Shakespeare Verbatim: The Reproduction of Authenticity and the 1790 Apparatus* (Oxford: Clarendon Press, 1991).

— — 'What is a Work? What is a Document?', in Hill (ed.), *New Ways of Looking at Old Texts*, 199–207.

DEMARIA, Robert, Jr., *Samuel Johnson and the Life of Reading* (Baltimore: Johns Hopkins University Press, 1997).

DENING, Greg, *Performances* (Chicago: University of Chicago Press, 1996).

DENNIS, John, *The Critical Works of John Dennis*, ed. Edward Niles Hooker, 2 vols. (Baltimore: Johns Hopkins Press, 1939–43).

DERRIDA, Jacques, *Of Grammatology*, trans. Gayatri Chakravorty Spivak (Baltimore: Johns Hopkins University Press, 1976).

— — 'Signature Event Context', *Glyph*, 1 (1977), 172–97. (Cf. reply by John R. Searle, ibid. 198–208.)

DESSEN, Alan C., *Elizabethan Stage Conventions and Modern Interpreters* (Cambridge: Cambridge University Press, 1984).

— — *Recovering Shakespeare's Theatrical Vocabulary* (Cambridge: Cambridge University Press, 1995).

DILLON, George L., *Constructing Texts: Elements of a Theory of Composition and Style* (Bloomington: Indiana University Press, 1981).

DOCHERTY, Thomas, *Alterities: Criticism, History, Representation* (Oxford: Clarendon Press, 1996).

DOLAN, Jill, *The Feminist Spectator as Critic* (Ann Arbor: UMI Research Press, 1988).

DOLLIMORE, Jonathan, *Radical Tragedy: Religion, Ideology and Power in the Drama of Shakespeare and his Contemporaries* (2nd edn., Hemel Hempstead: Harvester Wheatsheaf, 1989).

— — and SINFIELD, Alan (eds.), *Political Shakespeare: Essays in Cultural Materialism* (2nd edn., Manchester: Manchester University Press, 1994).

DONOHUE, Joseph, 'Evidence and Documentation', in Postlewait and McConachie (eds.), *Interpreting the Theatrical Past*, 177–97.

DRAY, William, *Laws and Explanation in History* (London: Oxford University Press, 1957).

— — *History as Re-enactment: R. G. Collingwood's Idea of History* (Oxford: Clarendon Press, 1995).

DRYDEN, John, *The Letters of John Dryden*, ed. Charles E. Ward (Durham: Duke University Press, 1942).

— — *The Works of John Dryden*, xvii, ed. Samuel Holt Monk, A. E. Wallace Maurer, and Vinton A. Dearing (Berkeley: University of California Press, 1971).

DUSSEN, W. J. van der, and RUBINOFF, Lionel (eds.), *Objectivity, Method and Point of View: Essays in the Philosophy of History* (Leiden: E. J. Brill, 1991).

EAGLETON, Terry, *Criticism and Ideology: A Study in Marxist Literary Theory* (London: NLB, 1976).

— — *Marxism and Literary Criticism* (London: Methuen, 1976).

— — *The Illusions of Postmodernism* (Oxford: Blackwell, 1997).

ECO, Umberto, *The Role of the Reader: Explorations in the Semiotics of Texts* (Bloomington: Indiana University Press, 1979).

— — 'Intentio lectoris: The State of the Art', *Differentia*, 2 (1988), 147–68.

— — with RORTY, Richard, CULLER, Jonathan, and BROOKE-ROSE, Christine, *Interpretation and Overinterpretation*, ed. Stefan Collini (Cambridge: Cambridge University Press, 1992).

EHRENPREIS, Irvin, *Swift: The Man, his Works, and the Age*, 3 vols. (London: Methuen, 1962–83).

ELLIS, John M., *The Theory of Literary Criticism: A Logical Analysis* (Berkeley: University of California Press, 1974).

— — *Against Deconstruction* (Princeton: Princeton University Press, 1989).

ELLRODT, Robert, 'Literary History and the Search for Certainty', *New Literary History*, 27 (1996), 529–43.

EMPSON, William, *Seven Types of Ambiguity* (1930; 2nd edn., London: Chatto and Windus, 1947).

ERDMAN, David V., *Blake: Prophet against Empire: A Poet's Interpretation of the History of his own Times* (Princeton: Princeton University Press, 1954).

EVELYN, John, *The Diary and Correspondence of John Evelyn*, ed. William Bray, 4 vols. (London: H. G. Bohn, 1889–95).

EZELL, Margaret J. M., *Writing Women's Literary History* (Baltimore: Johns Hopkins University Press, 1993).

— — and O'KEEFFE, Katherine O'Brien (eds.), *Cultural Artifacts and the Production of Meaning: The Page, the Image, and the Body* (Ann Arbor: University of Michigan Press, 1994).

FARR, James, 'Situational Analysis: Explanation in Political Science', *Journal of Politics*, 47 (1985), 1085–107.

FELL, A. P., '"Epistemological" and "Narrativist" Philosophies of History', in van der Dussen and Rubinoff (eds.), *Objectivity, Method and Point of View*, 72–86.

FELPERIN, Howard, *Beyond Deconstruction: The Uses and Abuses of Literary Theory* (Oxford: Clarendon Press, 1985).

— — *The Uses of the Canon: Elizabethan Literature and Contemporary Theory* (Oxford: Clarendon Press, 1990).

FERGUSON, Niall (ed.), *Virtual History: Alternatives and Counterfactuals* (1997; London: Papermac, 1998).

FERRARIS, Maurizio, *History of Hermeneutics* (1988), trans. Luca Somigli (Atlantic Highlands, NJ: Humanities Press, 1996).

FETTERLEY, Judith, *The Resisting Reader: A Feminist Approach to American Fiction* (Bloomington: Indiana University Press, 1978).

FISCHER, David Hackett, *Historians' Fallacies: Toward a Logic of Historical Thought* (New York: Harper and Row, 1970).

FISH, Stanley, *Self-Consuming Artifacts: The Experience of Seventeenth-Century Literature* (Berkeley: University of California Press, 1972).

— — *Is There a Text in this Class? The Authority of Interpretive Communities* (Cambridge, Mass.: Harvard University Press, 1980).

FOXON, David, *Alexander Pope and the Early Eighteenth-Century Book Trade*, ed. James McLaverty (Oxford: Clarendon Press, 1991).

FRANKLIN, H. Bruce, '*Billy Budd* and Capital Punishment: A Tale of Three Centuries', *American Literature*, 69 (1997), 337–59.

FRANKO, Mark, *Dance as Text: Ideologies of the Baroque Body* (Cambridge: Cambridge University Press, 1993).

FREUND, Elizabeth, *The Return of the Reader: Reader-Response Criticism* (London: Methuen, 1987).

FRYE, Northrop, *Anatomy of Criticism: Four Essays* (Princeton: Princeton University Press, 1957).

FRYER, Peter, *Staying Power: The History of Black People in Britain* (London: Pluto Press, 1984).

FRYKENBERG, Robert Eric, *History and Belief: The Foundations of Historical Understanding* (Grand Rapids, Mich.: William B. Eerdmans Publishing Co., 1996).

FURBANK, P. N., and OWENS, W. R., *The Canonisation of Daniel Defoe* (New Haven: Yale University Press, 1988).

— — — *Defoe De-Attributions: A Critique of J. R. Moore's Checklist* (London: Hambledon Press, 1994).

— — — *A Critical Bibliography of Daniel Defoe* (London: Pickering and Chatto, 1998).

GADAMER, Hans-Georg, *Truth and Method* (2nd rev. edn., trans. revised by Joel Weinsheimer and Donald G. Marshall, New York: Continuum, 1995).

— — (ed.), *Truth and Historicity* (The Hague: Nijhoff, 1972).

GARDINER, Patrick, *The Nature of Historical Explanation* (Oxford: Oxford University Press, 1952).

GEERTZ, Clifford, 'Thick Description: Toward an Interpretive Theory of Culture', ch. 1 of *The Interpretation of Cultures: Selected Essays* (New York: Basic Books, 1973).

— — *Local Knowledge: Further Essays in Interpretive Anthropology* (New York: Basic Books, 1983).

GEERTZ, Clifford, 'History and Anthropology', *New Literary History*, 21 (1990), 321–35.

GILBERT, Sandra M., and GUBAR, Susan, *The Madwoman in the Attic: The Woman Writer and the Nineteenth-Century Literary Imagination* (New Haven: Yale University Press, 1979).

GOLDBERG, Jonathan, 'The Politics of Renaissance Literature: A Review Essay', *ELH* 49 (1982), 514–42.

GOLDSTEIN, Leon J., *Historical Knowing* (Austin: University of Texas Press, 1976).

GORMAN, J. L., *The Expression of Historical Knowledge* (Edinburgh: Edinburgh University Press, 1982).

GOTTSCHALK, Louis, *Understanding History: A Primer of Historical Method* (2nd edn., New York: Knopf, 1969).

GRAFF, Gerald, 'The Pseudo-Politics of Interpretation', *Critical Inquiry*, 9 (1983), 597–610.

GRAFTON, Anthony, *Commerce with the Classics: Ancient Books and the Renaissance Reader* (Ann Arbor: University of Michigan Press, 1997).

GRAHAM, Gordon, *Historical Explanation Reconsidered* (Scots Philosophical Monographs, 4; Aberdeen: Aberdeen University Press, 1983).

GREENBLATT, Stephen J., *Renaissance Self-Fashioning from More to Shakespeare* (Chicago: University of Chicago Press, 1980).

— — *Shakespearean Negotiations: The Circulation of Social Energy in Renaissance England* (Oxford: Clarendon Press, 1988).

— — *Learning to Curse: Essays in Early Modern Culture* (New York: Routledge, 1990).

— — (ed.), *The Power of Forms in the English Renaissance* (Norman, Okla.: Pilgrim, 1982).

GREENE, Donald, 'Latitudinarianism and Sensibility: The Genealogy of the "Man of Feeling" Reconsidered', *Modern Philology*, 75 (1977), 159–83.

GREENLAW, Edwin, *The Province of Literary History* (Baltimore: Johns Hopkins Press, 1931).

GROSSBERG, Lawrence, NELSON, Cary, and TREICHLER, Paula A. (eds.), *Cultural Studies* (London: Routledge, 1992).

GRUMLEY, John E., *History and Totality: Radical Historicism from Hegel to Foucault* (London: Routledge, 1989).

HALL, Anne D., 'The Political Wisdom of Cultural Poetics', *Modern Philology*, 93 (1996), 423–44.

HAMILTON, Paul, *Historicism* (London: Routledge, 1996).

HARARI, Josué V. (ed.), *Textual Strategies: Perspectives in Post-Structuralist Criticism* (Ithaca: Cornell University Press, 1979).

HARDISON, O. B., Jr., *Christian Rite and Christian Drama in the Middle Ages: Essays in the Origin and Early History of Modern Drama* (Baltimore: Johns Hopkins Press, 1965).

HARRIS, Wendell V., *Dictionary of Concepts in Literary Criticism and Theory* (Westport, Conn.: Greenwood Press, 1992).

— — 'What is Literary "History"?', *College English*, 56 (1994), 434–51.

— — 'Moving Literary Theory On', *Philosophy and Literature*, 20 (1996), 428–35.

— — 'The Discourse of Literary Criticism and Theory', *Social Epistemology*, 10 (1996), 75–88.

— — *Literary Meaning: Reclaiming the Study of Literature* (London: Macmillan, 1996).

— — 'Marxist Literary Theory and the Advantages of Irrelevance', *Sewanee Review*, 104 (1996), 209–28.

HART, H. L. A., and HONORÉ, Tony, *Causation in the Law* (2nd edn., Oxford: Clarendon Press, 1985).

HART, Jonathan, 'New Historical Shakespeare: Reading as Political Ventriloquy', *English*, 42 (1993), 193–219.

HART, Lynda, *Fatal Women: Lesbian Sexuality and the Mark of Aggression* (Princeton: Princeton University Press, 1994).

HARTH, Phillip, *Contexts of Dryden's Thought* (Chicago: University of Chicago Press, 1968).

— — *Pen for a Party: Dryden's Tory Propaganda in its Contexts* (Princeton: Princeton University Press, 1993).

HAUN, Eugene, *But Hark! More Harmony: The Libretti of Restoration Opera in English* (Ypsilanti: Eastern Michigan University Press, 1971).

HAWKINS, Harriett, *Likenesses of Truth in Elizabethan and Restoration Drama* (Oxford: Clarendon Press, 1972).

— — *The Devil's Party: Critical Counter-interpretations of Shakespearian Drama* (Oxford: Clarendon Press, 1985).

HEILMAN, Robert B., 'Historian and Critic: Notes on Attitudes', *Sewanee Review*, 73 (1965), 426–44.

HEMPEL, Carl G., 'The Function of General Laws in History', *Journal of Philosophy*, 39 (1942), 35–48.

HENIGE, David, *Oral Historiography* (London: Longman, 1982).

HEXTER, J. H., *The History Primer* (New York: Basic Books, 1971).

HIGHFILL, Philip H., Jr., BURNIM, Kalman A., and LANGHANS, Edward A., *A Biographical Dictionary of Actors, Actresses, Musicians, Dancers, Managers, and Other Stage Personnel in London, 1660–1800*, 16 vols. (Carbondale: Southern Illinois University Press, 1973–93).

HILL, W. Speed (ed.), *New Ways of Looking at Old Texts: Papers of the Renaissance English Text Society, 1985–1991* (Medieval &

Renaissance Texts & Studies, 107; Binghamton: Renaissance English Text Society, 1993).

HIMMELFARB, Gertrude, *The New History and the Old* (Cambridge, Mass.: Harvard University Press, 1987).

HIRSCH, E. D., Jr., *Validity in Interpretation* (New Haven: Yale University Press, 1967).

— — *The Aims of Interpretation* (Chicago: University of Chicago Press, 1976).

— — 'Past Intentions and Present Meanings', *Essays in Criticism*, 33 (1983), 79–98.

— — 'Meaning and Significance Reinterpreted', *Critical Inquiry*, 11 (1984), 202–25.

HOGAN, Charles Beecher, *Shakespeare in the Theatre, 1701–1800*, 2 vols. (Oxford: Clarendon Press, 1952–7).

HOLLAND, Norman N., *The Critical I* (New York: Columbia University Press, 1992).

HOLLAND, Peter, *The Ornament of Action: Text and Performance in Restoration Comedy* (Cambridge: Cambridge University Press, 1979).

HOLUB, Robert C., *Reception Theory: A Critical Introduction* (London: Methuen, 1984).

HORWITZ, Henry, *A Guide to Chancery Equity Records and Proceedings 1600–1800* (Public Record Office Handbook No. 27, 1995; rev. ed. Kew: PRO Publications, 1998).

HOTSON, Leslie, *The Commonwealth and Restoration Stage* (Cambridge, Mass.: Harvard University Press, 1928).

HOUGHTON, Walter E., *The Victorian Frame of Mind, 1830–1870* (New Haven: Yale University Press, 1957).

HOWARD, Jean E., 'The New Historicism in Renaissance Studies', *English Literary Renaissance*, 16 (1986), 13–43.

HOWARD, Sir Robert, and VILLIERS, George, Second Duke of Buckingham, *The Country Gentleman*, ed. Arthur H. Scouten and Robert D. Hume (Philadelphia: University of Pennsylvania Press, 1976).

HUGHES, Derek, 'Providential Justice and English Comedy 1660–1700: A Review of the External Evidence', *Modern Language Review*, 81 (1986), 273–92.

HUIZINGA, Johan, 'The Task of Cultural History', in his *Men and Ideas*, trans. James S. Holmes and Hans van Marle (New York: Meridian, 1959), 17–76.

HUME, Kathryn, *Pynchon's Mythography: An Approach to Gravity's Rainbow* (Carbondale: Southern Illinois University Press, 1987).

HUME, Robert D., *Dryden's Criticism* (Ithaca: Cornell University Press, 1970).

— — *The Development of English Drama in the Late Seventeenth Century* (Oxford: Clarendon Press, 1976).

– – '"The Change in Comedy": Cynical versus Exemplary Comedy on the London Stage, 1675–1693', *Essays in Theatre*, 1 (1983), 101–18.

– – *Henry Fielding and the London Theatre, 1728–1737* (Oxford: Clarendon Press, 1988).

– – 'Before the Bard: "Shakespeare" in Early Eighteenth-Century London', *ELH* 64 (1997), 41–75.

– – 'The Politics of Opera in Late Seventeenth-Century London', *Cambridge Opera Journal*, 10 (1998), 15–43.

HUNT, Lynn (ed.), *The New Cultural History* (Berkeley: University of California Press, 1989).

HYMAN, Stanley Edgar, *The Armed Vision: A Study in the Methods of Modern Literary Criticism* (New York: Knopf, 1948).

IGGERS, Georg G., *New Directions in European Historiography* (Middletown, Conn.: Wesleyan University Press, 1975).

INGRAM, William, *The Business of Playing: The Beginnings of the Adult Professional Theater in Elizabethan London* (Ithaca: Cornell University Press, 1992).

ISER, Wolfgang, *The Implied Reader: Patterns of Communication in Prose Fiction from Bunyan to Beckett* (Baltimore: Johns Hopkins University Press, 1974).

– – *Act of Reading: A Theory of Aesthetic Response* (Baltimore: Johns Hopkins University Press, 1978).

JACKSON, J. R. de J., *Historical Criticism and the Meaning of Texts* (London: Routledge, 1989).

JAMESON, Fredric, 'Marxism and Historicism', *New Literary History*, 11 (1979), 41–73.

– – *The Political Unconscious: Narrative as a Socially Symbolic Act* (London: Methuen, 1981).

JARDINE, Lisa, *Reading Shakespeare Historically* (London: Routledge, 1996). Cf. Review by Lois Potter in *TLS*, 14 June 1996.

JAUSS, Hans Robert, *Toward an Aesthetic of Reception*, trans. Timothy Bahti, Introduction by Paul de Man (Theory and History of Literature, 2; Minneapolis: University of Minnesota Press, 1982), esp. ch. 1, 'Literary History as a Challenge to Literary Theory'.

– – *Aesthetic Experience and Literary Hermeneutics*, trans. Michael Shaw (Minneapolis: University of Minnesota Press, 1982).

– – *Question and Answer: Forms of Dialogic Understanding*, trans. Michael Hays (Minneapolis: University of Minnesota Press, 1989), esp. 'Horizon Structure and Dialogicity', 197–231.

JENKINS, Keith, *On 'What is History?' From Carr and Elton to Rorty and White* (London: Routledge, 1995).

JOHNSON, Barbara, *A World of Difference* (Baltimore: Johns Hopkins University Press, 1987).

JOHNSON, Maurice, 'A Literary Chestnut: Dryden's "Cousin Swift"', *PMLA* 67 (1952), 1024–34.

JOHNSTONE, Robert, 'The Impossible Genre: Reading Comprehensive Literary History', *PMLA* 107 (1992), 26–37.

JONES, Ernest, *Hamlet and Oedipus* (London: Victor Gollancz, 1949).

KAMPF, Louis, and LAUTER, Paul (eds.), *The Politics of Literature* (New York: Pantheon, 1972).

KEMP, Anthony, *The Estrangement of the Past: A Study in the Origins of Modern Historical Consciousness* (New York: Oxford University Press, 1991).

KERR, David, *African Popular Theatre from Pre-Colonial Times to the Present Day* (Oxford: James Currey, 1995).

KEWES, Paulina, *Authorship and Appropriation: Writing for the Stage in England, 1660–1710* (Oxford: Clarendon Press, 1998).

KEYMER, Tom, *Richardson's Clarissa and the Eighteenth-Century Reader* (Cambridge: Cambridge University Press, 1992).

KINNEY, Arthur F., 'Revisiting *The Tempest*', *Modern Philology*, 93 (1995), 161–77.

KLANCHER, Jon P., *The Making of English Reading Audiences, 1790–1832* (Madison: University of Wisconsin Press, 1987).

KOLODNY, Annette, 'The Integrity of Memory: Creating a New Literary History of the United States', *American Literature*, 57 (1985), 291–307.

KUBLER, George, *The Shape of Time: Remarks on the History of Things* (New Haven: Yale University Press, 1962).

KUHN, Thomas S., *The Structure of Scientific Revolutions* (2nd edn., Chicago: University of Chicago Press, 1970).

LACAPRA, Dominick, *Rethinking Intellectual History: Texts, Contexts, Language* (Ithaca: Cornell University Press, 1983).

— — *History and Criticism* (Ithaca: Cornell University Press, 1985), esp. 'Writing the History of Criticism Now?', 94–114.

— — *Soundings in Critical Theory* (Ithaca: Cornell University Press, 1989).

LANGHANS, Edward A., *Restoration Promptbooks* (Carbondale: Southern Illinois University Press, 1981).

LEACROFT, Richard, *The Development of the English Playhouse* (London: Eyre Methuen, 1973).

LEE, Dwight E., and BECK, Robert N., 'The Meaning of "Historicism"', *American Historical Review*, 59 (1954), 568–77.

LEHAN, Richard, 'The Theoretical Limits of the New Historicism', *New Literary History*, 21 (1990), 533–53.

LEINWAND, Theodore B., 'Negotiation and New Historicism', *PMLA* 105 (1990), 477–90.

LERER, Seth (ed.), *Literary History and the Challenge of Philology: The Legacy of Erich Auerbach* (Stanford: Stanford University Press, 1996).

LERNER, Laurence, 'Against Historicism', *New Literary History*, 24 (1993), 273–92.

LEVENSTON, E. A., *The Stuff of Literature: Physical Aspects of Texts and their Relation to Literary Meaning* (Albany: State University of New York Press, 1992).

LEVIN, Harry, 'Reflections on the Final Volume of *The Oxford History of English Literature*', in *Refractions: Essays in Comparative Literature* (New York: Oxford University Press, 1966), 151–70.

LEVIN, Richard, *New Readings vs. Old Plays: Recent Trends in the Reinterpretation of English Renaissance Drama* (Chicago: University of Chicago Press, 1979).

— — 'The Problem of "Context" in Interpretation', in W. R. Elton and William B. Long (eds.), *Shakespeare and Dramatic Tradition: Essays in Honor of S. F. Johnson* (Newark: University of Delaware Press, 1989), 88–106.

— — 'Unthinkable Thoughts in the New Historicizing of English Renaissance Drama', *New Literary History*, 21 (1990), 433–47.

— — 'The Poetics and Politics of Bardicide', *PMLA* 105 (1990), 491–504.

— — 'The New and the Old Historicizing of Shakespeare', *Yearbook of Research in English and American Literature*, 11 (1995), 425–48.

— — '(Re)Thinking Unthinkable Thoughts', *New Literary History*, 28 (1997), 525–37. Cf. reply by Valerie Traub, ibid. 539–42.

LEVINSON, Marjorie, BUTLER, Marilyn, McGANN, Jerome, and HAMILTON, Paul, *Rethinking Historicism: Critical Readings in Romantic History* (Oxford: Blackwell, 1989).

LIU, Alan, 'The Power of Formalism: The New Historicism', *ELH* 56 (1989), 721–71.

LLOYD, Christopher, *Explanation in Social History* (Oxford: Blackwell, 1986).

LODGE, David, 'Historicism and Literary History: Mapping the Modern Period', in *Working with Structuralism* (London: Routledge and Kegan Paul, 1981), 68–75.

The London Stage, 1660–1800, 5 parts in 11 vols., ed. William Van Lennep, Emmett L. Avery, Arthur H. Scouten, George Winchester Stone, Jr., and Charles Beecher Hogan (Carbondale: Southern Illinois University Press, 1960–8).

LORENZ, Chris, 'Historical Knowledge and Historical Reality: A Plea for "Internal Realism"', *History and Theory*, 33 (1994), 297–327.

LOVE, Harold, 'Was Congreve a Christian?', *Themes in Drama*, 5 (1983), 293–309.

LOVE, Harold, *Scribal Publication in Seventeenth-Century England* (Oxford: Clarendon Press, 1993).

LOVEJOY, Arthur O., 'The Parallel of Deism and Classicism' (1932; repr. in *Essays in the History of Ideas*; Baltimore: Johns Hopkins Press, 1948).

LOWENTHAL, David, *The Past is a Foreign Country* (Cambridge: Cambridge University Press, 1985).

LUKÁCS, Georg, *The Historical Novel* (1937), trans. Hannah and Stanley Mitchell (London: Merlin Press, 1962).

McALEER, Joseph, *Popular Reading and Publishing in Britain 1914–1950* (Oxford: Clarendon Press, 1992).

McCANLES, Michael, 'The Authentic Discourse of the Renaissance', *diacritics*, 10:1 (1980), 77–87.

McCONACHIE, Bruce A., 'Towards a Postpositivist Theatre History', *Theatre Journal*, 37 (1985), 465–86.

McCULLAGH, C. Behan, 'Can our Understanding of Old Texts be Objective?' *History and Theory*, 30 (1991), 302–23.

MACE, Nancy A., *Henry Fielding's Novels and the Classical Tradition* (Newark: University of Delaware Press, 1996).

McGANN, Jerome J., 'The Meaning of *The Ancient Mariner*', *Critical Inquiry*, 8 (1981), 35–67.

— — *The Beauty of Inflections: Literary Investigations in Historical Method and Theory* (Oxford: Clarendon Press, 1985).

— — (ed.), *Historical Studies and Literary Criticism* (Madison: University of Wisconsin Press, 1985).

— — *Social Values and Poetic Acts: The Historical Judgment of Literary Work* (Cambridge, Mass.: Harvard University Press, 1988).

MACK, Maynard, *The Garden and the City: Retirement and Politics in the Later Poetry of Pope, 1731–1743* (Toronto: University of Toronto Press, 1969).

— — *Alexander Pope: A Life* (New Haven: Yale University Press, 1985).

McKENZIE, D. F., *Bibliography and the Sociology of Texts* (Panizzi Lectures, 1985; London: The British Library, 1986).

— — *'What's Past is Prologue': The Bibliographical Society and History of the Book* (The Bibliographical Society Centenary Lecture 14 July 1992; Hearthstone Publications, 1993).

McKEON, Michael, *The Origins of the English Novel, 1600–1740* (Baltimore: Johns Hopkins University Press, 1987).

— — 'Historicizing *Absalom and Achitophel*', in Felicity Nussbaum and Laura Brown (eds.), *The New Eighteenth Century* (London: Methuen, 1987).

— — 'What Were Poems on Affairs of State?' *1650–1850: Ideas, Aesthetics, and Inquiries in the Early Modern Era*, 4 (1998), 368–82.

MAILLOUX, Steven, *Interpretive Conventions: The Reader in the Study of American Fiction* (Ithaca: Cornell University Press, 1982).
— — *Rhetorical Power* (Ithaca: Cornell University Press, 1989).
MAKKREEL, Rudolf A., 'Traditional Historicism, Contemporary Interpretations of Historicity, and the History of Philosophy', *New Literary History*, 21 (1990), 977–91.
MANDELBAUM, Maurice, *The Problem of Historical Knowledge: An Answer to Relativism* (New York: Liveright, 1938).
— — *The Anatomy of Historical Knowledge* (Baltimore: Johns Hopkins University Press, 1977).
MARCUS, Jane, 'The Asylums of Antaeus: Women, War, and Madness— Is there a Feminist Fetishism?' in Veeser (ed.), *The New Historicism*, 132–51.
MARCUS, Leah S., *Puzzling Shakespeare: Local Reading and its Discontents* (Berkeley: University of California Press, 1988).
MARKLEY, Robert, 'What isn't History: The Snares of Demystifying Ideological Criticism', *Critical Inquiry*, 15 (1989), 647–57. (Cf. reply by Oscar Kenshur, ibid. 658–68.)
MARSAK, Leonard M. (ed.), *The Nature of Historical Inquiry* (New York: Holt, Rinehart, 1970).
MARTIN, Raymond, *The Past within Us: An Empirical Approach to Philosophy of History* (Princeton: Princeton University Press, 1989).
— — 'Objectivity and Meaning in Historical Studies: Toward a Post-Analytic View', *History and Theory*, 32 (1993), 25–50.
MARTIN, Rex, *Historical Explanation: Re-enactment and Practical Inference* (Ithaca: Cornell University Press, 1977).
MATTER, E. Ann, *The Voice of My Beloved: The Song of Songs in Western Medieval Christianity* (Philadelphia: University of Pennsylvania Press, 1990).
MAYO, Robert, 'The Contemporaneity of the *Lyrical Ballads*', *PMLA* 69 (1954), 486–522.
MEILAND, Jack W., *Scepticism and Historical Knowledge* (New York: Random House, 1965).
MILHOUS, Judith, 'United Company Finances, 1682–1692', *Theatre Research International*, 7 (1981–82), 37–53.
— — and HUME, Robert D., 'Dating Play Premières from Publication Data, 1660–1700', *Harvard Library Bulletin*, 22 (1974), 374–405.
— — — 'Lost English Plays, 1660–1700', *Harvard Library Bulletin*, 25 (1977), 5–33.
— — — 'New Light on Handel and the Royal Academy of Music in 1720', *Theatre Journal*, 35 (1983), 149–67.
— — — *Producible Interpretation: Eight English Plays, 1675–1707* (Carbondale: Southern Illinois University Press, 1985).

M ILHOUS , Judith, and HUME , Robert D. , 'A Drury Lane Account Book for 1745–46', *Theatre History Studies*, 10 (1990), 67–104.

— — and HUME, Robert D., 'The Drury Lane Theatre Library in 1768', *Yale University Library Gazette*, 68 (1994), 116–34.

— — — 'Eighteenth-Century Equity Lawsuits in the Court of Exchequer as a Source for Historical Research', *Historical Research*, 70 (1997), 231–46.

— — — 'Profits from Play Publication: The Evidence of *Murphy v. Vaillant*', *Studies in Bibliography*, 51 (1998), 213–29.

— — — 'Heidegger and the Management of the Haymarket Opera, 1713–1717', *Early Music*, forthcoming.

— — — 'Playwrights' Remuneration in Eighteenth-Century London', *Harvard Library Bulletin*, forthcoming.

MILLER, J. Hillis, *The Disappearance of God: Five Nineteenth-Century Writers* (Cambridge, Mass.: Harvard University Press, 1963).

MILLER, Richard W., *Fact and Method: Explanation, Confirmation and Reality in the Natural and the Social Sciences* (Princeton: Princeton University Press, 1987).

MINK, Louis O., *Historical Understanding*, ed. Brian Fay, Eugene O. Golob, and Richard T. Vann (Ithaca: Cornell University Press, 1987).

MONTROSE, Louis, 'Renaissance Literary Studies and the Subject of History', *English Literary Renaissance*, 16 (1986), 5–12.

MOORE, John Robert, *A Checklist of the Writings of Daniel Defoe* (2nd edn., Hamden, Conn.: Archon, 1971).

MORRIS, Wesley, *Toward a New Historicism* (Princeton: Princeton University Press, 1972).

MUNZ, Peter, *The Shapes of Time: A New Look at the Philosophy of History* (Middletown, Conn.: Wesleyan University Press, 1977).

MURPHEY, Murray G., *Our Knowledge of the Historical Past* (Indianapolis: Bobbs-Merrill, 1973).

— — *Philosophical Foundations of Historical Knowledge* (Albany: State University of New York Press, 1994).

MYERS, Norma, *Reconstructing the Black Past: Blacks in Britain 1780– 1830* (London: Frank Cass, 1996).

NOKES, David, *John Gay: A Profession of Friendship* (Oxford: Oxford University Press, 1995).

NORRIS, Christopher, *Deconstruction: Theory and Practice* (London: Methuen, 1982).

— — *Reclaiming Truth: Contribution to a Critique of Cultural Relativism* (London: Lawrence and Wishart, 1996).

NUSSBAUM, Felicity A., *Torrid Zones: Maternity, Sexuality, and Empire in Eighteenth-Century English Narratives* (Baltimore: Johns Hopkins University Press, 1995).

OAKESHOTT, Michael, *Experience and its Modes* (1933; Cambridge: Cambridge University Press, 1966).

O'BRIEN, Patricia, 'Michel Foucault's History of Culture', in Hunt (ed.), *The New Cultural History*, 25–46.

OGDEN, James, 'Lear's Blasted Heath', *Durham University Journal*, 80 (1987), 19–26.

OLÁBARRI, Ignacio, '"New" New History: A *Longue Durée* Structure', *History and Theory*, 34 (1995), 1–29.

OLAFSON, Frederick A., *The Dialectic of Action: A Philosophical Interpretation of History and the Humanities* (Chicago: University of Chicago Press, 1979).

OLSEN, Bjørnar, 'Roland Barthes: From Sign to Text', in Tilley (ed.), *Reading Material Culture*, 163–205.

PALMER, William G., 'The Burden of Proof: J. H. Hexter and Christopher Hill', *Journal of British Studies*, 19:1 (1979), 122–9. (Cf. reply by Hexter, ibid. 130–6.)

PARRY, Milman, 'The Historical Method in Literary Criticism' (1936), repr. in *The Making of Homeric Verse: The Collected Papers of Milman Parry*, ed. Adam Parry (Oxford: Clarendon Press, 1971), 408–13.

PATTERSON, Annabel M., *Censorship and Interpretation: The Conditions of Writing and Reading in Early Modern England* (1984; Madison: University of Wisconsin Press, [1990]).

PATTERSON, Lee, 'Literary History', in *Critical Terms for Literary Study*, ed. Frank Lentricchia and Thomas McLaughlin (Chicago: University of Chicago Press, 1990), 250–62.

PAYNE, Michael, *Reading Theory: An Introduction to Lacan, Derrida, and Kristeva* (Oxford: Blackwell, 1993).

PECHTER, Edward, 'The New Historicism and its Discontents: Politicizing Renaissance Drama', *PMLA* 102 (1987), 292–303.

– – *What Was Shakespeare? Renaissance Plays and Changing Critical Practice* (Ithaca: Cornell University Press, 1995).

PECKHAM, Morse, 'Toward a Theory of Romanticism', *PMLA* 66 (1951), 5–23.

PERKINS, David, *Is Literary History Possible?* (Baltimore: Johns Hopkins University Press, 1992).

– – (ed.), *Theoretical Issues in Literary History* (Harvard English Studies, 16; Cambridge, Mass.: Harvard University Press, 1991).

PERRY, Ruth, 'De-Familiarizing the Family; or, Writing Family History from Literary Sources', *Modern Language Quarterly*, 55 (1994), 415–27.

PETERS, Sally, *Bernard Shaw: The Ascent of the Superman* (New Haven: Yale University Press, 1996).

POCOCK, J. G. A., 'Texts as Events: Reflections on the History of Political Thought', in Kevin Sharpe and Steven N. Zwicker (eds.), *Politics of Discourse: The Literature and History of Seventeenth-Century England* (Berkeley: University of California Press, 1987), 21–34.

POCOCK, J. G. A., 'Within the Margins: The Definitions of Orthodoxy', in Roger D. Lund (ed.), *The Margins of Orthodoxy: Heterodox Writing and Cultural Response, 1660–1750* (Cambridge: Cambridge University Press, 1995), 33–53.

POPPER, Karl R., *The Poverty of Historicism* (Boston: Beacon Press, 1957).

— — *The Logic of Scientific Discovery* (London: Hutchinson, 1959).

— — *Conjectures and Refutations: The Growth of Scientific Knowledge* (London: Routledge and Kegan Paul, 1963).

PORTER, Carolyn, 'Are We being Historical Yet?' *South Atlantic Quarterly*, 87 (1988), 744–86.

— — 'History and Literature: "After the New Historicism"', *New Literary History*, 21 (1990), 253–72.

PORTER, Dale H., *The Emergence of the Past: A Theory of Historical Explanation* (Chicago: University of Chicago Press, 1981).

POSTLEWAIT, Thomas, 'Historiography and the Theatrical Event: A Primer with Twelve Cruxes', *Theatre Journal*, 43 (1991), 157–78.

— — and MCCONACHIE, Bruce A. (eds.), *Interpreting the Theatrical Past: Essays in the Historiography of Performance* (Iowa City: University of Iowa Press, 1989).

POTTER, Lois, *Secret Rites and Secret Writing: Royalist Literature, 1641–1660* (Cambridge: Cambridge University Press, 1989).

PRICE, Curtis, MILHOUS Judith, and HUME, Robert D., *Italian Opera in Late Eighteenth-Century London*, i: *The King's Theatre, Haymarket, 1778–1791* (Oxford: Clarendon Press, 1995).

QUILLIGAN, Maureen, *Milton's Spenser: The Politics of Reading* (Ithaca: Cornell University Press, 1983).

QUINN, Michael L., '*Theaterwissenschaft* in the History of Theatre Study', *Theatre Survey*, 32 (1991), 123–36.

RAJAN, Balachandra, *Paradise Lost and the Seventeenth-Century Reader* (London: Chatto and Windus, 1947).

RAWSON, C. J., *Henry Fielding and the Augustan Ideal under Stress* (London: Routledge, 1972).

— — *Gulliver and the Gentle Reader: Studies in Swift and our Time* (London: Routledge, 1973).

RÉE, Jonathan, 'The Vanity of Historicism', *New Literary History*, 22 (1991), 961–83.

RENZA, Louis A., 'Exploding Canons', *Contemporary Literature*, 28 (1987), 257–70. [Rev. art. on *Canons*, ed. Robert von Hallberg (University of Chicago Press, 1984).]

RICHARDS, I. A., *Practical Criticism: A Study of Literary Judgment* (London: Routledge & Kegan Paul, 1929).

RICHTER, David H., *The Progress of Romance: Literary Historiography and the Gothic Novel* (Columbus: Ohio State University Press, 1996).

RICOEUR, Paul, *History and Truth*, trans. Charles A. Kelbley (Evanston: Northwestern University Press, 1965).

RIFFATERRE, Michael, 'Intertextuality vs. Hypertextuality', *New Literary History*, 25 (1994), 779–88.

RIGBY, S. H., 'Historical Causation: Is One Thing more Important than Another?', *History*, 80 (1995), 227–42.

RINGER, Fritz K., 'Causal Analysis in Historical Reasoning', *History and Theory*, 28 (1989), 154–72.

ROACH, Joseph R., *The Player's Passion: Studies in the Science of Acting* (1985; repr. Ann Arbor: University of Michigan Press, 1993).

— — *Cities of the Dead: Circum-Atlantic Performance* (New York: Columbia University Press, 1996).

ROBERTS, Clayton, *The Logic of Historical Explanation* (University Park: Pennsylvania State University Press, 1996).

ROBERTSON, D. W., Jr., *A Preface to Chaucer: Studies in Medieval Perspectives* (Princeton: Princeton University Press, 1962).

ROGERS, Pat, *Grub Street: Studies in a Subculture* (London: Methuen, 1972).

RORTY, Richard, SCHNEEWIND, J. B., and SKINNER, Quentin (eds.), *Philosophy in History: Essays on the Historiography of Philosophy* (Cambridge: Cambridge University Press, 1984).

ROSMARIN, Adena, *The Power of Genre* (Minneapolis: University of Minnesota Press, 1985).

ROSS, Marlon B., 'Contingent Predilections: The Newest Historicisms and the Question of Method', *Centennial Review*, 34 (1990), 485–538.

ROSSELLI, John, *The Life of Bellini* (Cambridge: Cambridge University Press, 1996).

ROTHSTEIN, Eric, and KAVENIK, Frances M., *The Designs of Carolean Comedy* (Carbondale: Southern Illinois University Press, 1988).

SAID, Edward W., *The World, the Text, and the Critic* (Cambridge, Mass.: Harvard University Press, 1983).

SAUNDERS, David, and HUNTER, Ian, 'Lessons from the "Literatory": How to Historicise Authorship', *Critical Inquiry*, 17 (1991), 479–509.

SCHILLING, Bernard N., *Dryden and the Conservative Myth: A Reading of 'Absalom and Achitophel'* (New Haven: Yale University Press, 1961).

SCHOENBAUM, S., *William Shakespeare: A Documentary Life* (New York: Oxford University Press, 1975).

SCHOLES, Robert, 'Deconstruction and Communication', *Critical Inquiry*, 14 (1988), 278–95.

SCOUTEN, Arthur H., 'The Perils of Evelyn', *Restoration*, 16 (1992), 126–8.

SEARLE, John R., *Expression and Meaning: Studies in the Theory of Speech Acts* (Cambridge: Cambridge University Press, 1979).

— — *Intentionality: An Essay in the Philosophy of Mind* (Cambridge: Cambridge University Press, 1983).

— — 'Literary Theory and its Discontents', *New Literary History*, 25 (1994), 637–67.

— — *The Construction of Social Reality* (London: Penguin, 1995).

— — and Vanderveken, Daniel, *Foundations of Illocutionary Logic* (Cambridge: Cambridge University Press, 1985).

SELDEN, Raman, *Criticism and Objectivity* (London: George Allen and Unwin, 1984).

SHAKESPEARE, William, *Titus Andronicus*, ed. Jonathan Bate (London: Routledge, 1995).

SIEGEL, Paul N., 'The New Historicism and Shakespearean Criticism: A Marxist Critique', *Clio*, 21 (1991), 129–44.

SIMPSON, David, 'Literary Criticism and the Return to "History"', *Critical Inquiry*, 14 (1988), 721–47.

— — (ed.), *Subject to History: Ideology, Class, Gender* (Ithaca: Cornell University Press, 1991).

SINFIELD, Alan, *Faultlines: Cultural Materialism and the Politics of Dissident Reading* (Berkeley: University of California Press, 1992).

SITTER, John, *Literary Loneliness in Mid-Eighteenth-Century England* (Ithaca: Cornell University Press, 1982).

SKINNER, Quentin, 'Meaning and Understanding in the History of Ideas', *History and Theory*, 8 (1969), 3–53.

— — 'Motives, Intentions and the Interpretation of Texts', *New Literary History*, 3 (1972), 393–408.

— — '"Social Meaning" and the Explanation of Social Action', in Patrick Gardiner (ed.), *The Philosophy of History* (Oxford: Clarendon Press, 1974), 106–27.

— — 'Some Problems in the Analysis of Political Thought and Action', *Political Theory*, 23 (1974), 277–303.

— — *The Foundations of Modern Political Thought*, 2 vols. (Cambridge: Cambridge University Press, 1978).

— — (ed.), *The Return of Grand Theory in the Human Sciences* (Cambridge: Cambridge University Press, 1985).

— — *Liberty before Liberalism* (Cambridge: Cambridge University Press, 1998).

SLAWIŃSKI, Janusz, 'Reading and Reader in the Literary Historical Process', *New Literary History*, 19 (1988), 521–39.

SMITH, Ruth, *Handel's Oratorios and Eighteenth-Century Thought* (Cambridge: Cambridge University Press, 1995).

SPACKS, Patricia Meyer, *Imagining a Self: Autobiography and Novel in Eighteenth-Century England* (Cambridge, Mass.: Harvard University Press, 1976).

SPENCE, Joseph, *Observations, Anecdotes, and Characters of Books and Men*, ed. James M. Osborn, 2 vols. (Oxford: Clarendon Press, 1966).

STERN, Laurent, 'Narrative versus Description in Historiography', *New Literary History*, 21 (1990), 555–68. Cf. exchange between Haskell Fain and Stern, ibid. 569–77.

STRIER, Richard, *Resistant Structures: Particularity, Radicalism, and Renaissance Texts* (Berkeley: University of California Press, 1995).

SULEIMAN, Susan R., and CROSMAN, Inge (eds.), *The Reader in the Text: Essays on Audience and Interpretation* (Princeton: Princeton University Press, 1980).

The Tatler (by Richard Steele *et al.*), ed. Donald Bond, 3 vols. (Oxford: Clarendon Press, 1987).

TAYLOR, Aline Mackenzie, *Next to Shakespeare: Otway's Venice Preserv'd and The Orphan and their History on the London Stage* (Durham: Duke University Press, 1950).

TAYLOR, Charles, *The Explanation of Behaviour* (London: Routledge & Kegan Paul, 1964).

THIHER, Allen, 'The Tautological Thinking of Historicism', *Texas Studies in Literature and Language*, 39 (1997), 1–26.

THOMAS, Brook, *The New Historicism and Other Old-Fashioned Topics* (Princeton: Princeton University Press, 1991).

THOMAS, Gary C., '"Was George Frideric Handel Gay?" On Closet Questions and Cultural Politics', in Philip Brett, Gary Thomas, and Elizabeth Wood (eds.), *Queering the Pitch: The New Gay and Lesbian Musicology* (London: Routledge, 1994), 155–203.

THOMPSON, E. P., *The Making of the English Working Class* (London: Victor Gollancz, 1963).

— — *The Poverty of Theory and Other Essays* (London: Merlin Press, 1978).

THOMPSON, James, 'What's Left of the Left?' *Eighteenth Century*, 32 (1991), 195–202. [Introduction to a special issue.]

TILLEY, Christopher (ed.), *Reading Material Culture: Structuralism, Hermeneutics and Post-Structuralism* (Oxford: Blackwell, 1990).

TILLOTSON, Kathleen, *Novels of the Eighteen-Forties* (Oxford: Clarendon Press, 1954).

TILLYARD, E. M. W., *The Elizabethan World Picture* (London: Chatto and Windus, 1943).

TOPOLSKI, Jerzy, 'Towards an Integrated Model of Historical Explanation', *History and Theory*, 30 (1991), 324–38.

TULLY, James (ed.), *Meaning and Context: Quentin Skinner and his Critics* ([Cambridge]: Polity Press, 1988). See esp. Skinner's 'A Reply to my Critics', 231–88.

UNGAR, Steven, 'Against Forgetting: Notes on Revision and the Writing of History', *diacritics*, 22:2 (1992), 62–9.

VEESER, H. Aram (ed.), *The New Historicism* (New York: Routledge, 1989).

– – *The New Historicism Reader* (New York: Routledge, 1994).

WALLACE, John M., 'Dryden and History: A Problem in Allegorical Reading', *ELH* 36 (1969), 265–90.

– – '"Examples Are Best Precepts": Readers and Meanings in Seventeenth-Century Poetry', *Critical Inquiry*, 1 (1974), 273–90.

WARD, Charles E., *The Life of John Dryden* (Chapel Hill: University of North Carolina Press, 1961).

WARNER, William B., 'Realist Literary History: McKeon's New Origins of the Novel', *diacritics*, 19:1 (1989), 62–81. Cf. further exchange with McKeon, ibid. 83–96 and 20:1 (1990), 104–7.

WASSERMAN, Earl R., *The Subtler Language: Critical Readings of Neoclassic and Romantic Poems* (Baltimore: Johns Hopkins Press, 1959).

WATKINS, Daniel P., *A Materialist Critique of English Romantic Drama* (Gainesville: University Press of Florida, 1993).

WATSON, Walter, *The Architectonics of Meaning: Foundations of the New Pluralism* (Albany: State University of New York Press, 1985).

WATT, Ian, *The Rise of the Novel* (1957; repr. Berkeley: University of California Press, 1964).

WEIMANN, Robert, *Structure and Society in Literary History: Studies in the History and Theory of Historical Criticism*, rev. edn. (Baltimore: Johns Hopkins University Press, 1984).

WEINBROT, Howard D., 'Johnson, Jacobitism, and the Historiography of Nostalgia', *The Age of Johnson*, 7 (1996), 163–211.

– – 'Johnson and Jacobitism Redux: Evidence, Interpretation, and Intellectual History', *The Age of Johnson*, 8 (1997), 89–125.

– – 'Johnson, Jacobitism, and Swedish Charles: *The Vanity of Human Wishes* and Scholarly Method', *ELH* 64 (1997), 945–91.

WELLEK, René, 'Literary History', in Norman Foerster *et al.*, *Literary Scholarship: Its Aims and Methods* (Chapel Hill: University of North Carolina Press, 1941), 89–130.

— — 'Six Types of Literary History', *English Institute Essays 1946* (New York: Columbia University Press, 1947), 107–26.

— — 'The Concept of "Romanticism" in Literary History', *Comparative Literature*, 1 (1949), 1–23, 147–72.

— — 'A New History of English Literature', *Modern Philology*, 47 (1949), 39–45. [Review article of *A Literary History of England*, ed. Albert C. Baugh.]

— — *Concepts of Criticism*, ed. Stephen G. Nichols, Jr. (New Haven: Yale University Press, 1963), esp. 'Literary Theory, Criticism, and History' (1–20) and 'The Revolt Against Positivism in Recent European Literary Scholarship' (256–81).

— — *The Attack on Literature and Other Essays* (Chapel Hill: University of North Carolina Press, 1982), esp. 'The Fall of Literary History' (64–77) and 'Reflections on my *History of Modern Criticism*' (135–45).

— — and WARREN, Austin, *Theory of Literature* (1949; London: Jonathan Cape, 1961).

WHITE, Hayden, *Metahistory: The Historical Imagination in Nineteenth-Century Europe* (Baltimore: Johns Hopkins University Press, 1973).

— — 'The Problem of Change in Literary History', *New Literary History*, 7 (1975), 97–111.

— — *Tropics of Discourse: Essays in Cultural Criticism* (Baltimore: Johns Hopkins University Press, 1978).

— — 'The Value of Narrativity in the Representation of Reality', *Critical Inquiry*, 7 (1980), 5–27.

— — 'New Historicism: A Comment', in Veeser (ed.), *The New Historicism*, 293–302.

WHITE, Morton, *Foundations of Historical Knowledge* (New York: Harper and Row, 1965).

WILKINSON, D. R. M., *The Comedy of Habit: An Essay on the Use of Courtesy Literature in a Study of Restoration Comic Drama* (Leiden: Universitaire Pers, 1964).

WILLEY, Basil, *The Seventeenth-Century Background* (London: Chatto and Windus, 1934).

WILLIAMS, Aubrey L., *An Approach to Congreve* (New Haven: Yale University Press, 1979).

WILLIAMS, Raymond, *Marxism and Literature* (Oxford: Oxford University Press, 1977).

WIMSATT, W. K., Jr., and BEARDSLEY, M. C., 'The Intentional Fallacy', *Sewanee Review*, 54 (1946), 468–88.

WINN, James Anderson, *John Dryden and his World* (New Haven: Yale University Press, 1987).

WINN, James Anderson, 'An Old Historian Looks at the New Historicism', *Comparative Studies in Society and History*, 35 (1993), 859–70.

WOMERSLEY, David, 'Gibbon's *Memoirs*: Autobiography in Time of Revolution', *Studies on Voltaire and the Eighteenth Century*, 355 (1997), 347–404.

WORDEN, Blair, *The Sound of Virtue: Philip Sidney's Arcadia and Elizabethan Politics* (New Haven: Yale University Press, 1996).

Index

Garrick, David:
  acting style 168
  acting theory 169
  as Lothario 166
  charged with papering house 122
  contrasted with Quin 167
  debut in London 166
  initiates supposed paradigm
    shift 166–70
  performances of Hamlet 56
  purchase of plays 190
  purchase of share in Drury Lane 107
Gay, John:
  sexual preferences 127
  What d'ye Call It 113
Geertz, Clifford 17, 75, 116
  on 'scientific' history 17
Geistesgeschichte 109, 148
generic history:
  denial of feasibility of 110
  principles governing 110
genesis *v.* reception 84
genetic analysis 84
genre 129–37
Gentleman's Journal 33
George I 122
Gervinius, Georg Gottfried 19
Gibbes, Phebe 182
Gibbon, Edward:
  Memoirs 87–8
Gilbert, Sandra 140
Gilbert, W. S. and Sir Arthur Sullivan:
  Pirates of Penzance 176
Gildon, Charles 126
Goethe, Johann Wolfgang von 3
Goldstein, Leon J. 17, 141
Gorgias of Leontini 11
Grafton, Anthony 78
Graham, Reverend Billy 91
Grant, Kerry S. 125
Gray, Thomas 139
Great Books Fallacy 110
Greenblatt, Stephen J. ix, 5, 7, 191
  champions cultural poetics 7
  denies doctrine in New Histori-
    cism 152
  practices close reading 6
  view of old historicism 5
Greene, Donald 70, 97
Greenleaf, W. H. 68
Greg, W. W. 158
Guardian 123
Gubar, Susan 140

Hamilton, Paul 3
Handel, George Frideric 189
  1730s documentation 53
  finances 41
  orchestra 31
  Rinaldo: popularity of 121
  sexual preferences 127
Hardison, O. B. Jr. 50
Hardy, Henry 18
Harootunian, Harry 142
Harris, Wendell V. 3, 4, 11
  on distinguishing historical scholar-
    ship and literary history 114
  on hermeticism 11
  on historicism 4
  on literary history 102
Hart, Charles 39, 66
Hart, Lynda 184
Harth, Phillip 34, 96
Harvey, James Robinson 144
Haun, Eugene 96
Hawkins, Harriett 63, 93
Hawthorne, Nathaniel 88
Haymarket Theatre 122
Hays, Michael 71
Heath, Stephen 175
Hegel, Georg Wilhelm Friedrich 14
  on progress in history 151
hegemony 109
Heidegger, J. J. 122
Heidegger, Martin 94
Hemingway, Ernest:
  For Whom the Bell Tolls 86
Hempel, Carl G. 15, 150
  demand for covering law 15
hermeticism 11–12, 14, 28, 193
Hexter, J. H. 99, 104
  on coherence of history 104
Heywood, Thomas:
  Woman Killed with Kindness 83
Highfill, Philip H. Jr. 60
Hill, Christopher 165
Hill, W. Speed 181
Hirsch, E. D., Jr. 27, 86, 176
  meaning/significance distinction 27
Historical Manuscripts Commis-
    sion 56
historical materialism:
  claim to stand outside ideology 162
historicism:
  concepts of 2–5
  meanings of term 2, 4
  not innately uniformitarian 36